AF600651

THE CATHOLIC UNIVERSITY OF AMERICA
CANON LAW STUDIES
No. 148

VIOLATION OF THE CLOISTER

AN HISTORICAL SYNOPSIS AND COMMENTARY

BY THE

REV. GARRETT FRANCIS BARRY, O.M.I., J.C.L.
Oblate of Mary Immaculate of the First American Province

A DISSERTATION

Submitted to the Faculty of Canon Law of the Catholic University of America in Partial Fulfillment of the Requirements for the Degree of Doctor of Canon Law

THE CATHOLIC UNIVERSITY OF AMERICA PRESS
WASHINGTON, D. C.
1942

Imprimi Potest:
JACOBUS T. MCDERMOTT, O.M.I.,
Superior Provincialis.
Washingtonii, D. C., die I maii, 1942.

Nihil Obstat:
HIERONYMUS D. HANNAN, S.T.D., J.C.D.,
Censor Deputatus.
Washingtonii, D. C., die XV maii, 1942.

Imprimatur:
✠ MICHAEL J. CURLEY, D.D.,
Archiepiscopus Baltimorensis et Washingtonensis.
Baltimorae, Md., die XV maii, 1942.

Printed by
THE PAULIST PRESS
New York, N. Y.
51

IN MEMORY

OF MY FATHER AND OF MY MOTHER

TABLE OF CONTENTS

CHAPTER VI

CHAPTER VII

CHAPTER VIII

FOREWORD

THE happy position of the Church as a Holy Mother is very consciously portrayed in the solicitude which she has exercised over those whose aspirations and vocation have directed them to traverse, within the sheltered confines of the cloistral life, the higher pathway to perfection and salvation. Supplying the zeal which all too frequently has been found wanting in some of those who have freely undertaken passage along that road, and dispelling the curiosity and over-zealousness of those externs whose entry within the cloister spelled disaster to its very purpose, the Church has ever striven by her legislation, severe at times, to preserve intact and inviolate the sanctity of the cloister and its occupants.

The purpose of the historical portion of the present study will be to trace the development of those efforts as they have unfolded throughout the centuries. Concentration will be more sharply focused upon ecclesiastical enactments in contradistinction to those constitutional provisions originating in the various Rules of Religious Communities. Justifying this procedure is the fact that it is the former legislation from which has evolved the law as it exists today.

The existence of separate monasteries for men and for women, each with its own specific legislation, will necessitate the pursuance of a twofold course in considering this historical conspectus.

The second portion of this study will consist in a commentary upon the canons of the Code which are pertinent to the cloister. A clear understanding of what constitutes cloistral violation postulates a knowledge of the notion of the cloister. This fact justifies the inclusion of an entire chapter relative to cloistral confines and their establishment.

The greatest portion of this commentary will be directed to a consideration of the cloister of regulars and of nuns. It is for the violation of these cloisters that explicit penalties have been stated in the canons. Much that will be said concerning the cloister of these monasteries will be applicable also to the cloister of men and women religious of simple vows. Repetition of those principles will not be made but proper references will be noted.

This discussion will be directed solely to the violation of the cloister. No effort will be made to state the character, necessity and benefits of the cloister.

The writer wishes to express his sincere gratitude to his Provincial, Very Reverend James T. McDermott, O.M.I., for the opportunity of pursuing advanced study in Canon Law; to the faculty of the School of Canon Law of the Catholic University of America for their instruction and guidance; to all who have generously given of their time and energies in assisting him in the composition of this study.

Part One

Historical Synopsis

CHAPTER I

EARLY LEGISLATION TO BONIFACE VIII

Article I. Early Legislation to the Year 500

A. Monastic Legislation

To form a proper frame for the ecclesiastical legislation of this period, a brief sketch of the regulations pertinent to this matter in the Rules of St. Pachomius (c. 292-346) and of St. Basil (329-379) will be outlined.

In his Rule [1] St. Pachomius was the first to effect order and system in monastic life.[2] Only when permission was granted by the *Praepositus,* or second in command,[3] was any monk allowed to go outside of the monastery.[4] Usually this permission was granted to allow visits to sick parents or attendance at their funerals.[5] On such occasions the precaution of having another monk accompany him was to be taken.[6] For going into the village general permission was granted only to those monks who were occupied in the official capacity of herdsmen, ploughmen or farmers.[7]

[1] P. J. Migne, *Patrologiae Cursus Completus, Series Latina* (221 vols., Parisiis: 1858-1864), XXIII, 65-78. Hereafter cited as *MPL.*

[2] Montalembert, *The Monks of the West* (2 vols., Boston: 1872), I, 180; Butler, *Benedictine Monachism* (2. ed., London: Longmans, Green & Co., 1924), p. 14.

[3] Butler, *op. cit.,* pp. 161, 261; Ladeuze, *Étude sur Le Cénobitisme Pakhomien* (Louvain, 1898), p. 287, note 3.

[4] Rule, 84—*MPL,* XXIII, 74.

[5] Rule, 53, 55—*MPL,* XXIII, 71; Ladeuze, *op. cit.,* p. 292.

[6] Rule, 56—*MPL,* XXIII, 71; Ladeuze, *op. cit.,* p. 292, note 5.

[7] Rule, 108—*MPL,* XXIII, 75.

In the early days of his monastic life, St. Pachomius was opposed to the reception of visits, even parental, by the monks. Subsequently this rule was mitigated, but only on infrequent occasions, and always the visit had to be spent in the presence of another monk.[8] Though friends and wayfarers who came to the monastery were to be treated with true Christian hospitality, yet they were not permitted entry into the monastery. A short distance from the monastery was situated the *xenodochium* or guest house and therein all such visitors were fed and given lodging. A special place was to be provided for women and, if possible, they were to be sent to a nearby monastery of sisters.[9]

It can well be said, however, that the Pachomian Rule did not enjoin a strict cloister.[10] Though no specific punishments can be found for violation of the cloister, chastisements were provided for those who disobeyed the Rule.[11] In the opinion of Dom Cuthbert Butler ". . . the Rule of Pachomius is little more than a monastic 'Don't.' "[12]

In the mind of Suarez (1548-1617) the Rule of Pachomius which forbade leaving the cloister without permission had no more binding force than the rules which forbade talking or wandering about the monastery.[13]

Though St. Basil's Rule was likewise enacted for monks in the East, it found its way into the West through the translation into Latin by Rufinus of Aquileja (c. 345-410) about the year 400.[14] Subsequently some of its legislation was incorporated into the Rule of St. Benedict which, as will be evident, played an important rôle in the story of monastic life. To the mind of Dom Butler, "St.

[8] Rule, 52—*MPL,* XXIII, 70-71; Ladeuze, *op. cit.,* p. 292.

[9] Rule, 51—*MPL,* XXIII, 70; Ladeuze, *op. cit.,* pp. 275, 283.

[10] Ladeuze, *op. cit.,* p. 292.

[11] *Regula, Praecepta et Instituta,* 150-153—*MPL,* XXIII, 79.

[12] *Benedictine Monachism,* p. 163.

[13] *Opera Omnia* (ed. nova, a Carolo Berton, 26 vols., Parisiis: Apud Ludovicum Vives, 1856-1866), tom. XVI, *De religione,* tract. VIII, lib. I, cap. VI, n. 3. Henceforth cited as *De religione.*

[14] Schaaf, *The Cloister,* The Catholic University of America Canon Law Studies, n. 13 (Washington, D. C.: The Catholic University of America, 1921), p. 19.

Benedict owed more of the ground ideas of his Rule to St. Basil than to any other monastic legislator." [15]

A few examples from his Rule [16] will serve adequately to portray the mind of St. Basil concerning the subject under discussion. No monk was permitted to depart from the monastery except in case of emergency.[17] The permission of the superior was necessary, and if it was not obtained the guilty monk was subject to punishment.[18] Since it was both unbecoming and dangerous for a monk to leave the monastery alone, one or more companions were to accompany him always.[19] St. Basil was opposed to all visiting, whether on the part of the monks themselves or on the part of their relatives.[20] A more lenient interpretation of this rule was always adopted, however, if the motive of the visit was supernatural.[21]

St. Basil did not absolutely forbid the institution of the twofold monastery whereby the buildings of the monks and the nuns were adjacent to one another. But all association between the inhabitants of these houses was to be scrupulously disciplined. Thus, according to the regulations which he had enacted, they were not to reside in one building and they were forbidden all conversation except in the presence of others.[22]

Though this Rule of St. Basil is lacking in strict legislation on

[15] *Benedictine Monachism*, p. 16; cf. also Schaaf, *loc. cit.*

[16] P. J. Migne, *Patrologiae Cursus Completus, Series Graeca* (161 vols., Parisiis: 1856-1866), XXXI, 889-1306. Hereafter cited as *MPG*. This Rule is divided into two sections: *Regulae Fusius Tractatae*, 889-1052; *Regulae Brevius Tractatae*, 1051-1306. *Poenae in Monachos Delinquentes*, 1305-1314, follows the Rule.

[17] *Reg. brev. tract.*, 120—*MPG*, XXXI, 1062.

[18] *Poenae*, 12—*MPG*, XXXI, 1307.

[19] *Reg. fus. tract.*, 39, 44—*MPG*, XXXI, 1018, 1030.

[20] *Reg. fus. tract.*, 32—*MPG*, XXXI, 994; *Reg. brev. tract.*, 188-189—*MPG*, XXXI, 1207-1210.

[21] *Reg. brev. tract.*, 189—*MPG*, XXXI, 1210.

[22] *Reg. fus. tract.*, 33—*MPG*, XXXI, 998; *Reg. brev. tract.*, 108-111—*MPG*, XXXI, 1155-1158; II General Council of Nice (787), c. 20—J. D. Mansi, *Sacrorum Conciliorum Nova et Amplissima Collectio* (53 vols. in 59, Paris, Leipzig, Arnhem, 1901-1927), XIII, 755. Hereafter cited as Mansi. Cf. also cc. 21, 22, C. XVIII, q. 11; E. F. Morison, *St. Basil and His Rule* (London: 1912), pp. 101-108.

the cloister, it was the mind of its founder that the monks remain close to the monastery under the guidance of their superiors.[23]

B. Conciliar Legislation

The history of conciliar activity in reference to the particular phase of coenobitical life under consideration dawns with the I General Council of Nice held in the year 325. When one couples the fact that monastic life was then an institution of only a few years [24] with the knowledge that the Church strove in the beginning rather to encourage than to correct the spiritual efforts of her faithful, one can understand the paucity of corrective conciliar law found during this period. In treating of monks, the Fathers who were congregated at Nice canonized the coenobitical rules which forbade the porter to allow any exit from the monastery unless the permission of the Abbot had first been obtained.[25]

Even before the beginnings of monasticism some virgins followed the custom of vowing themselves to God while yet remaining in the world living in private homes.[26] The I Council of Carthage (348) was most solicitous for these women and warned that they must not live with men who were not of their own family.[27] Later on the Fathers of Carthage in 397 ordained that when these virgins were placed under the guidance of the bishop in monasteries, or commended to the care of prudent women, they should not be allowed to wander outside of the monastery.[28] In this prohibition Suarez [29]

[23] Schaaf, *The Cloister*, p. 19.

[24] St. Anthony, the founder of the coenobitic life, lived from the years 250-356—Montalembert, *The Monks of the West*, I, 176. St. Pachomius, author of the first written rule, lived during the years 292-346—Ladeuze, *Étude sur Le Cénobitisme Pakhomien*, pp. 240-241. Montalembert places the year of his death in the year 348—*op. cit.*, I, 179.

[25] Mansi, II, 1013.

[26] Cf. St. Cyprian, *De habitu virginum*, cc. IV, V—*MPL*, IV, 443-444.

[27] Cc. 3, 4—Mansi, III, 154.

[28] C. 33—Mansi, III, 885.

[29] *De religione*, tract. VIII, lib. I, cap. VIII, n. 11. Suarez cites this canon as probably the first ecclesiastical legislation forbidding to nuns egress from the monastery.

can find nothing absolute, but only a ban on too frequent departure from the monastery. A repetition of this canon is found in the Council of Africa held in the year 424.[30]

The mind of the founders of the monastic life was always that those who aspired to this state of perfection should use the means most apt for its attainment. The early monks were not priests charged with the duty of the guidance of others, but rather simple men who combined the contemplative life with the laboring life. There could be no reason why they should leave the monastery and subject themselves to temptations inimical to their chosen state. Consequently, when monks not only left the monastery but even were the cause of great disturbance in the cities, particularly in Constantinople, conciliar legislation was required to correct these abuses. Monks were reminded that their life was one of prayer, work and sacrifice within the monastery, and that they should remain there.[31] All monks guilty of entrance into Constantinople were commanded immediately to return to their monasteries.[32] Refusal to obey warranted the use of force to compel them to return.[33]

Worthy of consideration here is the commentary of Suarez[34] which attributes to the above-mentioned canon 4 of the Council of Chalcedon far greater importance and sanction than it seems to warrant. It is his opinion "that no decrees of the Councils or of the Popes could more rigidly legislate in introducing this obligation of the cloister than have the Fathers of Chalcedon." But it seems that he has predicated of this Council an excommunication which was never imposed by it, as will appear from the following consideration.

When this canon appears in Gratian[35] it is minutely commented upon by the Glossators, who divide it into its logical sections. First

[30] C. 11—Mansi, IV, 484.

[31] Council of Chalcedon (451), c. 4—Mansi, VII, 416; c. 12, C. XVI, q. 1.

[32] Council of Chalcedon (451), Actio XV, c. 23—Mansi, VI, 367; c. 17, C. XVI, q. 1.

[33] Cf. gloss to c. 17, C. XVI, q. 1.

[34] *De religione*, tract. VIII, lib. I, cap. VI, n. 5.

[35] C. 12, C. XVI, q. 1.

of all there is given a laudatory comment on monastic life when it is properly lived. Then follows the decree that monks are to be subject to their bishop and are to remain in their monasteries away from all interference in ecclesiastical or secular business, unless they are so exempted by the bishop. The Council then states that no slave is to be received into a monastery except with the permission of his master. Violation of *this* command is to be punished with excommunication. But Suarez cites *only* the second section of the canon and derives from this the severe penalty.[36]

Furthermore, in another citation [37] Gratian refers to a letter of Pope Alexander II (1061-1073) written to the laity and clergy of Florence, in which he commands monks to live according to the tenor of the Council of Chalcedon. Though it was not absolutely necessary, it does seem that the pope would have made mention of the excommunication had the enactment of Chalcedon been so understood at that time. Moreover, the absence of any reference to this severe penalty in subsequent legislation seems to give foundation to a logical refutation of the opinion and interpretation of Suarez.

This argument used to refute Suarez is recognized as being only secondary and, since drawn from times far removed from that of the Council of Chalcedon, not compulsory. It is given here, however, for any intrinsic value which it may possess.

The essential feature of monastic life was that the monks should live in common. The concession could be granted, however, by the abbot, either as a regard for long and faithful service, or as a necessary precaution in case of sickness, for monks to live in separate cells. But always the condition that these cells be within the monastery had to be observed.[38]

[36] Suarez has this wording, "In locis, in quibus se semel Deo dedicaverunt, permanentes; (et subditur infra) Praetereuntem vero haec decrevimus extra communionem esse, ne nomen Domini blasphemetur"—*De religione,* tract. VIII, lib. I, cap. VI, n. 5.

[37] C. 11, C. XVI, q. 1.

[38] Council of Vannes (465), c. 7—Mansi, VII, 953; Council of Agde (506), c. 38—Mansi, VIII, 331.

Article II. From the Year 500 to the *Decretum Gratiani*

A. *Monastic Legislation*

Consequent upon the rapid flourishing and eager acceptance of monasticism in the West came many Rules to guide the monks and nuns in their new life. Chief among these were the Rules of St. Benedict and of St. Caesarius of Arles (470-543). The present consideration will be confined to these two Rules because each was indicative at that early day of the trend which later ecclesiastical legislation followed in its attitude towards the cloistral life of monks and nuns.

The Rule[39] of St. Benedict (480-553, 5)[40] was the first Rule written in the West for the West.[41] The wisdom of its norms of religious guidance is eloquently attested by the fact that it enjoyed primary importance as the norm for all monastic life until the thirteenth century.[42] That the Church held this Rule in high regard is made sufficiently evident by the many councils which commanded monastic life to be lived according to its spirit.[43]

In the first chapter of his Rule St. Benedict indicates that his Rule has been composed only for the coenobitical form of life. In the spiritual wisdom of St. Benedict, leaving the monastery was

[39] C. Butler, *Sancti Benedicti Regula Monasteriorum* (ed. altera, Friburgi Brisgoviae: Herder & Co., 1927). Rule with commentary by Martène—*MPL*, LXVI, 215-962.

[40] J. Chapman, *Saint Benedict and the Sixth Century* (London: Sheed & Ward, 1929), Chapter VIII, *The Date of Saint Benedict.*

[41] Montalembert, *The Monks of the West*, I, 328.

[42] Montalembert, *op. cit.*, I, 328, note.

[43] Cf. Council of Autun (670), c. 15—Mansi, XI, 124; Council of Lobbes (743), c. 1—*Monumenta Germaniae Historica, Legum Sectio III*, tom. II, *Concilia Aevi Karolini I*, Pars 1 (recensuit Albertus Werminghoff, Hannoverae et Lipsiae: 1904), p. 6 (hereafter to be cited as *MGH*); Mansi, XII, 370; Council of Rheims (813), c. 9—*MGH, ibid.*, p. 255; Mansi, XIV, 79; Council-sur Saône (813), c. 22—Mansi, XIV, 98; Council of Tours (813), c. 25—*MGH, ibid.*, p. 290; Mansi, XIV, 87; II Council of Aachen (836), c. 15—*MGH, Legum, Sectio III*, tom. II, *Concilia Aevi Karolini I*, Pars 2 (recensuit Albertus Werminghoff, Hannoverae et Lipsiae: 1908), p. 713; Mansi, XIV, 683; II General Council of the Lateran (1139), c. 26—Mansi, XXI, 532.

harmful to the souls of the monks.[44] Contained in Chapter LXVI is the request, made by St. Benedict, that it be read and reread lest any monk proffer the excuse of ignorance for its violation. To counteract the prevalent practice of monks in transferring from one monastery to another, Benedict first of all bound his monks by vow to remain always in the monastery of their profession.[45] Strictly this rule was not pertinent to the cloister, but rather to the constant dwelling in the same monastery. This vow of stability was one of the most important factors in the Rule of St. Benedict, as well as one of his greatest contributions to Monasticism, definitely establishing, as it did, a juridic relationship between the monk and his monastery. Though this notion of stability was one which was characteristic of St. Benedict and of Benedictines, it cannot be said that it was original with St. Benedict. The idea was taken by St. Benedict from Caesarius of Arles who had incorporated it in his *Regula ad Monachos*.[46] While it is true that in Chapter LVIII of his Rule St. Benedict zealously decreed that the monk stay within the confines of his monastery, yet other chapters provided for journeys which the monks might be required to take.[47]

Thus, while it can certainly be said that the Rule of St. Benedict aimed at the object of stability within the precincts of one monastery, it would be a misinterpretation to attribute to this Rule the intention or force of a strict cloister prohibitive of all exit. Leaving the monastery, as has been said, was made contingent upon permission obtained from the abbot.[48] No one was to presume to leave the monastery without having first obtained the permission of the abbot. To leave without the requisite permission would bring pun-

[44] Chapter LXVI—*MPL*, LXVI, 899-900; Butler, *Sancti Benedicti Regula Monasteriorum*.

[45] Chapter LVIII—*MPL*, LXVI, 803-806.

[46] C. 1—*MPL*, LXVII, 1099-1104; Butler, *Benedictine Monachism*, p. 123, note 4.

[47] Chapter L—*MPL*, LXVI, 743-744; Chapter LXVII—*MPL*, LXVI, 913-914; Butler, *Sancti Benedicti Regula Monasteriorum*.

[48] Chapter LXVII—*MPL*, LXVI, 913-914. For excellent references and treatments of the notion of stability as contained in the Rule of St. Benedict, confer Butler, *Benedictine Monachism*, pp. 123-124 and W. F. Ullathorne *Ecclesiastical Discourses* (London: 1876), pp. 305, 306, 310.

ishment. St. Benedict forbade further that those who had been outside relate anything on their return that they may have seen or heard.[49] Each monastery was to be so constructed that all necessities, *e. g.*, water, mill, garden, were within its walls. Thus would the obligations of leaving the monastery be reduced to a minimum.[50]

The absence of any mention concerning communications with women and their admittance within the monastery is conspicuous. An indication that this was forbidden may be drawn from the famous story related by Pope Gregory the Great (590-604) concerning the meeting of St. Benedict and his sister, St. Scholastica, *outside* of the monastery.[51] St. Benedict's great insistence that he and his companions should not remain overnight outside of the monastery is indicative of the great importance he placed in the security of the cloister. Centuries later when the Cistercian Monks recalled the pristine spirit of the Benedictine Rule they noted that both in his Rule and in his life St. Benedict reflected the practice of not admitting women into his monastery.[52]

St. Caesarius of Arles (470-543) was a contemporary of St. Benedict.[53] The Rule which he composed for nuns [54] established a very strict cloistral life and was marvelously akin to the common law as it now stands.[55] Once a nun entered the monastery she was to remain there until death.[56] In one of his sermons to the nuns, however, St. Caesarius seems to mitigate this strictness by admitting egress from the monastery in the case of great necessity.[57] No man was allowed entry into the private parts of the monastery or of the

[49] Chapter LXVII—*MPL,* LXVI, 913-914; Butler, *Sancti Benedicti Regula Monasteriorum.*

[50] Chapter LXVI—*MPL,* LXVI, 899-900; Butler, *loc. cit.*

[51] Dialogorum S. Greg. Magni excerpta—*MPL,* LXVI, 193-196; Montalembert, *The Monks of the West,* I, 325-327.

[52] *Exordium Coenobii et Ordinis Cisterciencis,* Chapter XV—*MPL,* CLXVI, 1507.

[53] A. Malnory, *St. Césaire, Évêque D'Arles* (Paris: 1894), p. 1.

[54] *MPL,* LXVII, 1103-1116; *Recapitulation, MPL,* LXVII, 1115-1120.

[55] Malnory, *op. cit.,* p. 263.

[56] Rule, Chapter I—*MPL,* LXVII, 1107; *Recapitulation,* Chapter I,—*MPL,* LXVII, 1117.

[57] *Sermo ad Sanctimoniales*—*MPL,* LXVII, 1122.

oratory. Exception was made, during the time of Mass and other divine services, for the bishop, procurator, priest, deacon, subdeacon, and two lectors of commendable character. When necessity demanded, artisans were also permitted entry to any part of the monastery.[58] Women were likewise excluded from the monastery.[59] The indulgence of visits from relatives were granted, but always in the presence of another nun.[60] At only certain times were the doors of the monastery to be left unlocked. At all other times the keys were to be kept by the abbess.[61]

B. *Justinian Legislation*

Within the confines of his jurisdiction Justinian restricted religious life to the coenibitical form alone. It was his desire that all adherents to that life live together, eat together, work together and pray together.[62] In this matter Justinian desired to follow the example and guidance of the ancient Fathers and the sacred laws, for there was, as he said, nothing of which a worthy Emperor was not solicitous.[63]

Wishing to combine his own legislation with that of the Church, Justinian sanctioned as laws in his realm the decrees of the Councils of Nice, Constantinople, Ephesus and Chalcedon.[64] For the present consideration the adoption of the rulings of the Council of Chalcedon is important, since it gave civil sanction to all the cloistral legislation enacted by that Council.

Though Justinian did not speak explicitly of the cloister, his legislation pertinent to the regulation of monasteries implicitly contained this notion. The institution of a twofold monastery was declared foreign to his empire.[65] Wherever this evil, *i. e.*, the living together of men and women religious, already existed, immediate

58 Rule, Chapter XXXIII—*MPL,* LXVII, 1114.
59 Rule, Chapter XXXIV—*MPL, loc. cit.*
60 Rule, Chapter XXXVII—*MPL, loc. cit.*
61 *Recapitulation,* Chapter IX—*MPL,* LXVII, 1118.
62 N. (5, 3); N. (133, pr.); N. (123, 36).
63 N. (133, pr.).
64 N. (133, 1).
65 N. (123, 36); C. (1, 3) 43, 1.

separation had to be effected. The nuns were to remain in their monastery and the monks were to go to another. In the event that the nuns were outnumbered by the monks, then under the guidance of the bishop a new monastery was to be provided for the nuns. Thus all occasions of mixed conversation and visiting would be avoided and the foundation for any suspicion of wrongdoing would be vitiated.[66] Lest any delay be caused in effecting this change, Justinian allowed one year for the desired separation to be made. This time element had to be observed under the sanction of incurring the consequent penalties.[67]

Having thus separated the monasteries, Justinian forbade men to enter the monasteries of women, and women to enter the monasteries of men. His legislation was most exacting and specific. Since the thought and occupations of those within the monastery walls were not of this world, the presence of a brother, a sister, or some other relative in a monastery was not a valid excuse for affording entry to the laity or to other religious. Men were not to possess burial places within the monasteries of women, nor were women to have sepulchers within the confines of the monasteries of monks. Even on the occasion of burial services or of any anniversaries these rules were not permitted to be broken. Justinian wished to forestall all endeavors to veil evil in this regard under the cloak of religion or under the guise of a love for dear ones. For what other reason would one seek entry, he asked, than to do that which has been declared wrong? This was a strict ruling, but one which he regarded as a necessary means in order to prevent all sad lapses and to render more easy the living of the true monastic life. Though it was necessary that certain men conduct the nun's funeral, they were to leave the monastery immediately after the service was completed. With the exception of the ostiary and the abbess, no nuns were permitted to be present at these functions. The men who made the necessary arrangements for the funeral service were to guard not merely against observing the nuns, but also against being seen by them.[68]

[66] C. (1, 3) 43, 2, 3, 4; N. (123, 36); cf. c. 22, C. XVIII, q. 11.
[67] C. (1, 3) 43, 13.
[68] N. (133, 3).

To each monastery were assigned *apocrisiarii* whose duty it was to administer the temporal interests and affairs of the religious. Those assigned to the convents of nuns were, if possible, to be eunuchs, or at least men of proved virtue. With the abbess alone were the *apocrisiarii* permitted to converse.[69] Choice of a priest or deacon to administer Holy Communion was left to the nuns with the approval of the bishop. If the nuns selected a man who was neither a priest nor a deacon, then in the judgment of the bishop he could be ordained for that purpose.[70] But the *apocrisiarii* were never permitted to eat, converse or live within the monastery.[71]

Monastic discipline in the future was to be more rigid than in the past. Consequently Justinian decreed that monasteries should possess at the very most only two entrances and exits. Moreover, each monastery was to be surrounded by strong walls. All exits and entrances were to be made possible through the proper gates alone. Men of advanced age and proved virtue were to be stationed at the door to prevent all exit except to those who had the permission of the abbot, and to forbide entry to any strangers at all times, and especially when these were of such a character that they did not encourage the maintenance of the true monastic life.[72]

Justinian stressed the prohibition which forbade monks to leave the monastery. Especially did it apply to those whose wont it had been to go into the city of Antioch or to any other city. Permission was granted only to the *apocrisiarii,* and then only on affairs of business.[73]

Search for any definite punishments as applying specifically to the violation of the rules of the cloister will be in vain. Upon abbots and abbesses rested the obligation of correcting the slightest fault and deviation from the rule. Bishops, Patriarchs and Metropolitans were likewise charged with the maintenance of discipline.

[69] N. (133, 5).

[70] N. (123, 36); C. (1, 3) 43, 5.

[71] N. (123, 36); C. (1, 3) 43, 5.

[72] N. (133, 1). Though Justinian was legislating specifically for the monasteries of monks, it seems permissible to apply that legislation likewise to the convents of nuns.

[73] C. (1, 3) 29.

One of the duties of the *apocrisiarii* was that of being the defender of the monastery and, upon the order of the proper superior, the corrector of faults.[74] No negligence in the correction and punishment of monks by the proper authorities was countenanced by the civil government.[75]

C. Conciliar Legislation

The great impetus which St. Benedict had given to monasticism resulted in the rapid growth of that institution throughout the West.[76] As monasticism progressed, conciliar legislation relative to the safeguarding of its cloistral feature became more and more extensive. This legislation was all particular in scope, designed to meet the needs arising in individual countries and dioceses. Since the activity of the councils directed itself now to monks and now to nuns, it will be feasible to distinguish under separate headings the legislation which was enacted.

1. Legislation Pertaining to Monks

While it is true that the purpose of the cloister was to provide an atmosphere of quiet, peace and semi-solitude in order to facilitate the advancement of the monks on the road to perfection, it was likewise ordained as a safeguard of the precious virtue of chastity. Women, consequently, were excluded from the monastery. Any negligence in this matter on the part of an abbot by delaying to command a women to leave when she had entered the monastery resulted in excommunication.[77]

Writing in August of the year 594 to the abbot Valentine, Pope Gregory I forbade him to allow women freely to enter the monastery. It was customary to grant such permission since it seems to have been a prevalent usage at that time to choose monks as god-fathers.

[74] N. (133, 4); C. (1, 3) 43, 9-12.

[75] N. (133, 5) 7.

[76] Montalembert, *The Monks of the West*, I, 344.

[77] II Council of Tours (567), c. 16—*MGH, Legum Sectio III*, tom. I, *Concilia Aevi Merovingici* (recensuit F. Maassen: Hannoverae: 1893), p. 126; Mansi, IX, 796.

Pope Gregory warned Valentine that failure to discontinue this practice would result in severe punishment.[78]

Prudently fearful of the dangers involved in the presence of great crowds of people, and especially of women, at public solemn Masses celebrated in the Monastery of SS. Andrew and Thomas at Rimini in Italy, Pope Gregory commanded not only Castorius, the ruling bishop, but all future bishops absolutely to forbid these Masses. The presence of women in a monastery was an occasion of real harm to the spirit of that monastery and therefore it was never to be allowed.[79]

The Council of Autun (seventh century) forbade monks to go into the cities except for a reasonable cause dictated by the needs of the monastery. And then the permission of the abbot had to be expressed in writing and shown to the archdeacon of the city.[80] This Council strongly repeated the prohibition aimed at excluding women from the monasteries of men.[81] Any abbot guilty of transgressing these rules was suspended from his office for the period of a year. Disregard for these enactments by a *praepositus* merited suspension from office for two years. A guilty monk was either to be subjected to bodily punishment or else to be barred from Communion, from Mass and from the association of others for a period of three years.[82]

Mention has been made in relation to the Pachomian Rule of the

[78] *Gregorii I Regestrum Epistolarum,* lib. IV, ep. 40—*MGH, Epistolae,* tom. I, pars 1, lib. I-IV (ed. Paulus Ewald, Berolini: 1887), p. 276; *MPL,* LXXVII, 717; c. 20, C. XVIII, q. 11; P. Jaffé, *Regesta Pontificum Romanorum ab condita Ecclesia ad annum post Christum natum 1198* (editionem secundam correctam et auctam auspiciis Guliemi Wattenbach curaverunt S. Loewenfeld, F. Kaltenbrunner, P. Ewald, 2 vols. in 1, Lipsiae: 1885-1888), n. 1312. Hereafter cited as Jaffé.

[79] *Regestrum Epistolarum,* lib. II, ep. 41—*MPL,* LXXVII, 578; Jaffé, n. 1362; c. 6, C. XVIII, q. 11.

[80] C. 6—*MGH, Legum Sectio III,* tom. I, *Concilia Aevi Merovingici,* p. 221; Mansi, XI, 123. In Mansi this Council is attributed to the year 670. However, in *MGH* it is simply attributed to the reign of Bishop Leodegarius of Autun who is said to have ruled from the year 663-680. Thus the Council is dated as falling sometime during this period.

[81] C. 10—*MGH, ibid.,* p. 221; Mansi, XI, 123.

[82] C. 15—*MGH, loc. cit.*; Mansi, *loc. cit.*

institution of *xenodochia* or guest houses wherein visitors and others were to receive their food and lodging. That this generous provision proved to become but the stepping stone to a further encroachment upon the tranquillity of the monasteries of monks is evident from the tenor of subsequent legislation. The III Council of Saragossa (691) found it necessary to be most explicit in recalling to the attention of monks and externs the absolute demand for quiet and solitude which should prevail within the monastery. Thenceforth only those men who, in the judgment of the abbot, were very needy and poor could be permitted the shelter of the monastery. The abbot and the monks were strictly forbidden to grant entry for such a purpose to any others. Only in this way could the proper spirit of the monastic life be maintained.[83] That the contrary practice must have been widespread is evidenced by the legislation of the Trullan Synod (692) which found it necessary to excommunicate women who slept in the monasteries of monks.[84]

For the next one hundred years there is little to relate in the form of conciliar legislation. Monasteries were again the haven of seculars with the consequence that the monastic spirit was infected with a very unhealthy and decidedly unspiritual atmosphere. In the middle of the eighth century, one Council raised its voice in an effort to stem the tide of abuses. But possibly in view of its failure to sanction its laws with any effective penalties, the desired result was not obtained.[85]

With the advent of the Carolingian Reform in the early years of the ninth century came a revival of discipline regarding the morals within the Church. Much of this reform effort was directed toward monastic life. An immediate return to the Rule of St. Benedict was demanded in those places where it was either forgotten or where it had been allowed to fall into disuse. The pristine fervor of the monastic life was to be restored.[86] Again abbots and monks were commanded to remain within their cloister unless true necessity de-

[83] C. 3—Mansi, XII, 43.

[84] C. 47—Mansi, XI, 996.

[85] II Council of Clovesho (747), c. 20—Mansi, XII, 401.

[86] III Council of Tours (813), cc. 24-26—*MGH, Legum Sectio III*, tom. II, *Concilia*, Pars 1, pp. 289-290; Mansi, XIV, 87.

manded that they leave it. Their absence was always to be conditioned on the permission of the abbot or of the bishop.[87] *Missi* of the King went about from diocese to diocese in company with the proper bishop to ascertain whether the monasteries were suitably situated and adaptably constructed for the safeguarding of the cloistral life.[88]

To prevent all surreptitious violation of the cloister, each monastery was to be so constructed that entry and egress would be possible only through the proper door. The dormitories, refectory, storage room and other places essential for the daily life of the monks were to occupy the innermost quarters of the monastery. The responsibility for carrying out these commands rested upon the headmaster. Failure to do what was in his power resulted not only in his unworthiness to attain other ecclesiastical offices but also in his subjection to the punishment of the Council. This was the first explicit conciliar legislation relative to the structural plan of the monastery and, in particular, with regard to its division into suites of rooms of which some were more inviolate than the others.[89]

The chapel of the monastery could be entered by women. But they were absolutely forbidden to enter further and thus pass into the monastery. If it happened, however, that charity dictated that a woman be permitted entry into the monastery, she always had to be received in a special room outside of the cloister. And even then a monk was not permitted to converse with her except in the presence of witnesses. Any violation of these enactments met with the severe correction of the bishop and of the authorities of the monastery. Such punishment was to stand as an example not only for the guilty party but also for the others.[90]

With this revival of legislation all further progressive conciliar activity pertinent to this subject ceased until after the time of Gratian. Though there had been evident a legal development relative to the cloister in monasteries of men, it never attained to the stage of a perpetual cloister. Many of the monks during the later period

[87] Council of Mainz (813), c. 12—*MGH, ibid.*, p. 264; Mansi, XIV, 68.
[88] Council of Mainz (813), c. 20—*MGH, ibid.*, p. 266; Mansi, XIV, 70.
[89] Council of Aachen (816), c. 117—*MGH, ibid.*, p. 389; Mansi, XIV, 230.
[90] Council of Aachen (816), c. 144—*MGH, ibid.*, p. 418; Mansi, XIV, 243.

were priests, and their work demanded that they spend some time outside of the monastery. The legislation which was designed to preserve intact the inviolability of the cloister from entry by externs, especially by women, was more rigid than that which prohibited the monks themselves to leave the cloister. Their departure from the cloister could be authorized with the permission of the abbot for any reasonable cause. Severe penalties for the simple breaking of the cloister rules by egress without the proper permission were few.

2. Legislation Pertaining to Nuns

Evidently the evil consequences deriving from the proximity of the monasteries of women to those of men far outweighed the good results, for at a very early period it was deemed necessary to separate at some distance the two kinds of monasteries.[91] Only men of probity and of advanced age were permitted entry into the monasteries of nuns when necessity or the various acts of the Church's ministry demanded it. And then they had to leave immediately upon the completion of their work or of the divine services. The exceptions were those which were granted at certain times to parents and other relatives.[92] The requisite of probity combined with advanced age extended not only to lay persons, regardless of rank and position, but even to bishops.[93] Those who were allowed to enter had to confine their conversations with the nuns to the greeting room, beyond which they were not permitted to go. In this distinction there is evidence of an early endeavor to render more inviolate certain parts of the monastery.[94] That some monasteries—evidently those which professed the Rule of Caesarius of Arles—required the nuns upon receiving the habit to remain perpetually enclosed was recognized by the V Council of Orleans in the year 549.[95]

When Pope Gregory I (590-604) was informed that Agnella, an

[91] I Council of Agde (506), c. 28—Mansi, VIII, 329; c. 23, C. XVIII, q. 11.

[92] Council of Epaone (517), c. 38—*MGH, Legum Sectio III*, tom. I, *Concilia*, Pars 1, p. 28; Mansi, VIII, 564.

[93] I Council of Mâcon (581), c. 2—*MGH, ibid.*, p. 156; Mansi, IX, 932.

[94] I Council of Mâcon (581), c. 2—*loc. cit.*

[95] C. 19—*MGH, Legum Sectio III*, tom. I, *Concilia*, Pars 1, p. 107; Mansi, IX, 133.

abbess, was housing soldiers in her monastery, he wrote immediately to Bishop Fortunatus and commanded that this source of great danger be obviated at once. In view of the fact that the laws of the cloister were then well known, Pope Gregory wondered at the delay of the bishop in taking action in this case.[96]

When the monasteries in the Province of Baetica in Spain were entrusted to the spiritual and temporal care of some monks, exact rules of conduct were outlined. Associations were to be as infrequent as possible, most brief and always in the presence of others. Any contempt or neglect of this ruling brought the penalty of excommunication.[97]

It was the right and duty of the bishop, in company with other pious and trustworthy persons, frequently to visit monasteries and make inquiries relative to religious life there. Nuns who were guilty of sins which could result only upon a violation of the cloister were to be punished with flogging. Great care was to be exercised that laymen and clerics could have no secret access to the monastery.[98] This legislation was not heeded, as is evident from the fact that later on the Trullan Council (692) found it necessary to excommunicate men who undertook to sleep in the monasteries of nuns.[99] This same Council employed very strong and precise language in decreeing that nuns must not leave the monastery. Once women had chosen the religious life they absolutely had to remain within the cloister and only an inexorable necessity was deemed a sufficient reason for them to leave it. Strict though this was, the right of granting permission was reserved merely to the abbess. Disregard for this law of the cloister brought punishment proportionate to the guilt.[100] Suarez finds here an obligation which appears to be absolute and yet at the same time dependent upon the will of the abbess. Thus, as he says, the efficacy of this canon in its binding force is not sufficiently evident.[101]

[96] *Regestrum Epistolarum,* lib. IX, ep. 103—*MPL,* LXXVII, 1026.
[97] II Council of Seville (619), c. 9—Mansi, X, 560; c. 24, C. XVIII, q. 11.
[98] Council of Rouen (c. 646), c. 10—Mansi, X, 1201.
[99] C. 46—Mansi, XI, 996.
[100] C. 46—Mansi, XI, 966.
[101] *De religione,* tract. VIII, lib. I, cap. VIII, n. 11.

The prohibition against leaving the monastery applied equally to the abbess. The Council of Verneuil (755) permitted abbesses to visit the king once a year when he commanded this, but only after having previously obtained the consent of her bishop. Once the visit had been completed, the abbess had to return to the monastery by means of the least populated route. To this law were attached penances to be imposed by the bishop for any violation of its spirit.[102]

When the II General Council of Nice (787) enacted legislation which forbade twofold monasteries, it allowed to continue those monasteries which were already in existence and which followed the Rule of St. Basil. However, nuns were not allowed to live in the same building with monks. It was at that time the common practice for monks and nuns to chant the office in the same choir, thus giving occasion for sin.[103] The practice of permitting a monk to sleep in a monastery of women in order the more readily to be present for the religious exercises in the early morning had to be eliminated. When food was carried from the monastery of the monks to that of the nuns, it was to be received at the door by two nuns. Visits of any monk with a nun were to be completed quickly and always in the presence of the abbess. Yet, despite these detailed regulations, the law of the Council was not fortified with any penal sanction.[104]

The legislation and penalties to the contrary notwithstanding, the laws of the cloister were not taken seriously by everybody. Consequently, the Council of Friuli (796-797) found it necessary to reiterate the precaution of strongly fortifying all monasteries against entry by outsiders. Only with the permission of the bishop did any laymen or clerics enjoy the necessary authorization to enter the cloister. And the injunction was placed upon the bishop that he should give consent only to persons who were above all suspicion and then only when there was a case of true necessity. Nuns were all warned against leaving the enclosure on the pretext of making

[102] C. 6—*MGH, Legum Sectio II,* tom. I, *Capitularia Regum Francorum* (edidit A. Boretius, Hannoverae: 1883), p. 34; Mansi, XII, 580.

[103] Cf. Gloss to c. 21, C. XVIII, q. 11.

[104] C. 20—Mansi, XIII, 755; c. 21, C. XVIII, q. 11.

pilgrimages to shrines and other venerated places. In view of this limitation, the placing of an absolute prohibition upon the nuns seems not to have been present. There was, however, a severe sanction attached to the enforcement of this law. Excommunication, or deprivation of any office and honor possessed, followed upon the disregard of any of these enactments. The penalty was to be meted out in proportion to the circumstances and character of the fault committed.[105]

With the advent of Charles the Great as emperor in the year 800 came the Carolingian Reform of subsequent years. Conciliar legislation as well as enactments of the civil power bearing on the subject under discussion increased. Much of it was just the reaffirmation and re-enactment of what had been either forgotten or willfully disobeyed. Nuns and abbesses had to remain within the walls of the cloister. Priests who entered to say Mass had to leave immediately upon the completion of the service. Permission of the bishop was needed before any men could enter the cloister. There was stressed the necessity of safeguarding the monasteries against the evil designs of men. *Missi* of the king were sent about in company with the proper bishop to examine carefully each monastery and to make provisions, if necessary, for improvements and more efficacious precautions.[106]

The Council held at Aachen in the year 816 outlined in a specific manner that it was within the interior rooms and apartments of the monastery that the refectory, dormitory, storage quarters and other frequently used rooms were to be situated. Thus the inviolability of the cloister could be more certainly assured. Moreover, it was outside of the monastery itself that the home of the ministering

[105] C. 12—*MGH, Legum Sectio III*, tom. II, *Concilia*, pars 1, p. 194; Mansi, XIII, 850.

[106] *First Chapter of Charlemagne* (802), cc. 18, 20—*MGH, Legum Sectio II*, tom. I, *Capitularia Regum Francorum*, p. 95; Council of Chalon-sur-Saône (813), cc. 55-65—*MGH, Legum Sectio III*, tom. II, *Concilia*, pars 1, pp. 284-5; Mansi, XIV, 105-106; VI Council of Arles (813), c. 7—*MGH, ibid.*, p. 251; Mansi, XIV, 60; Council of Mainz (813), cc. 13, 20—*MGH, ibid.*, pp. 264, 266; Mansi, XIV, 68, 70; III Council of Tours (813), cc. 29, 30—*MGH, ibid.*, p. 290; Mansi, XIV, 87-88.

priest, or a room which served him and his ministers as a place of preparation for the divine services, was to be erected. Only at the stated time were they allowed to enter the monastery. The Council further decreed that a nun of advanced age and of proved virtue was to be assigned as portress. Only at the stated hours was she to allow anyone to enter into the monastery. All personal discrimination was to be avoided. Failure to fulfill her position worthily after one warning brought removal from her office.[107]

Whatever meager legislation existed from this time until the period of Gratian was only repetitive. It did not reflect any development in the trend of the legal institution which dealt with the question of cloistral observance. The development up to this stage clearly manifested that this feature of monasticism was begotten of custom,[108] was nursed by the founders of religious and monastic life, and was finally aided in its growth by conciliar legislation. There was no definite ruling which was everywhere adopted. From the sources which could be consulted no absolute and fixed law of the cloister could be derived. Constant exceptions were made in favor of person of proved virtue and of upright motives; at times necessary situations were quite leniently interpreted. The prime intent with regard to exclusion from the cloister was directed to the barring of the other sex, but the permitted exceptions were sometimes pushed to disadvantageous and dangerous limits. In general, the growth of the institution was slow. It was retarded not only by laxity in discipline, but likewise by the encountered difficulties of educating lay persons to the point of a proper recognition of and a due appreciation for the monastic cloister. The legislation thus far considered presupposed, perhaps, more than it imposed the direct obligation of the cloistral observance. That it was universal and absolute cannot be evidenced from historical research. Rather it was an obligation of which the desired fulfillment was ever strongly safeguarded, first by custom and later also by law. It became a precept

[107] Cc. 11, 26, 27—*MGH, ibid.*, pp. 336, 355; Mansi, XIV, 276, 279.

[108] Suarez, *De religione*, tract. VIII, lib. I, cap. VIII, n. 11; F. Ferraris, *Prompta Bibliotheca, Canonica, Iuridica, Moralis, Theologica, nec non Ascetica, Polemica, Rubricistica, Historica* (ed. Migne, 8 vols., Parisiis: 1863-1865), s. v. "Moniales," art. III, n. 1. Hereafter cited as *Bibliotheca*.

which for its observance had as yet not abstracted from the concomitant legitimate faculty which the abbess possessed for the granting of dispensations.

Article III. From the *Decretum Gratiani* to Pope Boniface VIII

A. The Decretum Gratiani

The legislation which appears in the *Decretum Gratiani* (c. 1140) pertinent to the subject under consideration is confined mostly to the enactments of the early councils which have already been cited. However, the inclusion of these in the *Decretum Gratiani* reflects the canon law which was prevalent at that time.[109] In the *Decretum* there is found little change which affects radically and essentially the legislation of these councils. There is nothing to warrant the assumption that during Gratian's time the legislation on this topic was generally more severe.

It is interesting to note that Gratian included in his *Decretum* the enactment of Justinian which forbade the twofold monastery.[110] Immediately preceding this included enactment in the *Decretum* is the precept of the II General Council of Nice (787), which likewise forbade the institution and maintenance of such monasteries.[111] Perhaps there is significance in the fact that Gratian linked with these enactments the decree of the Council of Agde (506) which ordered that the monasteries of men and women be widely separated.[112]

Beyond the canons found in the *Decretum* which refer to early legislation, there is one important canon which dates from Gratian's own time. This is the severe enactment of Pope Innocent II (1130-1143) which was issued in the II General Lateran Council in the

[109] For information relative to the date, composition, juridic force and authority of the *Decretum Gratiani,* cf. A. Van Hove, *Prolegomena ad Codicem Iuris Canonici,* Commentarium Lovaniense in Codicem Iuris Canonici, Vol. I, tom. I (Mechliniae et Romae: Dessain, 1928), pp. 160-167.

[110] C. 22, C. XVIII, q. 11; N. (123, 36); C. (1, 3) 43, 2, 3, 4.

[111] C. 28—Mansi, XIII, 755; c. 21, C. XVIII, q. 11.

[112] C. 28—Mansi, VIII, 329; c. 23, C. XVIII, q. 11.

year 1139.[113] There had arisen the pernicious and scandalous custom, as practiced by some nuns, which witnessed on the one hand the relegation of the monastic life and rule to a position of secondary importance and on the other hand the elevation of extreme social activity to a degree of prime import. Nuns either had forgotten or just wantonly disobeyed their rules and were living outside of the monasteries and in a manner which, to say the least, was not befitting their state in life. Pope Innocent II commanded these nuns to return to their monasteries and to live there the community life which was prescribed in their rules. Persistence in their current form of life outside of the monastery became branded with the sentence of excommunication.

Pope Innocent II forbade, likewise, that nuns and monks convene in the same choir for the purpose of chanting the Divine Office. Refusal to obey this decree also brought the dire consequence of excommunication.

Gratian himself seems not to have inserted into his *Decretum* any further information which would justify the assertion that during his time the obligation of the cloister was subjected to any new legislative impetus or disciplinary enactment.

B. *Conciliar Legislation*

From the time of Gratian to the ascent of Pope Boniface VIII (1294-1303) to the throne of St. Peter there was a mild revival in the history of conciliar legislation concerning the cloister and its observance. The picture which can be drawn from this legislation portrays a scene of lapsed monastic life which was in need of strict restoration.

1. Legislation Pertaining to Monks

Monks at this time were so desirous of advancing in the intellectual pursuits of the secular sciences that they frequently attended schools outside of their monasteries. This attendance prevented their nightly return to the monastery and the proper adherence to the monastic and religious spirit. Thus it was that the Council of

[113] Cc. 26, 27—Mansi, XXI, 532; c. 25, XVIII, q. 11.

Tours (1103) commanded that monks no longer be permitted to leave the monastery for this purpose. The rigor of this law was greatly mitigated, however, through the fact that the sanction of excommunication took effect only after the monks had been absent for a period of two months. Those who did return to the monastery were relegated to the lowest place in all things and deprived of all hope of promotion except by the intervention of the Holy See.[114]

In the year 1238 Gerald, the Archbishop of Bordeaux, commanded that only with the special permission of the abbot or prior were monks to leave the cloister. The doors of the cloister were to be firmly locked at the proper hours.[115] Similar to this legislation was that of the Council of Cologne (1260), which forbade monks to leave the cloister except during the hours between Prime and Compline. In the case of a death in his family a monk was allowed to go home to chant the Office.[116] Moreover, the Council leniently granted permission to attend a wedding at home.[117]

That the practice of admitting women into monasteries was once again prevalent is evidenced by the enactment of the Council of Treves (1277) which forbade any woman, regardless of position or dignity, to be admitted into the cloister. Though women were never permitted to eat in the monastery, it was nevertheless the privilege of the abbot to grant permission for them to visit. Loss of vote in the Chapter, coupled with demotion to the last place in choir, was the punishment for those monks who left the cloister without the necessary permission.[118]

All of this legislation did not effect any marked change in the obligation of the cloister of monks. The observance of the cloistral regulations was made contingent in part upon the permissions which could be granted by the abbot. Once again severe sanctions were invoked against the entry of women into the cloister rather than against the unauthorized exit of the monks from the monastery.

[114] C. 8—Mansi, XXI, 1179; cf. also Council of Paris (1212), c. 20—Mansi, XXII, 831.

[115] Cc. 21, 22—Mansi, XXIII, 492.

[116] C. 16—Mansi, XXIII, 1027.

[117] C. 26—Mansi, XXIII, 1028.

[118] Cap. 17, nn. 138-139—Mansi, XXIV, 205.

2. Legislation Pertaining to Nuns

An important and far-reaching canon was issued in the III General Lateran Council (1179) and was later included in the Decretals of Pope Gregory IX (1227-1241).[119] Because clerics were frequenting too often and without cause the monasteries of nuns, the III General Lateran Council decreed that persistence in that practice after they had been warned by the bishop would result in deprivation of their ecclesiastical benefice. The Council likewise declared that lay persons guilty of sins against nature suffered excommunication. However, when canon 11 subsequently appeared in the Decretals of Pope Gregory IX, the penalty of excommunication against lay persons was applied in the case of their frequentation of the monasteries of nuns. No reference was made to the case of sins against nature.

Before the punishment of excommunication could set in, a twofold element was prerequisite: the material factor of frequentation and the formal factor of the absence of a manifest and reasonable cause for the frequentation.[120] The word *"frequentare"* gave possible rise to a double acceptation in its meaning. One sense of the word had reference to numerical value; the other related rather to the physical approach or entry which it connoted. In endeavoring to determine the meaning of the word *"frequentare"* in relation to the idea of approach or visiting, Hostiensis (Henricus de Segusio +1271) appealed to the common usage which that word had among men.[121] Ioannes Andreae (+1348) adopted as his own the meaning employed by Hostiensis.[122]

The meaning of this word as considered in the light of the mathematical notion which it implied was interpreted in the *Glossa* as implying more than one visit.[123] Ioannes Andreae [124] and Hos-

[119] C. 11—Mansi, XXII, 224; c. 8, X *de vita et honestate clericorum,* III, 1.

[120] Cf. Gloss to c. 8, X *de vita et honestate clericorum,* III, 1.

[121] *Commentaria in Quinque Decretalium Libros,* 5 vols. in 3 (Venetiis: 1581), lib. III, *de vita et honestate,* cap. VIII, s. v. "monasteria."

[122] *In VI Libros Decretalium Novella Commentaria,* 6 vols. in 5 (Venetiis: 1581), lib. III, *de vita et honestate,* cap. VIII, n. 6.

[123] Cf. c. 8, X *de vita et honestate clericorum,* III, 1.

[124] Lib. III, *de vita et honestate,* cap. VIII, n. 3.

tiensis[125] were in full agreement in this matter, both holding a view which was opposed to the one presented in the *Glossa*. Both were of the opinion that even one visit to the monastery after a warning by the bishop would result in the punishment.

The Provincial Council of Mainz (1261) found it necessary to repeat that legislation. Again the warning to clerics was necessary in order to put an end to their visits to the monasteries of women. But once more the prohibition allowed for the exception which was provided by the presence of a good cause and of proved virtue in the one who frequented the monastery. Punishments followed upon any refusal to abide by the commands of the Council. The penalties were to be proportioned in accordance with the gravity of the committed misdeed.[126]

The Council of Sens (1239) admitted only rare instances when the nuns might be allowed to leave the cloister. Particular stress was attached to the prohibition of overnight absences.[127]

In England the Council of London (1268) was adamant in decreeing that only to abbesses, in their pursuance of the necessary duties relative to the monastery, was it permitted to be absent from the monastery, and then only for the necessary time. All other nuns were to remain within the cloister except when the usual grave reasons demanded otherwise. Of course the nuns who lawfully left the cloister were to be accompanied by companions. The custom which had allowed nuns to leave the cloister on the occasion of solemn and public processions was thenceforth abolished. To ensure the maintenance of the observance of the cloister, bishops were gravely obliged to be most meticulous in this matter on the occasion of their visitation.[128]

It is evident that there was great need of strict regulation in this matter. Nevertheless it seems that no Council deemed it imperative to sanction its enactments with severe penalties. However,

[125] Lib. III, *de vita et honestate*, cap. VIII, s. v. "monasteria," n. 2.

[126] C. 22—Mansi, XXIII, 1087.

[127] C. 5—Mansi, XXIII, 509; cf. Council of Paris (1248), c. 12—Mansi, XXIII, 766.

[128] C. 53—Mansi, XXIII, 1256.

when in the year 1287 Bishop John of Tusculum as legate of the Holy See convened the Council of Wuerzburg in Bavaria, the sanction of excommunication was attached to its decree concerning the cloister. Ecclesiastical persons, especially those possessing dignities and sacred orders, were too frequently guilty not only of violating the cloister of convents, but likewise of giving themselves to speech and actions therein which could no longer be countenanced. Thenceforth all those who were guilty of such misdeeds were to be excommunicated by the bishop. The importance of this decree was enhanced by the fact that its force applied not only to all communities of religious, but embraced in its scope the territories of Bohemia, Wallachia, Moravia, Poland, Pomerania, Prussia, Russia, etc.[129]

C. *Monastic Legislation for Nuns*

In the Rule which St. Francis of Assisi (1181-1226) gave to his spiritual sons there was contained no prohibition against leaving the cloister. The purpose of the Friars Minor was to work among the faithful, and this necessitated their absence from the cloister as the ordinary procedure. But though the Friars were permitted to leave their own monastery, they were allowed entry into the monastery of nuns only with special permission from the Holy See.[130]

Definitely to settle doubts and misinterpretations which arose concerning this prohibition, Pope Gregory IX (1227-1241) made it clear that this prohibition extended to all monasteries of nuns and not alone to the monasteries of the Poor Clares. Without special permission from the Holy See they were allowed to enter, for the purposes of preaching and collecting alms, those quarters of other monasteries which were outside the cloister proper.[131] This same

[129] C. 3—Mansi, XXIV, 851.

[130] Cf. Honorius III, Bulla "*Solet annuere,*" 29 nov. 1223, cap. XI—*Bullarium Diplomatum et Privilegiorum Sanctorum Romanorum Pontificum, Taurinensis Editio,* 24 vols., et Appendix (Augustae Taurinorum: 1857-1872), III, 394. Hereafter cited as *Bull. Rom.* A. Potthast, *Regesta Pontificum Romanorum,* 2 vols. (Berolini: 1874-1875), n. 7108. Hereafter cited as Potthast.

[131] Bulla "*Quo elongati a saeculo,*" 17 oct. 1230—*Bull. Rom.*, III, 452; Potthast, n. 8627.

interpretation was repeated a few years later by Pope Innocent IV (1243-1254).[132]

The foundation of the Order of St. Clare was occasioned in view of the striking example of poverty which so forcibly struck St. Clare as she observed her contemporary St. Francis. Discussion of the rise and spread of this Order, as well as the much discussed origin of the Rule of St. Clare, is beyond the ambit of this treatise.[133]

Within this Order, strict and perpetual cloister was vowed by the nuns. However, the establishing of a new house, one's being elected as a superioress for another house, and the serving of a period of correction in another house were all reasons which enabled the General Superior of the Friars Minor, to whom these nuns were subject, or the Provincial Superior of the place where the convent was situated, to grant the necessary permission for the nuns to leave the enclosure.[134]

To these causes Urban IV (1261-1264) added the cases of emergency arising from fire and other dangerous situations which could not be avoided. But always the nuns had to retreat to a more suitable location and there continue to observe the cloister as much as possible.[135] The legislation which forbade the entry of externs into the monastery was very rigid. Regardless of dignity or personage, this prohibition extended to all who had not the proper permission from the Apostolic See, from the General of the Friars Minor, or from the proper Provincial.[136] Exceptions were made for the Cardinal Protectors who wished to enter the cloister of the nuns. But always they were reverently requested to reduce their companions to a very few. The same exception was enjoyed by the General of

[132] Bulla *"Ordinem vestrum,"* 14 nov. 1245—*Bull. Rom.*, III, 522; Potthast, n. 11,962; cf. also Pope Nicholas III (1277-1280)—c. 3, *de verborum significatione*, V, 12, in VI°.

[133] Cf. Wauer, *Entstehung und Ausgreitung des Klarissenordens* (Leipzig: 1906); Paschal Robinson, *The Rule of St. Clare* (Philadelphia: Dolphin Press: 1912).

[134] Innocentius IV, Bulla *"Cum omnis vera religio,"* 6 aug. 1247—*Bull. Rom.*, III, 528; Potthast, n. 12,635.

[135] Bulla *"Beata Clara,"* 18 oct. 1264, cap. II—*Bull. Rom.*, III, 710.

[136] Innocentius IV, Bulla *"Cum omnis vera religio,"* 6 aug. 1247—*Bull. Rom.*, III, 530; Potthast, 12,635.

the Friars Minor whenever he desired to celebrate Mass or to preach to the nuns within the cloister. In his case also the retinue was to be small and it was to be composed of persons of integrity. Whenever bishops obtained the proper permission to enter the cloister, which was very rare, the same rules were binding upon them. Before the abbess could allow anyone to enter the cloister, she had to make certain that he possessed permission from the proper authorities.[137] The law which forbade entry into the cloister admitted exceptions for doctors and for others whose work in the cloister was absolutely necessary. But in all these situations strict precautions had to be observed and immediate exit had to follow the completion of the work performed.[138]

Attached to the nuns' monasteries were other women who were occupied as servants. Though they were obliged to the rules of monastic life as were the nuns, the strict observance of the cloister did not pertain to them. They were allowed to be absent from the cloister with the permission of the abbess. Usually such absence was occasioned by the needed performance of some duty relative to the utility of the monastery.[139] In these rules which the Popes approved, there were not attached to the violation of the cloister, whether it was perpetrated by the exit of the nuns or by the entry of outsiders, any serious penalties approaching excommunication. At the most there was the indication that properly suited punishments were to follow upon infractions of the rule.

Up to the second half of the thirteenth century, however, the monasteries of the Daughters of St. Clare were alone in possessing and observing the strict cloister imposed by Pontifical precept.[140]

[137] Urbanus IV, Bulla "*Beata Clara*," 18 oct. 1264, cap. XVIII—*Bull. Rom.*, III, 716.

[138] Innocentius IV, Bulla "*Cum omnis vera religio*," 6 aug. 1247—*Bull. Rom.*, III, 530; Innocentius IV, Bulla "*Solet annuere*," 9 aug. 1253, cap. XI—*Bull. Rom.*, III, 576; Urbanus IV, Bulla "*Beata Clara*," 18 oct. 1264, cap. XVIII—*Bull. Rom.*, III, 716.

[139] Innocentius IV, Bulla "*Cum omnis vera religio*," 6 aug. 1247—*Bull. Rom.*, III, 529; Bulla "*Solet annuere*," 9 aug. 1253, cap. IX—*Bull. Rom.*, III, 575; Urbanus IV, Bulla "*Beata Clara*," 18 oct. 1264, cap. XVIII—*Bull. Rom.*, III, 717.

[140] *Analecta Juris Pontificii* (Romae: 1855), III (1857-1858), 431.

It is interesting to note how well defined was the concept of the cloister as portrayed in the Rule of the Order of St. Clare. The minutest details were considered, and all precautions were employed to render the cloister the place of solitude and safety that it was intended to be.

Contemporaneous with the founding of the Friars Minor and of the Order of St. Clare was the birth of the Order of St. Dominic. As a result of the eloquent preaching and saintly example of St. Dominic (c. 1170-1221) nine women were converted from the Albigensian heresy and under his guidance confined themselves in a convent in Prouille in the Diocese of Toulouse.[141] Bernard de la Guyenne (c. 1260-1331) stated that these nuns were under perpetual cloister.[142]

As this community grew, other convents were founded in Madrid [143] and at Rome, to which many came willingly and joyfully to become nuns.[144] On October 23rd in the year 1232, Pope Gregory IX confirmed the Rule under which these nuns lived.[145] In this Rule the enactments concerning the cloister detailed that the perpetual cloister was always to be observed. Permission to transfer to another convent of the same Order was to be granted when a necessary cause merited this. Only with the permission of the Cardinal Protector, of the bishop, or of the Legate of the Holy See were any of the sons of St. Dominic allowed entry into the cloister of these monasteries. Only once a year, on the occasion of the visitation, was the Provincial Prior of the Dominicans free to enter the cloister. A cause approved by the General Superior could, however, permit more frequent entry.

Writing to the nuns in the convent of St. Lawrence in the diocese of Plasencia in Spain, Pope Gregory X (1271-1276) commanded

[141] *Acta Sanctorum Bollandiana,* August, tom. I (Parisiis et Romae: 1867), pp. 410-412.

[142] Innocentius III, Bulla *"Iustis petentium,"* 8 oct. 1215—*Bullarium Ordinis FF. Praedicatorum,* 8 vols. (Romae: 1729-1740), I, p. 1, note 3 (hereafter cited *Bull. O. P.*) ; Potthast, n. 4997.

[143] *Acta Sanctorum Bollandiana, ibid.,* p. 474, n. 604.

[144] *Acta Sanctorum Bollandiana, ibid.,* p. 376, n. 98.

[145] Bulla *"Ne hostis antiquus"*—*Bull. O. P.,* VII, 410.

them not to leave the cloister after profession except with the permission of the prioress.[146] Thus it seems that, although these nuns observed a perpetual cloister, it was not one which was imposed by papal authority, but rather one which was accepted voluntarily. The granting of permission for egress from the monastery on rare occasions was left to the good judgment and wisdom of the prioress.[147] In this rule, as in that of the Order of St. Clare, no severe punishments for the violation of the cloister were in evidence.

[146] Bulla "*Religiosam vitam,*" 7 mart. 1274—*Bull. O. P.*, I, 518; Potthast, n. 20,800.

[147] *Analecta Juris Pontificii,* III (1857-1858), 431.

CHAPTER II

BONIFACE VIII TO THE COUNCIL OF TRENT

ARTICLE I. THE *Liber Sextus* OF POPE BONIFACE

WITH the advent of Pope Boniface VIII (1294-1303) to the throne of Peter there was ushered in a new era in the historical life of the cloister for women. It was an era in which definite steps were taken to control the monastic life of all nuns. Departing from the hitherto provincial and diocesan legislation, the new enactments comprehended in their scope all monasteries of nuns regardless of where they might be. For the first time in the history of the Church a universal obligation of strict enclosure within the confines of the cloister proceeded from the authoritative Chair of Peter.[1]

The history of the cloister up to this period has betrayed the fact that all too frequently nuns had forgotten the necessity of seeking safety within the sheltering walls of their monasteries. Constant prodding was demanded on the part of the various councils to remind them of this necessary feature of religious life. But even after so many centuries conditions were not universally improved. The true picture of conditions as they existed when the fourteenth century approached the horizon can be told by no greater authority than the Holy Father himself. This he has done in the opening words of his Constitution *"Periculoso."* [2]

[1] C. un., *de statu regularium,* III, 16, in VI°; Suarez, *De religione,* tract. VIII, lib. I, cap. VIII, n. 11; Navarrus (Martin de Azpilcueta), *Opera Omnia* (6 vols., Venetiis: 1618), tom. II, *Comment. IV de regularibus,* n. 39. Hereafter cited as *Comment. IV de regularibus.* Benedict XIV, *De Synodo Dioecesana* (Venetiis: 1775), tom. I, lib. XIII, cap. XII, n. XXIV; Ferraris, *Bibliotheca,* s. v. "Moniales," art. III, n. 2; Hollweck, *Die kirchlichen Strafgesetze* (Mainz: 1899), § 149, note 1.

[2] "Periculoso et detestabili quarandam Monialium statui (quae, honestatis laxatis habenis et monachali modestia sexusque verecundia impudenter abiectis, extra sua monasteria nonnumquam per habitacula secularium personarum discurrunt, et frequenter infra eadem monasteria personas suspectas admittunt, in illius, cui suam integritatem voluntate spontanea devoverunt, gravem offensam, in religionis opprobrium et scandalum plurimorum) providere salubriter cupientes . . . sancimus . . . c. un., *de statu regularium,* III, 16, in VI°.

In an effort to correct this lamentable condition Boniface VIII imposed upon all nuns, present and future, the strict obligation of thenceforth observing the rigorous and perpetual cloister. There was only one necessary condition, and that was based on profession. If, therefore, women had not yet made profession at the time this Constitution was promulgated, they were not bound by its obligation.[3]

Boniface VIII, however, extended this Constitution to include even those who were tacitly professed.[4] And profession, whether it was expressed or tacit, was still to be regarded as profession.[5] When Boniface VIII imposed this obligation upon professed members, he did not legislate for those nuns who before had professed the vow of the cloister. His law was not one which supposed a previous obligation and then restored it. This law was meant to impose the obligation. That there can be no question about this is evident from the fact that in inaugurating this obligation he used the words "*Presenti constitutione perpetuo irrefragabiliter valitura sancimus.*"[6] Moreover, the obligation extended to all nuns of every order.[7]

There was only one reason, as admitted by this Constitution, which enabled a nun to leave the cloister. That was a severe sickness or malady which did not permit the victim to live with the other nuns without grave danger.[8]

So rigorous was this law that only in virtue of a dispensation could there exist any other reason which permitted a nun to leave the monastery. And the dispensation had to proceed from the giver of the law, because no inferior could dispense from so absolute a

[3] Cf. Gloss to c. un., *de statu regularium,* III, 16, in VI°.

[4] ". . . ita quod nulli earum religionem tacite vel expresse professae . . ."—c. un., *de statu regularium,* III, 16, in VI°.

[5] Suarez, *De religione,* tract. VIII, lib. I, cap. VIII, n. 13.

[6] C. un., *de statu regularium,* III, 16, in VI°.

[7] ". . . universas et singulas moniales, praesentes atque futuras, cuiusque religionis sint vel ordinis, in quibuslibet mundi partibus existentes, sub perpetua in suis monasteriis debere de coetero permanere clausura . . ."—c. un., *de statu regularium,* III, 16, in VI°.

[8] ". . . nisi forte tanto et tali morbo evidenter earum aliquam laborare constaret, quod non posset cum aliis absque gravi periculo seu scandalo commorari . . ."—c. un., *de statu regularium,* III, 16, in VI°.

prohibition.[9] If, however, a nun desired for spiritual reasons to transfer to a more strict monastery, or if it was expedient that a nun be made superior of another monastery, then this Constitution permitted exit from the cloister. Its rigor was not so extensive as to include even these situations.[10]

Moreover, Boniface allowed abbesses and prioresses to leave the monastery when there arose the occasion of paying necessary homage and fidelity to the owner of the property on which the monastery was situated. Always, however, she had to be accompanied by other worthy persons, and there was to be absolutely no delay in returning. If this duty of homage could be performed by a procurator, then it was to be done in that way. The reason for the granted concession was founded on the fact that the common good of the nuns was imperiled if this homage and fidelity was not given.[11]

All temporal rulers were severely warned that any litigation affecting the monastery was to be carried out through procurators. Thus would the necessity of leaving the cloister be reduced to a minimum. Officials who refused to observe this command could be censured by their bishops. Citing women, and especially religious women, to civil trial was contrary to the law.[12]

But this Constitution was not confined to enclosing nuns within their cloisters. It likewise forbade persons to enter, or even to visit, the monasteries. Whereas in preceding legislation the exception was usually made for persons of proved integrity and of right intention, even these were now excluded from entering or visiting the monasteries of women. There was no distinction of sex. Men and women were included in this prohibition. No exceptions in favor of dignities were admitted. Consequently all clerics, even bishops, were included here. Whereas persons of ill fame and of dishonest intentions were always to be excluded, others were allowed this privilege when they

[9] Suarez, *De religione*, tract. VIII, lib. I, cap. VIII, n. 11.

[10] Cf. Gloss to c. un., *de statu regularium*, III, 16, in VI°.

[11] C. un., *de statu regularium*, III, 16, in VI°, § *Verum*; M. Bonacina, *Opera Omnia* (3 vols., Venetiis: 1775), *Tractatus De Clausura*, q. 1, p. IX, n. 9. Hereafter this work will be cited as *De Clausura*.

[12] C. un., *de statu regularium*, III, 16, in VI°; c. 2, *de iudiciis*, II, 1, in VI°. This question will be treated more at length in the following pages.

had a *rationabilis et manifesta causa*" PLUS the special permission of the proper authority.[13] The reason which Boniface VIII gave for this protection to nuns by the exclusion of externs from their monasteries succinctly epitomizes the life which they were to lead.[14]

Whereas Alexander III (1159-1181) had strongly forbidden frequent visiting of monasteries by clerics and laymen,[15] Boniface VIII went further and forbade absolutely not only the visiting (*accessus*), but also the entering (*ingressus*) of monasteries. There seems to be no foundation for any different interpretation of Boniface VIII, since he used the disjunctive phrase "*ingressus vel accessus*" in stating this prohibition.[16]

The causes which merited a grant of permission for entering the cloister had to be understood in the sense of causes which were necessary for the good of the monastery itself.[17]

To all patriarchs, primates, archbishops and bishops was confided under obedience the strict obligation of bringing to fulfillment each enactment of this Constitution. It was their duty to watch over the monasteries which were subject to themselves, and also over those monasteries which were directly subject to the Holy See. Jurisdiction over the latter was delegated to them by the Holy See. In convents subject to regulars, the superiors were bound in holy obedi-

[13] C. un., *de statu regularium,* III, 16, in VI°; cf. Gloss to c. un., *de statu regularium,* III, 16, in VI°; Suarez, *De religione,* tract. VIII, lib. I, cap. X, n. 2.

[14] "Ut sic a publicis, et mundanis conspectibus separatae, omnino Deo servire valeant liberius, et lasciviendi opportunitate sublata, eidem corda sua et corpora in omni sanctimonia diligentius custodire"—cf. c. un., *de statu regularium,* III, 16 in VI°.

[15] C. 8, X, *de vita et honestate clericorum,* III, 1.

[16] ". . . nullique aliquatenus inhonestae personae nec etiam honestae (nisi rationabilis et manifesta causa existat, ac de illius, ad quem pertinuerit, speciali licentia) ingressus vel accessus pateat ad easdem . . ."—c. un., *de statu regularium,* III, 16, in VI°; Suarez, *De religione,* tract. VIII, lib. I, cap. X, n. 24.

[17] Cf. Gloss to c. un., *de statu regularium,* III, 16, in VI°—". . . sicut in medicis, barbitonsoribus, sartoribus, carpentoribus cum eguerint, et his similibus . . ."; Suarez, *De religione,* tract. VIII, lib. I, cap. X, nn. 10, 16; Fagnanus, *Commentaria in Quinque Libros Decretalium* (4 vols., Venetiis: 1696), lib. III, *De Conver. Conjug.,* c. *Praeterea,* n. 18. Hereafter this work will be cited as *Commentaria.*

ence to erect a fitting cloister and enforce the law of enclosure for nuns. If these superiors appealed or resisted, they could, in order to make them comply with the law, be compelled by means of ecclesiastical censures which left no way open for appeal and, if necessary, the aid of the secular power could be invoked against them.[18]

Despite the full force and rigor of this Constitution, plus the fact that it was introducing for the first time a universal obligation to correct widespread abuses, Pope Boniface VIII did not incorporate in it the sanction of excommunication for the violation of this law by exit from or entry into the cloister.

When Boniface VIII decreed that women were not to be brought personally to civil judgment or trial, he made explicit mention of those nuns who were obliged to live within the cloister.[19] This was the special reason on account of which they were prohibited from appearing in person before a trial. Boniface VIII by his very reference to the obligation of the cloister implied that this decree was enacted before the time of his Constitution "*Periculoso.*"[20] Thus it appears certain that he made reference in the earlier decretal simply to those women who had vowed themselves to perpetual cloister at the time. Ioannes Andreae is authority for the statement that this decretal of Boniface VIII was issued before the compilation of *Liber Sextus.* It is true, on the other hand, that another gloss to this decretal cites "*Periculoso*" as authority for the extant obligation of the cloister. But it seems impossible to establish from this gloss in itself that its writer necessarily intended to imply that the cloistral obligation of which mention is made in the decretal "*Mulieres*" actually derived from the decretal "*Periculoso*" as the earlier law in this matter. It is quite conceivable that the writer of the gloss simply wanted to point to these two decretals as mutually corrobo-

[18] Suarez, *ibid.,* n. 10.

[19] C. 2, *de iudiciis,* II, 1, in VI°.

[20] "Coeterum foeminae religiosae, praesertim quae debent sub clausura morari . . ."—c. 2, *de iudiciis,* II, 1, in VI°. In their edition of the *Corpus Juris Canonici* Friedberg-Richter, in a footnote related to this decretal ("*Mulieres*"), vouch for the date of April 8, 1295. They accept March 3, 1298 (the date of promulgation of the *Liber Sextus*) as the date of the issuance of the decretal "*Periculoso.*"

rative enactments which obtained their binding force upon the promulgation of the *Liber Sextus*.[21]

In his decretal "*Mulieres,*" Boniface VIII prohibited the nuns' appearance at trials even when of themselves the nuns were willing to appear in person. And Ioannes Andreae (+1348) explained that some nuns even endeavored to be brought to civil trial in order that they might leave the cloister for a time.[22] The prohibition of Boniface VIII and the apposite remark of Ioannes Andreae throw light on the attitude which some nuns of that period entertained towards the law of cloistral observance. While the law did not attach any sanction of punishment for those who left the cloister under such circumstances, yet all the consequent judicial acts were declared to be void if in violation of the cloistral law the nuns appeared in court.

Article II. From the Constitution *Periculoso* to the Council of Trent

The difficulties encountered up to this time in confining the adherents of the monastic life to abiding residence within the cloister have been outlined. With reference to the nuns, there exists no doubt that the enactment of Boniface VIII was intended as a strict obligation which was to be zealously fulfilled and scrupulously obeyed by all. Since this Constitution did not incorporate any severe penal sanction directed specifically against the violation of the cloister, regardless of whether the violation occurred through prohibited entry or interdicted egress, and since its desired enforcement was confided to the watchful jurisdiction of the proper ecclesiastical authorities, the subsequent influence, reception and fate of this Constitution up to the time of the Council of Trent can best be manifested by a study of the conciliar and monastic legislation. It can well be surmised that the vast majority of cloistral laws enacted between the time of Pope Boniface VIII and the celebration of the Council of Trent concerned the convents of nuns.

21 Cf. Gloss to c. 2, *de iudiciis*, II, 1, in VI°.

22 *Loc. cit.*

A. Conciliar Legislation

1. Legislation Pertaining to Nuns

This legislation commenced a short time after the promulgation of the Constitution of Boniface VIII [23] with the salutary decree which emanated from the Synod of Autun in 1299.[24] Citing *Periculoso,* this Synod warned all nuns to live within the cloister. Only under pain of excommunication could any men, regardless of dignity and status, enter the monasteries of nuns, unless they had a necessary cause and the proper permission. Though not punishing nuns for illicit egress from the cloister, this Synod warned that severe penalties would befall anyone offering the shelter of his or her home to them.

In France the permission of the abbess coupled with a grave cause sufficed for a nun to leave the cloister. Permission could be given only under the requisite condition of an immediate return as soon as the reason for the absence ceased. Instruction given to boys and girls within the monastery was proscribed.[25]

Any nun guilty of leaving the cloister without proper permission incurred the sentence of excommunication in the archdiocese of Treves. As a means of reducing to a minimum any and all opportunities and temptations for leaving the cloister, the prioresses were charged with the strict guarding of all the keys of the cloistral portals. Special reference to nocturnal egress from the cloister was deemed necessary by this Council.[26]

That the profession of solemn vows was synonymous with the observance of the strict and perpetual cloister was reiterated by the Council of Cologne (1310), as it repeated in part the words of Boniface VIII. Those nuns whose monastic life was not in harmony with this statute within three months after its publication were regarded as having fallen into a state of excommunication.[27]

[23] The date of this Constitution was March 3, 1298—Cf. c. un., *de statu regularium,* III, 16 in VI°.

[24] C. 11—Mansi, XXXII, 312.

[25] Council of Bayeux (1300), c. 92—Mansi, XXV, 77.

[26] Council of Treves (1310), c. 47—Mansi, XXV, 261.

[27] C. 28—Mansi, XXV, 245.

In 1314 the III Council of Ravenna strictly distinguished between the act of visiting and the act of entering the cloister. Any lay man guilty of the former, inasmuch as he had not sought and obtained the permission of the bishop, incurred a pecuniary penalty which, if it was not paid within one month, broadened into immediate excommunication. A strict fast on bread and water twice a week for a month was the penalty incurred by an equally guilty monk. Failure to begin the fulfillment of this punishment within a month, as well as the refusal ever fully to complete it, involved the further penalty of excommunication for a wayward monk. The penalty of excommunication was suffered immediately, however, by those who entered within the cloister. A sentence of penance to be performed for a month in solitary confinement befell the nun who left the cloister but not the monastery. Excommunication was suffered by the nun who went farther and left even the monastery. Other penalties, humiliations and deprivations awaited her upon her return to the cloister.[28]

Three years later, however, the IV Council of Ravenna acceded to the supplications of many persons who, while possessing no evil intentions, had visited monasteries and thereby incurred the dire spiritual consequences enacted in the current legislation. The Council abrogated its previous enactments relative to the visiting of monasteries. The sole permission of the abbess or prioress was sufficient to enable any person who was not obviously malicious to converse with a nun.[29]

The institution of guards, appointed by the exempt superior or by the bishop, for the protection of the monasteries was established in Spain. Strangely enough, to these guards was delegated the faculty of granting all the needed permissions relative to the entering of or leaving from the cloister. Failure to obtain this permission brought excommunication for all who in a consequently unauthorized manner entered or left the monastery.[30]

Any aid or assistance given by an abbess or prioress to facilitate

[28] C. 11—Mansi, XXV, 544.

[29] IV Council of Ravenna, Rubr. 23—Mansi, XXV, 622.

[30] Council of Palencia (1322), c. 12—Mansi, XXV, 708.

the entry of a man into her monastery was visited with excommunication. A similar fate was experienced by the man.[31]

Recognizing and honoring the prerogatives of queens, of their retinue and of the sisters of the King, the Constitutions of the Diocese of Nicosia in Sicily graciously granted to these the privilege of entering the monasteries of nuns. Those who lacked such prerogatives when they entered the monastery, as well as those who introduced them, incurred excommunication. Exception was likewise made for the confessors of nuns specifically nominated by the bishop. The prerogative of this bishop to establish such exceptions may well be questioned here. It seems that the rights given to bishops by Pope Boniface VIII did not embrace this power.[32]

If there is any legislation which portrays in a vivid manner the dogged persistence in self-reliance and the utter disregard for authority as manifested by the actions of some nuns, it is the Synodal Statutes which emanated from the See of Cologne in the year 1327. Less than thirty years before, the decretal *"Periculoso"* of Pope Boniface VIII (1294-1303) had been rigorously promulgated in that diocese. Yet, despite sundry warnings, nuns were frequently leaving their cloister, disguising their identity in the garb of lay women and conducting themselves in a manner that not even charity when stretched to the utmost could excuse from grave sin. Consequently the Constitution of Boniface VIII and its specification of *one sole reason* for leaving the monastery was renewed. Permission was extended to abbesses and prioresses to leave the monastery on necessary business, but on the condition that they return without delay. Any cleric who celebrated divine services at which were present nuns who were illegitimately outside of their monastery was suspended *ab ingressu ecclesiae.* The extending of hospitality to any unwarrantedly absent nuns was punished with the severe penalty of excommunication. The nuns themselves were excommunicated *cum sententia vitanda.*[33]

[31] Synod of Perugia (1320)—Mansi, XXV, 641.

[32] Constitutions of June 17, 1321—Mansi, XXVI, 367.

[33] Synodal Statute of Henry, Archbishop of Cologne (1327)—*Concilia Germaniae* (11 vols., Coloniae Augustae Agrippinensium: 1759-1790), IV, 295.

In the Diocese of Ferrara in Italy a general permission to visit the monastery was extended to the immediate family of any nun professed therein. On each occasion an express permission of the bishop or of his delegate was demanded of all others under pain of fine for clerics, and of interdict *ab ingressu ecclesiae* for lay persons. Entry within the cloister merited excommunication for all.[34]

Similar penalties were enacted in the Council of Benevento (1331). Particular emphasis was given to the consideration of those chaplains and procurators who invoked false excuses and permissions for entering within the cloister.[35] The impression is conveyed that permissions allowing nuns to leave the monastery were freely given, for the Council inveighed against the actions of the nuns in eating outside the monastery. The license granted to anyone to enter within the cloister did not warrant the presumption that he also had the right to dine in the cloister, for if the latter act was not authorized by means of a specific permission it became punishable with excommunication.[36] A later council held at Benevento in the year 1378 listed the violations of the cloister, either on the part of the nuns or on the part of lay persons, among the sins which were deemed so pernicious that they were reserved for absolution to the bishop. Only *in articulo mortis* could the delinquents obtain absolution from others than the bishop.[37]

During the subsequent one hundred years few councils legislated on this aspect of monastic life. The councils which fortified their decrees with heavy sanctions were confined to Italy. Excommunication was imposed on those who violated the monastic cloister either from within or from without.[38]

[34] Constitutions of the Church of Ferrara (1334), Const. 40—Mansi, XXV, 921.

[35] C. 58—Mansi, XXV, 966.

[36] C. 59—Mansi, XXV, 967. Cf. also the Council of Benevento held in 1378 wherein these identical canons are repeated—Mansi, XXVI, 648-649.

[37] C. 42—Mansi, XXVI, 640.

[38] Cf. Council of Florence (1346)—Mansi, XXVI, 37; Council of Padua (1350)—Mansi, XXVI, 227; Constitutions of the Church of Lucca (1351), Const. 35—Mansi, XXVI, 269; Excommunications of the Bishop of Treviso (1390)—Mansi, XXVI, 762; Council of Constance (1414), tit. X, cap. XXI—Mansi, XXVIII, 333.

Navarrus attributes to Ioannes Andreae the statement that he himself had noted that the cloister, as regulated by Boniface VIII, was not observed in Venice.[39] While it is true that the statement which Navarrus attributes to Ioannes Andreae relative to the non-observance of the cloister in France is verifiable from the latter's writings, the contrary appears to obtain relative to the statement which is accredited to Ioannes Andreae concerning the practice in Venice.[40] Navarrus also cites the testimony of a literary work, known to him, which asserts that in Venice the authority of the civil law was employed against those who endeavored to constrain nuns to observe the perpetual cloister.[41]

A perusal of the councils held during the fifteenth century portrays the observance of the cloister in Venice at that time. Though it excommunicated nuns who left the cloister without permission, the I Synod of Venice extended the punishment of suspension from indulgences and from participation in the sacraments for entering the cloister only to those males whose ages ranged from twelve to sixty years.[42] Prescinding from the possibility that this Synod may have enjoyed special powers granted by the Holy See, the cited enactment appropriated to this Synod a power which certainly was not

[39] ". . . Ioan. Andreae dicit in Novell. super d. c. pri. (C. un. III, 16, in VI°) quod serebatur Galliam non recepisse clausuram Bonif. et quod ipse viderat Venetiis non servari . . ."—*Comment. IV de regularibus*, n. 41.

[40] ". . . Haec constitutio (periculoso) recepta non fuit in partibus Gallicanis, vidi etiam ipsam servari Venetiis quacumque ratione vel causa . . ."—Ioannes Andreae, *In Sextum Decretalium Librum*, c. un., de statu regularium, cap. I, in VI°. It is true that the obvious meaning of the words of Ioannes Andreae contradict Navarrus. It is possible, however, that the force of the word "*ipsam*" refers back to the non-reception of the cloister in France. Moreover, the phrase "*quacumque causa*" seems to leave at least possible room for a practice according to which lax dispensations were granted for any reason whatsoever.

[41] ". . . fictor casuum testatus ibidem (Venetiis) moniales quasdam defensas fuisse a perpetua clausura per senatum parlamenti a conantibus eas ad eam cogere."—Navarrus, *loc. cit.* The "*fictor casuum*" is referred to by Navarrus as commentating on the *Liber Sextus*. However, in view of the fact that no mention of this situation is contained in the "*casus*" appended to the Constitution "*Periculoso*," the conclusion is that Navarrus is citing some other work known to him.

[42] I Synod of Venice (1438)—Mansi, XXXIA, 346-347.

granted by Boniface VIII. The cause required by Pope Boniface was not to be judged, it seems, by the criterion of age.[43]

The II Synod of Venice (1438) allowed nuns to leave their cloister for the purpose of visiting the Cathedral Church and the Church of St. Mark in Venice.[44] Certainly this reason for leaving the enclosure was not implied in the one exception which Boniface allowed. And so, once again, this Synod appears to have taken unto itself unfounded authority and dispensatory powers.

Because some nuns complained vigorously about the imposition of this cloistral life which far exceeded that to which they had been accustomed and in which they had been initiated, the II Synod of Venice (1438) was forced once again to renew the Constitution of Boniface, and to invoke the sanction of excommunication against all nuns who refused to live according to its meaning. Moreover, the same penalty awaited those who extended hospitality to nuns who were violators of this decree.[45]

Since there arose some doubts concerning the extent and confines of the cloister, it was defined as being comprised by that section of the monastery which was required perpetually to be locked and barred. Entry into or egress beyond these limits constituted a violation of the cloister, punishable by excommunication.[46]

To insure its knowledge of all violations, the IV Synod of Venice (1438) enacted that under pain of incurring excommunication, suspension from office, interdict, incarceration, and other grave penalties, each abbess and prioress had to inform the bishop within six days of all the offenses committed in violation of the cloister in her monastery. At the risk of incurring the same penalties, each nun who knew of a violation was forced to inform the abbess within two days.[47]

During the last half of the fifteenth century, two councils in Germany recalled the obligation of the strict cloister and established

[43] "Nullique aliquatenus ingressus vel accessus pateat ad easdem . . ."—c. un., *de statu regularium*, III, 16, in VI°.

[44] Mansi, XXXIA, 347.

[45] Mansi, XXXIA, 348.

[46] III Synod of Venice (1438)—Mansi, XXXIA, 349.

[47] Mansi, XXXIA, 351.

severe punishments for all violations.[48] Though similar provisions were enacted in Bavaria [49] and in Austria [50] severe penalties were not invoked as penal sanctions.

The absence of conciliar legislation emanating from Spain during this period has been conspicuous. When the Council of Seville convened in the year 1512, the admission was voiced that many convents were not observing the strict cloister. Thenceforth, then, only with special permission of the archbishop could anyone enter or leave the cloister. Delegation of any faculties to minor officials to grant this permission was revoked. Excommunication was the sanction invoked to compel the observance of the cloistral regulations.[51]

The manner in which this legislation was observed was told by Suarez, himself a Spaniard, when he related that from his own experience he knew that the Constitution of Boniface VIII was not heeded in Spain.[52]

A similar story can be told about the conditions in France. The lack of French conciliar legislation on the observance of the cloister bespeaks an absence of initiative in ecclesiastical superiors in opposition to the wishes and command of Pope Boniface VIII. Ioannes Andreae (+1348) could testify to the non-observance of the decretal "*Periculoso*" in France during his time.[53] That this condition was not rectified in subsequent years may be concluded from the lack of conciliar legislation in that country. Only in 1528 did a council raise its voice in command to all bishops to renew within their dioceses the Constitution of Pope Boniface VIII. But since no penal sanction was attached to this law, one may readily deduce that the observance of the cloister was hardly urged with all the rigidity contemplated by Boniface VIII.[54]

[48] Council of Mainz (1451), cap. *de reformatione monasteriorum*—Mansi, XXXII, 139; Council of Magdeburg (1489)—Mansi, XXXII, 461.

[49] Council of Freising (1440), c. 12—Mansi, XXXII, 10.

[50] Council of Salzburg (1490)—Mansi, XXXII, 508.

[51] C. 25—Mansi, XXXII, 664.

[52] *De religione*, tract. VIII, lib. I, cap. VIII, n. 12.

[53] *In Sextum Decretalium Librum*, c. un., *de statu regularium*, cap. I, in VI°.

[54] Council of Sens, c. 28—Mansi, XXXII, 1195.

In an effort to justify the non-observance of the cloister in the diocese of Hildesheim in Germany, it was asserted that the Constitution of Boniface VIII had fallen into desuetude. Ignoring such assertions, the bishop renewed that Constitution under pain of suspension for ecclesiastics, and of excommunication for lay persons, if they refused to obey its enactments. Continuous persistence of superiors and procurators in disregarding this ruling also resulted in their excommunication.[55]

Closing the conciliar legislation prior to the Council of Trent are two councils in Germany and in France. Repeating the words of Boniface VIII, the bishops congregated at Mainz decreed excommunication for lay persons, and suspension for clerics, who freely entered the convents of women.[56] At the Councils celebrated in Treves and in Narbonne no penal sanctions were incorporated in the statutes, but the various enactments otherwise followed the rigid pattern of the "*Periculoso.*"[57]

2. *Legislation Pertaining to Monks*

(a) The *Clementinae*

The portrayal by Pope Clement V (1305-1314) of monastic life as it existed in some places is indeed a bleak and discouraging one. Not only had monks forgotten their pristine fervor, but, what was worse, they took refuge in the fallacy that life within the monastery was not secure. Pope Clement V, in the Council of Vienne (1311-1312), forbade monks to leave the cloister except in fulfillment of administrative duties which it was their task to perform. More time was being spent within the palaces of the secular powers than within the enclosure of the monastery. The obligation rested upon the superiors to enforce the monastic rule of life. Constant and unwarranted absence from the monastery was not a part of that pattern. Thus, severe penalties were necessary and these had necessarily to

[55] Council of Hildesheim (1539), cap. 30—*Concilia Germaniae*, VI, 329.

[56] Council of Mainz (1549), c. 79—Mansi, XXXII, 1429.

[57] Council of Treves (1549), c. 11—Mansi, XXXII, 1449; Council of Narbonne (1551), c. 55—Mansi, XXXIII, 1274.

be employed by the superiors in order to obtain the desired result of disciplinary reform.[58]

(b) Provincial Councils

A similar chaotic discipline in monastic life had occasioned the corrective legislation enacted by the Council of Treves in 1310. Only when the necessity of the monastery warranted an absence from it by any monk was it licit for the superior to grant permission for such an absence. Excessive liberality on the part of the abbot in his interpretation of what constituted a righteous cause for permitting a monk to be absent from his monastery resulted in the abbot's excommunication.[59] Moreover, any monk who left the monastery without having first obtained the needed permission was similarly excommunicated. The special permission of the abbot was essential before any woman could be introduced into the cloister of the monastery. This permission in no way included any license for her to dine therein.[60]

In the I Synod of Venice (1438) the legislation concerning the necessity on the part of the monks to procure the permission of the abbot before they left the monastery was repeated.[61] But the anomalous feature of this law was that in the III Synod there was need to censure the abbots themselves for frequent and delayed absence.[62]

The legislation which emanated from the Council of Seville in the year 1512 attained new heights of severity in its demands regarding the requisite residence within the cloister. Reserved excommunication befell not only nuns who left the cloister, but likewise monks. In view of all former enactments, this one was extremely severe.[63]

58 C. 1 (*Ne in agro,* § 5), *de statu monachorum,* III, 10, in Clem.

59 C. 28—Mansi, XXV, 257.

60 C. 47—Mansi, XXV, 261.

61 Cap. 29, *de regularibus*—Mansi, XXXIA, 346.

62 Mansi, XXXIA, 349.

63 Cap. 25: ". . . si aliquis reclusus seu reclusa foras exierit, ex nunc pro tunc et tunc pro nunc pronunciamus super eo sententiam excommunicationis maioris . . ."—Mansi, XXXII, 644.

B. Monastic Legislation

Within the Monastic Orders themselves the legislation became more rigid and drastic. A few citations from various Apostolic enactments will suffice to manifest that increase of rigor.

1. Legislation Pertaining to Nuns

Because apparently the Constitution *"Periculoso"* of Pope Boniface VIII (1294-1303) had been honored more in the breach than in the fulfillment, the abbess and nuns of the Convent of St. Dominic in Pisa pleadingly appealed to Pope Urban VI (1378-1389) for intervention. As a consequence, excommunication awaited any man who presumed to enter the monastery. Concessions were granted the Master General of the Dominicans and the Provincial to enter once a year with an aged companion for the purpose of canonical visitation. Moreover, at the time of the veiling ceremonies, as well as at the time when their services were required for administering the last rites and for assisting at funerals, a Dominican priest and an associate, who acted as his companion, were accorded the privilege of entering the monastery.

Excommunication reserved to the Holy Father himself was incurred by anyone who dared to remove the grate which was erected in the visiting room.[64] Later Pontiffs repeated the enactment of that Bull in its entirety.[65]

The exemption which had been granted for use at times of the veiling ceremonies and also at funerals, was the occasion of grave danger in the monastery at Pisa. At the instance of the abbess, that privilege was revoked and subsequent use of it meant excommunication reserved to the Holy See.[66]

It had been necessary for Pope Benedict XII (1334-1342) to warn the Poor Clares to live not only according to the dictates of

[64] Urbanus VI, Bulla *"Ut inter,"* 25 iul. 1387—*Bull. O. P.*, VII, 65.

[65] Cf. Martinus V, Bulla *"Ut inter,"* 19 febr. 1420—*Bull. O. P.*, II, 578; Eugenius IV, Bulla *"Iis quae pro,"* 21 maii 1435—*Bull. O. P.*, III, 36; Bulla *"Ex Apostolicae Sedis,"* 29 maii 1435—*Bull. O. P.*, III, 38; Pius II, Bulla *"Circumspecta,"* 1 febr. 1460—*Bull. O. P.*, III, 400.

[66] Martinus V, Const. *"Pia supplicum,"* 9 apr. 1426—*Bull. O. P.*, II, 665.

their Rule in reference to the cloister, but also to observe strictly the Constitution of Pope Boniface VIII. Once again the rigidity of the Rule was recalled in regard to the exclusion both of the laity and of the Friars Minor.

The punishments for those nuns who left the cloister without permission consisted in their absolute disqualification for the acquisition of any offices or dignities in the Order, and also in their subjection to the specified penalties contained in the Rule for serious offenses. Abbesses who left the cloister or who granted permission for other nuns to go out were subject to removal from office.[67]

A reiteration of the prohibition against the entry of Friars Minor within the cloister of any convents was issued by Pope Martin V (1417-1431).[68]

2. Legislation Pertaining to Monks

Foreshadowing future universal legislation was the Bull *"Regularem vitam,"* issued by Pope Eugene IV (1431-1447) to the Benedictine Monks of the Congregation of St. Justin. In virtue of that Bull the penalty of excommunication was incurred by any woman who entered the cloister of the monasteries of those monks. The same punishment awaited those monks who in any way co-operated in effecting the entry of women into the cloister. No exceptions were admitted regarding either persons or occasions. Absolution from these penalties could be given by the canonical visitors and the major superiors.[69]

[67] Bulla *"Redemptor noster,"* 28 nov. 1336, § 33—*Bull. Rom.*, IV, p. 391.
[68] Bulla *"Cum generale,"* 21 iun. 1430—*Bull. Rom.*, IV, p. 733, n. 11.
[69] 30 iun. 1436—*Bull. Rom.*, V, 21.

CHAPTER III

COUNCIL OF TRENT UP TO THE PRESENT CODE

Article I. The Council of Trent

A. Decree on the Cloister of Nuns

In its last session, held on the third and fourth of December in the year 1563, the Council of Trent legislated on the cloister of nuns.[1] Recognizing the lamentable failure of some nuns, lay persons, and bishops to fulfill perfectly the Constitution of Boniface VIII (1294-1303), the Council renewed that enactment and once again imposed upon all bishops the strict obligation of bringing it to its desired fruition.[2]

Invoking the aid of the civil power in effecting this desired result, the Council of Trent enacted an excommunication for any magistrates who refused to obey this command.[3]

The persistence of some nuns in seeking excuses in the law is manifested by the quibbling which arose from the apparent lack of clarity in the terminology employed by the Fathers of this Council. Basing their arguments on the words of the Council which stated:

> " . . . clausuram Sanctimonialium, ubi violata est, diligenter restitui; et ubi inviolata est, conservari maxime procuret . . . "

some nuns asserted that since in their monasteries the cloister never was observed and, consequently, never was violated, they were not

[1] Sess. XXV, *de regularibus*, c. 5.

[2] "Bonifacii Octavi constitutionem . . . renovans sancta Synodus universis Episcopis, sub obtestatione divini judicii, et interminatione maledictionis aeternae, praecipit, ut in omnibus monasteriis sibi subjectis, ordinaria, in aliis vero Sedis Apostolicae auctoritate clausuram Sanctimonialium, ubi violata fuerit, diligenter restitui; et ubi inviolata est, conservari maxime procuret; inobedientes atque contradictores per censuras ecclesiasticas . . . compescentes. . . ."—Sess. XXV, *de regularibus*, c. 5.

[3] "Quod auxilium ut praebeatur, omnes Christianos Principes hortatur sancta Synodus, et sub excommunicationis poena, ipso facto incurrenda, omnibus magistratibus secularibus injungit. . . ."—Sess. XXV, *de regularibus*, c. 5.

bound by the decree of the Council of Trent. Navarrus (1493-1586) related that this objection was thrust at him in Spain.[4] Moreover, had those nuns studied further into this Session of the Council of Trent, they would have found there the unequivocal answer to their objections.[5]

Though the Council of Trent forbade any professed nun to leave the cloister, it mitigated the severe regulation of Boniface VIII pertinent to the reason which justified her egress. Whereas Boniface in his legislation allowed only one severe exception, the Council of Trent extended this exception to include any legitimate cause approved by the bishop.[6]

The Council of Trent did not wish to confine its interpretation of a legitimate cause to the meaning contained in the Constitution of Boniface.[7] One of the causes permitting a nun to leave the

[4] *Comment. IV de regularibus,* n. 44. Cf. Suarez, *De religione,* tract. VIII, lib. I, cap. VIII, n. 14; Bonacina, *De Clausura,* q. 1, p. XI, n. 2.

[5] "Haec omnia et singula in superioribus decretis contenta, observari sancta Synodus praecipit in omnibus coenobiis ac monasteriis . . . quarumcumque Sanctimonialium virginum. . . ."—Sess. XXV, *de regularibus,* c. 22.

[6] ". . . Nemini autem Sanctimonialium licet post professionem exire a monasterio etiam ad breve tempus, quocumque praetextu, nisi ex aliqua causa, ab Episcopo approbanda; indultis quibuscumque et privilegiis non obstantibus. . . ."—Sess. XXV, *de regularibus,* c. 5.

". . . Sancimus universas et singulas moniales . . . sub perpetua in suis monasteriis debere de cetero permanere clausura ita, quod nulli earum, religionem tacite vel expresse professae, sit vel esse valeat quacumque ratione vel causa (nisi forte tanto et tali morbo evidenter earum aliquam laborare constaret, quod non posset cum aliis absque gravi periculo seu scandalo commorari) monasteria ipsa deinceps egrediendi facultas . . ."—c. un., *de statu regularium,* III, 16, in VI°.

[7] Suarez, *De religione,* tract. VIII, lib. I, cap. IX, n. 2. This was, Suarez relates, the mind of the Council and the common acceptation at that time. This mitigation introduced by the Council of Trent resulted from the weighty consideration given this question by the Fathers of the Council. Navarrus offers the suggestion that probably they considered the proverb of Solomon (Prov. xxx. 33) which counseled moderation, as well as the psychological nature of women which innately seems to demand company and consolation. Moreover, the Fathers, so he notes, undoubtedly recalled the observation of Ioannes Andreae that there was never compliance with the Constitution of Boniface in France and in Venice. These facts led them to adopt a different approach to

cloister and to take up residence in another monastery was the necessity of providing a worthy abbess for that monastery. This cause was stated explicitly by the Council itself.[8] But as subsequent legislation proved, the fulfillment of this transference necessitated a permission granted by the Holy See.[9]

Entry into the cloister (*septa*) of the monastery without the written permission of the bishop or of some superior meant excommunication for everybody involved.[10]

When the Council used the word *septa,* it referred this term to that part of the monastery which was enclosed by walls, or which was always kept firmly locked, and beyond which the nuns were not allowed to go.[11] Thus the permission to enter the monastery was to be given by the bishops in the case of monasteries which were subject directly to them or to the Holy See, and by the properly estab-

the problem. Cf. Navarrus, *Comment. IV de regularibus,* nn. 40-41. Suarez explained that the Council wisely considered that the nuns could more easily be induced to observe a precept which admitted of some relaxation than one which was unbendingly rigid.—*De religione,* tract. VIII, lib. I, cap. IX, n. 1.

[8] ". . . Quod si his qualitatibus non reperiatur in eodem monasterio, ex alio eiusdem Ordinis eligi possit. . . ."—Sess. XXV, *de regularibus,* c. 7.

[9] S. C. Concilii, resp. in dubium ad c. 5—S. Pallottini, *Collectio omnium Conclusionum et Resolutionum quae a causis propositis apud Sacram Congregationem Cardinalium S. Concilii Tridentini interpretum prodierunt* . . . (18 vols., Romae: 1868-1893), s. v. "Monasteria Monialium," § 11, n. 93. Hereafter cited as Pallottini, "Monasteria Monialium." If no date is given to decisions of the Sacred Congregation of the Council which are taken from Pallottini, it will be because he has not given any date. A. Bizzarri, *Collectanea in usum Secretariae Sacrae Congregationis Episcoporum et Regularium* (Romae: 1863), p. 230. Hereafter cited as Bizzarri, "Collectanea." Herein is given a reply of Gregory XIII (1572-1585) explaining that Pius V (1566-1572) had corrected this statement of the Council of Trent. Permission of the Holy See was necessary—cf. S. C. Ep. et Reg. *Hispaniarum,* 16 iul. 1884—*Codicis Iuris Canonici Fontes cura Emi. Petri Card. Gasparri Editi* (9 vols., Romae [postea Civitate Vaticana]: Typis Polyglottis Vaticanis, 1923-1939)—n. 2010. Hereafter cited as *Fontes.*

[10] Sess. XXV, *de regularibus,* c. 5.

[11] "Septa autem monasterii non appellantur cubiculum aliquod, sed murus quo habitatio monialium clauditur, ut constat ex communi usu vocis"—Suarez, *De religione,* tract. VIII, lib. I, cap. X, n. 8; cf. *ibid.,* n. 6; Bonacina, *De Clausura,* q. IV, p. I, n. 1; Reiffenstuel, *Jus Canonicum Universum* (5 vols. in 7, Parisiis: 1864-1870), lib. III, tit. XXXV, nn. 26, 27.

lished prelate who had jurisdiction over exempt monasteries. The bounds of each one's jurisdiction were thus established.[12] The requirement that this permission be in writing was absolutely to be fulfilled if the sentence of excommunication was to be avoided.[13] This condition was meant to apply, too, in ordinary cases (doctors, confessors, etc.) as well as in the extraordinary instances.[14] An exception from this rule was to be allowed, however, whenever there was danger consequent upon delay in obtaining the written permission.[15]

The Council of Trent, in demanding the presence of a necessary cause before admittance into the cloister could be allowed, seems to have required more than an equivalent of the *rationabilis et manifesta causa* which was demanded by Boniface VIII in his legislation regarding the entry of externs. Though the judgment concerning this cause rested with the bishops and superiors, they were not to be over-indulgent in interpreting what constituted necessity. On the other hand, not only physical but also moral necessity was sufficient. Moreover, the necessity had to be something which attached to the monastery itself, and not simply something which was connected with those who sought entry.[16]

In closing the present consideration of the legislation on the cloister one may note that the Council of Trent authorized bishops and monastic superiors to transfer to the city or to towns those nuns

[12] Bonacina, *De Clausura,* q. IV, p. II, nn. 1-3; Suarez, *De religione,* tract. VIII, lib. I, cap. X, nn. 13-15; Navarrus, *Comment. IV, de regularibus,* n. 60; Ferraris, *Bibliotheca,* s. v. "Moniales," art. III, n. 88.

[13] Suarez, *De religione,* tract. VIII, lib. I, cap. X, n. 15.

[14] Bonacina, *De Clausura,* q. IV, p. III, n. 2, contra Reiffenstuel, *ibid.,* n. 60, and Schmalzgrueber, *Ius Ecclesiasticum Universum* (5 vols. in 12, Romae: 1843-1845), lib. III, tit. XXXV, n. 124.

[15] Bonacina, *loc. cit.*; Reiffenstuel, *ibid.,* n. 59; Schmalzgrueber, *loc. cit.*

[16] "Dare autem tantum Episcopus vel Superior licentiam debet in casibus necessariis. . . ."—Sess. XXV, *de regularibus,* c. 5. ". . . nullique aliquatenus inhonestae personae, nec etiam honestae (nisi rationabilis et manifesta causa existat, ac de illius ad quem pertinuerit speciali licentia) ingressus vel accessus pateat ad easdem . . ."—c. un., *de statu regularium,* III, 16, in VI°. Cf. Bonacina, *De Clausura,* q. IV, p. IV, nn. 1, 2; Benedictus XIV, Const. "*Salutare,*" 3 ian. 1742, § 3—*Fontes,* n. 323.

whose convents were located in the country where they were exposed without protection to the wiles of wicked men. And resistance to this decree, whether by disobedience or through other modes of opposition, was punishable with ecclesiastical censures.[17]

B. *Decree on the Cloister of Monks*

The legislation of the Council of Trent relative to the cloister of men was very brief. The long-standing rule which demanded the obtaining of permission before any monk could rightfully leave the cloister was renewed by the Fathers of the Council. The employment of any pretexts for gaining egress from the monastery was rigidly prohibited. The plea of visiting one's superior was not to be employed unless the monk had been sent for or called upon to appear before his superiors. And then, of course, his leaving of the monastery was an act which was performed under obedience and not under an unjustifiable pretext. But it was absolutely necessary that he possess an indication in writing that his act was performed under obedience. Any monk who did not possess such a written vindication for his act of departure from the monastery could be punished by the local ordinary as a deserter of his community.[18]

Article II. The Council of Trent to the Constitution *Apostolicae Sedis*

A. *Legislation Pertaining to Monks*

1. Leaving the Monastery

Mention has been made of the various councils and decrees which insisted upon the observance of the cloister of monks. The binding force of this obligation had failed by far to approach the severity of the obligation which had been placed upon nuns. It was required

[17] Sess. XXV, *de regularibus,* c. 5.

[18] ". . . Nec liceat regularibus a suis conventibus recedere, etiam praetextu ad Superiores suos accedendi, nisi ab eisdem missi aut vocati fuerint. Qui vero sine praedicto mandato, in scriptis obtento, repertus fuerit, ab Ordinariis locorum tamquam desertor sui instituti puniatur."—Sess. XXV, *de regularibus,* c. 4.

always that proper permission be obtained from the superior. All of this was reaffirmed by Pope Clement VIII (1592-1605) in his Constitution "*Nullus omnino.*" [19] The purpose motivating this Constitution was the protection of the monks. In each monastery a trustworthy custodian appointed by the Superior was to guard the exits so diligently that only upon the obtaining of the proper permission was any monk allowed to go out. The necessary permission was granted by the superior only for a just cause. On each occasion specific permission was necessary to leave the house. General permissions were explicitly excluded, and even special permissions were not given except on the condition that the monk have a companion of the superior's choice. Moreover, the assignment of one and the same companion to any monk was proscribed.[20]

Those monks who disobeyed these rules, as well as the custodian who winked at their violation, were punished by grave penalties to be imposed as the superior judged fit. The penalty of incarceration was explicitly mentioned as one of those which the superior might well choose.[21]

Six years before, Pope Clement VIII indicated the possibility on the part of religious superiors of establishing as a reserved sin stealthy and nocturnal egress from the monastery.[22]

2. Entry of Women into the Cloister

The lack of the Council of Trent to legislate on the exclusion of women from the monasteries of men was provided for by Pope St. Pius V (1566-1572) in his Constitution "*Regularium.*" [23]

[19] 25 iul. 1599—*Bull. Rom.*, X, 662.

[20] Const. "*Nullus omnino,*" § 12: "Nullus e conventu egredi audeat, nisi ex causa et cum socio, licentiaque singulis vicibus impetrata . . . qui non aliter eam concedat, nisi causa probat; sociumque exituro adjungat, non petentis rogatu, sed arbitrio suo, neque eumdem saepius. Licentiae vero generales exeundi nulli omnino concedantur. . . ."—*Bull. Rom.*, X, 664-665.

[21] Const. "*Nullus omnino,*" § 12—*Bull. Rom.*, X, 664-665.

[22] Decr. "*Sanctissimus Dominus,*" 26 maii 1593, § 1, n. 2—*Fontes*, n. 177. Cf. S. Quaranta, *Summa Bullarii* (Venetiis: 1622), p. 423.

[23] 24 oct. 1566—*Fontes*, n. 115.

Heedless of the dictates inherent in their native sense of modesty, and taking refuge in the pretext that they were fulfilling religious duties, women were frequenting the monasteries of men all too often. This practice proved not only a source of annoyance for the monks, but it occasioned scandal as well. With such thoughts in mind, Pope Pius V determined to correct this abuse. His first step was to derogate each and every privilege which had ever been granted to any woman, regardless of her superior social standing and prerogatives, to permit her to enter into the monasteries of monks.[24] Desiring to insure once and for all the absolute observance of his revocation of past privileges in this regard, Pope Pius V declared

[24] "Nomine Clausurae Conventuum, in quam est foeminis interdictus ingressus, intelligitur totum illud spatium quod intra septa Monasterii, seu Conventus continetur, id est Claustra, Cellae, Officinae, Coenaculum, seu Refectorium, Dormitorium, Infirmaria, Coquina, et huiusmodi"—Ferraris, *Bibliotheca,* s. v. "Conventus," art. III, n. 9. Ferraris gives this statement as the common opinion of all. Cf. Bonacina, *De Clausura,* q. V, p. I, n. 1; Reiffenstuel, *Jus Canonicum,* lib. III, tit. XXXV, n. 26.

Gardens and fields are within the cloister if they are enclosed by the monastery wall—S. C. Ep. et Reg., *Ordinis Praedicatorum,* 24 apr. 1582—*Fontes,* n. 1394; *Arben.,* 3 iun. 1606—*Fontes,* n. 1640. Cf. Ferraris, *loc. cit.,* wherein other decisions of the Congregation of Bishops and Regulars are cited; Bonacina, *ibid.,* n. 6; Reiffenstuel, *loc. cit.*

Whether the sacristy had to be considered as being with the cloister was determined by the position of its door. If its one and only door led to the cloister, then the sacristy was included. Ferraris, *ibid.,* n. 12; Bonacina, *ibid.,* n. 4. These authors held the opposite view if the door led into the church. Cf. S. C. Ep. et Reg., *Aretina,* 8 aug. 1614—*Fontes,* n. 1661.

If the two doors led into the sacristy, one from the church and one from the cloister, the sacristy was to be considered as in the cloister. Cf. Bonacina, *loc. cit.* and Ferraris, *ibid.,* n. 14, wherein corroborative decisions of the Congregation of Bishops and Regulars are cited. Ferraris (+1763) notes, however, that it was not the practice in such a case to regard the sacristy as part of the cloister. And Bonacina (+1631) stated at an earlier time that there was no scrupulous observance which dealt with the sacristy as forming part of the cloister, for it was not entirely evident that the sacristy in such a case was within the cloister. The choir of the church was not to be considered as being within the cloister—F. Piatus, *Praelectiones Iuris Regularis* (3. ed., 2 vols., Tornaci: Casterman, 1906), I, p. 353, q. 6. Hereafter to be cited as *Praelectiones.* Cf. Bonacina, *ibid.,* n. 3. The opposite obtained if the choir could be entered only from the cloister—Piatus, *loc. cit.*; Ferraris, *loc. cit.*

that any women who had knowledge of the fact that their privilege was of no use and yet continued to employ it incurred an excommunication reserved to the Holy See in all cases outside of the danger of death.[25]

As a further precaution to effect the desired inviolability of the cloister, Pope Pius V saw himself compelled to legislate against the monks themselves. The sentence of suspension *a divinis*, and the privation of all present offices plus the incapacitation to receive any future offices awaited all those monastic superiors and monks who presumed to introduce or admit women into the monastery. It is noted that the element of presumption had to be present before these penalties were incurred.[26]

Prescinding, now, from the case in which some pretext of privilege was urged, one may well raise the question relative to the punishment incurred by those women who entered the monasteries absolutely on their own authority. Were they equally excommunicated? The query loses the aspect of mere theory in view of the fact that later in his reign Pope Pius V declared that it had been and in fact still was his intention to include in his prohibition even such women as had not at any previous time shared any privileges or prerogatives in the matter of entering the cloister.[27]

Even a further explanation and interpretation of his former Constitution "*Regularium*" was given by Pope Pius V. He declared that in that Constitution it had not been his intention to exclude women from attending Masses, processions, funerals, and other divine services conducted in the monasteries of monks. Moreover, he asserted that when the size of the congregation forbade easy entry and exit through the doors of the monastic church, it was perfectly licit for women to use an entrance which led into the cloister, provided al-

[25] Const. "*Regularium,*" 24 oct. 1566, § 3—*Fontes,* n. 115.

[26] Const. "*Regularium,*" 24 oct. 1566, § 4—*Fontes,* n. 115; Bonacina, *De Clausura,* q. V, p. III, n. 1.

[27] Const. "*Decet,*" 16 iul. 1570, § 2—*Fontes,* n. 136. Cf. Bonacina, *De Clausura, loc. cit.*; Fagnanus, *Commentaria,* lib. V, *De sent. excomm.*, c. XXIX, *Nuper.* n. 36; Suarez (*De religione,* tract. VIII, lib. I, cap. VII, n. 9) declares that his opinion was necessarily altered; Navarrus, *Comment. IV, de regularibus,* n. 62; Reiffenstuel, *Jus Canonicum,* lib. III, tit. XXXV, nn. 71-77.

ways that in so doing they continued immediately to the door of the monastery which led to the outside.[28]

It seems that the exception granted by Pope Pius V opened the door of the monasteries to women in a far different manner than he had either intended or expected. In view of the fact that within a very few years Pope Gregory XIII felt constrained to revoke all privileges previously given, and in view also of the fact that serious penalties again befell the users of these revoked privileges, it can well be surmized that there had been grave abuse of the generosity of Pope Pius V. In his Constitution *"Ubi gratiae,"* Gregory XIII declared that any presumptuous entering of monasteries under the pretext of privileges previously granted, but by him universally revoked, meant excommunication reserved exclusively to the Holy See in all cases which did not involve the *articulus mortis.*[29]

Whereas among the penalties decreed by Pope Pius V no excommunication had been threatened against monastic superiors and monks who co-operated in effecting entry of women into their monasteries, this most drastic of ecclesiastical punishments was added by Pope Gregory XIII. Moreover, no longer was it a requisite that the element of presumption be present. No mention of this added element of guilt was contained in the Constitution *"Ubi gratiae."*

It was the mind of Pope Gregory XIII to legislate against those women who continued to employ privileges to gain entry into monasteries in spite of the fact that they had been revoked either by Pope Pius V or by himself. It would have been futile, however, for any woman to think that, because in entering a monastery she was invoking no privilege, therefore she did not suffer the excommunication consequent upon the prohibited entry. Even if Pope Gregory XIII had not meant to include such a forbidden entry under his punitive sanctions, it certainly was so included in the Constitution

[28] Const. *"Decet,"* 16 iul. 1570, §§ 3, 4—*Fontes,* n. 136. Though the present Constitution was directed to the Carthusians of the Monastery of Monte Vergine, it must not be understood as applying solely to that monastery. Pope Pius V declared in this enactment that he intended to interpret his previous Constitution *"Regularium"* which, though likewise issued to the Carthusians, was specifically declared to embrace all Orders.

[29] 13 iun. 1575, §§ 1-2—*Fontes,* n. 147.

"Regularium" of Pope Pius V. The force of that Constitution was in no way diminished by the enactment of Gregory.[30]

Moreover, the Sacred Congregation of the Council invoked the Constitutions *"Regularium"* and *"Decet"* of Pius V as well as the enactment *"Ubi gratiae"* of Pope Gregory XIII as authority for declaring that even those women who entered monasteries under the pretext of hospitality were excommunicated together with those monks who permitted such entry to be made.[31]

Notwithstanding the evident sense of the revocatory words employed by Pope Gregory XIII in his Constitution *"Ubi gratiae,"* much unjustified discussion revolved about the continued validity of the privileges accorded to women by Pope Pius V to enter monasteries on certain designated occasions. Some authors conceded the continuance of those privileges.[32]

Quite the opposite is that which may be manifested by a perusal of several decisions of the Sacred Congregations. Certainly any processions which were to be held should not follow a course leading through the cloister.[33]

Only with special permission originating from the Holy See were women allowed to enter the monasteries of men—even on occasions of divine services, and, in particular, in the event of sacred processions. This was certainly the mind of the Bishop of Narni in petitioning for the faculty to absolve those women who had entered the cloister on the occasion of a procession. The faculty was granted to absolve *ad cautelam.*[34]

[30] Cf. Const. *"Regularium,"* 24 oct. 1566—*Fontes,* n. 115.

[31] 11 mart. 1623—*Fontes,* n. 2437; cf. also S. C. Ep. et Reg., *Ferrarien.,* 10 maii 1743—*Fontes,* n. 1859.

[32] Schmalzgrueber, *Ius Ecclesiasticum,* lib. III, tit. XXXV, n. 130; Reiffenstuel, *Jus Canonicum,* lib. III, tit. XXXV, n. 74; Ferraris, *Bibliotheca,* s. v. "Conventus," art. III, n. 26; Bonacina, *De Clausura,* q. V, p. IV, nn. 6-11. While declaring (q. V, p. IV, n. 1) that no privileges granted before the Pontificates of Pope Pius V and Gregory XIII were of any subsequent value, Bonacina does make an exception for those particular privileges which were granted afterwards, *i. e.,* by later Popes.

[33] S. C. Ep. et Reg., *Faventina,* 24 ian. 1595—*Fontes,* n. 1531; *Caven.,* 22 febr. 1595, ad 3—*Fontes,* n. 1533.

[34] S. C. Ep. et Reg., *Narnien.,* 21 apr. 1577—*Fontes,* n. 1329.

That this was the mind of the Sacred Congregation of Rites may be gathered from its proscription of a contrary custom which was reported from the diocese of Alicante in Spain.[35] When the bishop of that diocese asked persistently whether this proscription was true in spite of the privileges accorded by Pope Pius V, the Congregation retaliated with the firm reply that not only must its former decree be observed, but also that since Pius V's Constitution preceded that of Gregory XIII, the latter's revoked the former's.[36]

That this practice must have been widespread is indicated by the sweeping prohibition which the Sacred Congregation of Rites issued a few years later in an endeavor to stop such customs.[37]

With the advent of Pope Benedict XIV (1740-1758) to the throne of St. Peter, all doubts which any women might yet erroneously have entertained about the licitness of entry into the cloister of men were dissipated. Women were not only relieved of their doubts, but they were also deprived of any and all privileges which perhaps they had obtained relative to this matter.

Reasserting the rigor of the old law and renewing its full vigor, Benedict XIV in his Constitution "*Regularis disciplinae,*" determined once and for all to establish the inviolability of the monasteries of men.[38] He recalled the fact that before as well as after the Council of Trent women had been forbidden under penalty of excommunication to approach and enter the cloister of men. Wishing now to restore the security and privacy of monasteries, he renewed and confirmed all of the Constitutions and Decrees of his predecessors, whether they issued before or after the Council of Trent. Thenceforth, not only were those enactments to be observed

[35] S. R. C., *Oriolen,* 30 sept. 1628—*Fontes,* n. 5308.

[36] *Oriolen,* 11 iun. 1629—*Fontes,* n. 5308.

[37] "Emi DD. Patres mandarunt: 'Extrahi Decretum prohibitivum, consulto SS'mo, quod mulieres de cetero non possint occasione quarumvis Processionum ingredi septa Monasteriorum Regularium, et quod sub eadem poena comprehendantur ipsi Regulares permittentes foeminas ingredi septa eorum Monasteriorum."—S. R. C., *Urbis et Orbis Regularium,* 5 iul. 1631—*Fontes,* n. 5337. Cf. also similar decisions given in subsequent years. S. R. C., *Sulmonen.,* 24 nov. 1635—*Fontes,* n. 5360; *Cusentina,* 10 dec. 1667—*Fontes,* n. 5568.

[38] 3 ian. 1742—*Fontes,* n. 322.

rigidly, but also the sundry penalties were to be applied according to the full measure of their potential punitive force.[39]

Revoking, then, all faculties which any person might have enjoyed as permitting entry into the cloister, Benedict XIV declared that those who dared to make use of such voided faculties would incur ecclesiastical penalties reserved to the Holy See, for such grants and permissions, whether already given or yet to be bestowed, had thenceforth to be regarded as having neither force nor value. If anyone nevertheless used them, he suffered the same fate of excommunication as that which befell the unauthorized donor of the spurious concession.[40]

B. Legislation Pertaining to Nuns

1. Leaving the Cloister

The Council of Trent had not long become history when it was again necessary for the Church to act with regard to the cloister of nuns. Despite the fact that the Fathers of Trent had been truly considerate and mild in their regulations pertaining to the cloister of nuns, there were yet some nuns who refused to submit to the law which demanded cloister. They justified their actions with the assertion that new and unforeseen obligations had been imposed upon them. Mention of this trend of thought and action was made above.

In view of this situation Pope Pius V on May 29, 1566, outlined in clear and unmistakable language the true mind of the Church as opposed to the erroneous mind of these nuns. Renewing the decrees of Pope Boniface VIII and of the Council of Trent in his Constitution *"Circa pastoralis"* Pope Pius V declared that all nuns had to obey the enactments contained therein. There was a lack of all legal consequence in the allegations made by these nuns when they stressed the force of immemorial custom in opposition to this binding rigid observance, and when they asserted that the Rule under which they lived contained no prescription that called for the ob-

[39] Benedictus XIV, const. *"Regularis disciplinae,"* 3 ian. 1742, § 3—*Fontes*, n. 322.

[40] *Ibid.*, § 5—*Fontes*, n. 322.

servance of the cloister. Any further display of tenacity in adhering to these false principles was to be counteracted with ecclesiastical penalties. Therefore all nuns had to take solemn vows and observe the strict enclosure. Failure to inaugurate this procedure in any convent meant that it would soon become extinct, for any other type of professed vows was declared to be invalid.

Means of sustenance for these monasteries was to be obtained from the alms of the faithful, collected by extern sisters, or even by the professed, if they were over forty years of age. But these sisters had to live in a separate and adjacent house, could not enter the cloister, and were to leave their house to collect alms only with the permission of the bishop or of their superiors. This was an exception which Pope Boniface VIII and the Council of Trent did not make. If this method of seeking support did not suffice, then other suitable methods were to be instituted by the bishops and monastic superiors.[41]

But finally it became apparent to Pope Pius V [42] that two essential forms of legislation were necessary to effect the long sought enclosure of nuns. One of these was definiteness; the other was severity. The former was needed because once again nuns were leaving their enclosure for reasons which stood unwarranted by the preceding legislation.[43]

Thus, in an endeavor to dispel all doubts and to establish an absolute criterion by which a just cause for leaving the monastery could be judged, Pope Pius V defined three exceptions to the rule of the enclosure. These exceptions embraced leprosy, an epidemic and the grave situation of an extensive fire.[44] Wishing not to afford

[41] Const. "*Circa pastoralis,*" 29 maii 1566—*Fontes,* n. 112.

[42] Const. "*Decori,*" 1 febr. 1570—*Fontes,* n. 133.

[43] Const. "*Decori,*" § 1—*Fontes,* n. 133.

[44] Const. "*Decori,*" § 2: ". . . Unde . . . volumus, sancimus, et ordinamus nulli Abbatissarum, Priorissarum, aliarumve Monialium . . . nisi ex causa magni incendii, vel infirmitatis leprae, aut epidemiae . . . a Monasteriis exire . . ."—*Fontes,* n. 133 Navarrus observed that the latter two exceptions of Pope Pius V are really contained under the one cause given by Boniface VIII. Thus only the exception of fire was added by Pius V—cf. *Comment. IV, de regularibus,* n. 48.

any occasion for subsequent claims of exemption, Pope Pius V included in this decree all Orders of nuns, some of which he specifically named and the remainder of which he included under a general and universal classification.[45]

Obviously, it would have been unreasonable to expect the nuns to seek a qualified judgment regarding the seriousness of a fire before they could leave the enclosure. In the cases of sickness, however, the gravity of the infirmity, as well as the danger present, were factors which were withdrawn from the judgment of the nuns themselves, and committed to the disposal of the superiors of the Order to which the nuns were subject *plus* the discretion of the bishop or local ordinary. Their combined approbation had to be given in writing.[46]

But even this strict interpretation would have been of no avail had not Pope Pius V attached to it a most severe sanction. Experience and long unavailing efforts had taught this lesson. Consequently, for the first time in the history of the Church, a universal law was enacted which decreed excommunication for nuns who left the enclosure of their monastery without cause and permission. And it is interesting to note that this first penalty imposed by a Pope on all recalcitrant nuns was of the most severe type. Being reserved to the Holy Father himself, it could be absolved by others only when the recipient of the absolution was in imminent danger of death.[47] A like penalty was visited not only on the misapplied generosity of those who unauthoritatively granted permission for these

[45] Const. *"Decori,"* § 2—*Fontes,* n. 133.

[46] *Loc cit.* Cf. also S. C. C., 18 nov. 1713—Pallottini, s. v. "Monasteria Monialium," § 11, n. 99. Moreover, before the requisite permission for egress from the enclosure could be granted, it was essential that the monastery itself or one of the nuns was infected with the disease. The spread of an epidemic throughout the surrounding countryside constituted no reason for the nuns to leave the enclosure. On the contrary, it was more reasonable for them to remain within their enclosure.—S. C. Ep. et Reg., *Avenionen.,* 20 sept. 1720—*Fontes,* n. 1837; Benedictus XIV, *De Synodo Dioecesana,* lib. XIII, cap. XII, n. XXXI.

[47] Const. *"Decori,"* § 2: ". . . Aliter autem quam, ut praefertur, egredientes . . . excommunicationis maioris latae sententiae vinculo statim eo ipso absque aliqua declaratione subiacere, a quo praeterquam a Romano Pontifice, nisi in mortis articulo absolvi nequeant . . ."—*Fontes,* n. 133.

nuns to leave, but also on the presumption of those who assisted in that illegitimate egress or harbored the nun after she had left her enclosure.[48] The penalty against those who offered help and hospitality to the nuns who had left the enclosure applied only when there had been collusion and co-operation in the crime. Assistance or favor given to them from the motive of urbanity, friendship or relationship, was not included or meant in the decree of Pope Pius V.[49] In addition to the above-mentioned punishment, Pope Pius V rendered all persons involved incapable of possessing in the present or in the future any dignities of ecclesiastical offices.[50]

Pertinent to the force and proper interpretation of this Constitution was the answer furnished by the Holy Office on December 22, 1880, to the following question:

> Moniales e clausura exeuntes extra casus et formam a S. Pio PP. V in Constitut. Decori praescriptam, excommunicationi latae sententiae Romano Pontifici reservatae subiiciuntur. Sed in hac dioecesi, ut etiam in pluribus aliis, omnino ab immemorabili conceditur iisdem egressus ex causis gravibus, ab Episcopo recognitis et probatis, iuxta Concilium Trid. et nulla ratione habita Constitutionis Pianae. Quaeritur ergo utrum particularis ea et immemorabilis consuetudo per dictam novam Constitutionem abrogata censeri debeat, an continuari possit.

The reply was as follows:

> R. ad III—Affirmative ad primam partem; Negative ad secundam; nempe quoad egressum Monialium e clausura servandam esse Constitutionem S. Pii V *Decori*, contraria consuetudine non obstante.[51]

[48] *Loc. cit.*: ". . . seu licentiam exeundi quomodocumque concedentes, necnon comitantes, ac illarum receptatrices personas, sive laicas, aut saeculares, vel Ecclesiasticas, consanguineas, vel non, excommunicationis maioris, etc. . . . "

[49] Navarrus, *Comment. IV, De regularibus,* n. 51; Bonacina, *De Clausura,* q. I, p. IV, n. 5; Ferraris, *Bibliotheca,* s. v. "Moniales," art. III, n. 9; Schmalzgrueber, *Ius Ecclesiasticum,* lib. III, tit. XXXV, n. 110.

[50] Const. *"Decori,"* § 2—*Fontes,* n. 133. The office of confessor, preacher, professor, etc., were not meant to be excluded here. Cf. Schmalzgrueber, *ibid.,* n. 107.

[51] *Fontes,* n. 1068; cf. S. C. C., *Sabinen.* 3 iul. 1632, ad 3: "Decretis Conciliaribus et Constitutionibus Apostolicis clausuram praecipientibus nullam consuetudinem obstare."—*Fontes,* n. 2544.

This is proof that the legal arm of the Constitution reached down the centuries without losing any of its primitive force. It bound nuns in the nineteenth century even as it did in the sixteenth. That no change was introduced through the intervening years is apparent from the two decisions just cited.

The provision of Pius V which allowed some professed nuns and extern sisters to collect alms from the faithful was abrogated by Pope Gregory XIII in his Constitution *"Deo sacris,"* issued on December 30, 1572.[52] Thenceforth all nuns were to live secluded in perpetual enclosure.

Not until Pope Benedict XIV (1740-1758) occupied the Chair of St. Peter was it again necessary for any Pontiff to renew all the former decrees of the Council of Trent and the enactments of Pope Pius V relative to egress from the enclosure. The lamentable lapses from the true monastic and cloistral life, which are so sorrowfully described by Pope Benedict XIV, betray the unhappy fact that the entire gamut of excuses and pretensions for leaving the enclosure had been exhausted in such a manner that to a great extent convent life in the kingdoms of Portugal and Algarve[53] had been utterly destroyed. Nuns who had previously professed solemn vows which entailed the necessary consequence of perpetual enclosure were found to be absent from that same enclosure for months, and even for years. Though ostensibly they were absent to care for the sick, they could be seen attending the many entertainments staged for the people of the world.

Motivated solely by solicitude for the cloister, and not by any desire to fulminate censures against nuns who had strayed from the pathways of their first choice, Benedict XIV directed his Encyclical Letter to the bishops of Portugal and Algarve in an effort to root out these abuses.

Thus, to effect this result, all bishops were commanded upon official reception of that encyclical letter to notify the nuns that within the space of fifteen or twenty days they had to return to the

[52] *Fontes*, n. 143.

[53] What then constituted Algarve now constitutes the southernmost province of Portugal.

enclosure of their profession. Failure on the part of the nuns to fulfill these commands resulted in their subjection to all the penalties previously enacted against such violations. The same penalties befell all those who in any way hindered the attainment of that return. Beyond these penalties, all were likewise subject to any further punishments which the bishops deemed necessary to enact. Since all privileges theretofore conceded by any authority, including the Holy See, were no longer valid, recourse to them as a pretext for continuing to remain outside of the monastery was necessarily void. Moreover, such privileges no longer could be granted to nuns by any authority in those territories.[54]

2. Entry into the Cloister

As time progressed the Holy See had accorded to various persons certain privileges which permitted these persons to enter the monasteries of women. The unforeseen result was that much danger and many temptations were placed in the pathway of the nuns. For this reason, then, Pope Gregory XIII recalled, and for the future declared invalid, every single license and privilege which had been given in the past, and even those which had been given by himself.[55]

Moreover, the possession of a privilege offered the opportunity of more frequent visits to the monasteries, plus the assurance of a certain security in one's right to be there. From these very privileges sprang a more ready facility for abusing the concessions bestowed on them.[56] Those who continued to make use of such privileges as a pretext for gaining entry into the monastery incurred a *latae sententiae* excommunication reserved to the Holy See.[57]

A lengthy discussion arose as to whether this Constitution embraced even those who entered monasteries of women without a pretext of permission. It was certain that they were excommunicated

[54] *"Cum Sacrarum,"* 1 iun. 1741, § 2—*Fontes*, n. 310.

[55] Const. *"Ubi gratiae,"* 13 iun. 1575—*Fontes*, n. 147.

[56] Fagnanus, *Commentaria*, lib. V, *De sent. excomm.*, c. XXIX, *Nuper*, nn. 23-24.

[57] Const. *"Ubi gratiae,"* § 2—*Fontes*, n. 147.

by virtue of the Constitution *"Regularium"* [58] of Pope Pius V. But whether this penalty was reserved to the Holy Father himself was not so certain. Pallottini quoted a decision rendered by the Congregation of the Council stating that such persons were not included in the Constitution *"Ubi gratiae"* of Gregory XIII.[59] Fagnanus, moreover, made reference to the mind of Gregory XIII in this matter as expressed in a decision of the Sacred Congregation of Bishops and Regulars. In this decision Gregory XIII is cited as saying that in his Bull such persons were not included among those who incurred the excommunication in the nature of a papally reserved censure.[60]

On the other hand, Ferraris asserted the opposite opinion. He based it on a reply given by Gregory XIII to a query of St. Charles Borromeo. Gregory XIII asserted that it was his mind, as that of Pope Pius V, to include under the reserved censure mentioned in his Constitution even those who entered the monasteries of nuns apart from any pretext of permission.[61]

Confirming this opinion is a decision of the Congregation of Bishops and Regulars sent to the Archbishop of Braga on July 26, 1594. After due consideration and consultation with the Holy Father (Clement VIII) it was declared that always had the Constitutions of Pius V and Gregory XIII been so interpreted. Thus, those who entered the cloister even without any pretext of possess-

[58] 24 oct. 1566—*Fontes,* n. 115.

[59] "Ingredientes tamen clausuram monialium, sine licentia, non comprehenduntur in Bulla S. M. Greg. XIII contra abutentes licentia."—Pallottini, s. v. "Monasteria Monialium," § II, n. 89.

[60] ". . . et ita declaravit Gregorius XIII Constitutionis conditor, ut in subjecta declaratione, Episcopus *Çomen.* declarari petiit, an Bulla Sanctissimi imponens poenam excommunicationis ingredientibus monasteria vigore facultatum Apostolicarum, etiam eos comprehendat, qui absque talibus facultatibus ingrediuntur, ut sciri possit an absolutio sit reservata Summo Pontifici, Sac. Congregatio censuit agendum cum Sanctissimo, quia Concilium non reservavit Papae, et non videtur adesse majoritas rationis; quia abutentes litteris Apostolicis majori poena digni sunt. Sanctissimus declaravit Bullam non comprehendere eas personas, quae ingrediuntur propria auctoritate absque licentiis Sedis Apostolicae. . . ."—Fagnanus, *Commentaria,* lib. V, *De sent. excomm.,* CXXIX, *Nuper,* n. 26.

[61] Ferraris, *Bibliotheca,* s. v. "Moniales," art. III, n. 49.

ing privileges were likewise excommunicated with absolution reserved to the Holy See.[62]

Those who entered the cloister with evil motives undoubtedly incurred an excommunication reserved to the Holy See.[63] Those who permitted entry to violators of that type also incurred excommunication but its absolution was not reserved to the Holy See.[64]

Having rigidly legislated against those who entered the monastery, Gregory XIII then forbade all persons who were the inhabitants of monasteries, under pain of incurring the identical penalty, to grant entry to any persons who invoked the recalled privileges which had formerly been conceded to them.[65]

The Council of Trent had granted to bishops and monastic superiors the right to allow entry into convents whenever necessity dictated. It is manifest that they generously, though not juridically, stretched this right to comprehend even those situations which did not present the feature of necessity. As a result scandal and moral danger ensued. Recalling this lamentable situation and desiring to remedy it, Pope Gregory XIII strictly forbade all persons

62 Quaesitum fuit Amplitudinis tuae nomine ab hac Sacra Congregatione Cardinalium quos SS. D. N. Episcoporum et Regularium negotiis nominatim praefecit num scilicet poenae contentae in constitutione sanctae memoriae Pii V quae incipit *Regularium* et in alia fel. rec. Gregorii XIII quae incipit *Ubi gratiae* locum habeant solummodo contra ingredientes monasteriorum septa sanctimonialium literis Apostolicis suffultos an potius comprehendant etiam qui egrediuntur monasteria praedicta non ex auctoritate apostolica sed voluntate propria et alias nulla denuo ab hac S. Sede obtenta licentia; et omnibus hesitandi rationibus mature perpensis illud Amplitudini Tuae respondendum fore Patres Illmi censuerunt semper ita fuisse interpretatas constitutiones supradictas apud eandem S. Sedem ut utrumque omnino amplectantur casum. Quapropter tuae nunc erit Amplitudinis et idem sentire et contra inobedientes ex praescripto constitutionum in utroque casu procedere"—*Fontes*, n. 1513; cf. S. C. Ep. et Reg., *Papien.*, 28 apr. 1579—*Fontes*, n. 1357; S. C. Ep. et Reg., *Camerinen.*, 24 nov. 1597—*Fontes*, n. 1571. Fagnanus makes mention of a decree confirmed by Pope Clement VIII wherein the exact opposite is affirmed—Cf. second preceding footnote.

63 S. C. Ep. et Reg., 26 nov. 1602—*Fontes*, n. 1616; S. C. C., *Sabinen.*, 3 iul. 1632, ad 1—*Fontes*, n. 2544; cf. Fagnanus, *ibid.*, n. 26; Ferraris, *ibid.*, n. 49.

64 S. C. C., *ibid.*, ad 2.

65 Const. "*Ubi gratiae,*" § 3—*Fontes*, n. 147.

who possessed permissions which were not given in virtue of urgent necessity to enter the monasteries of women. To enforce this law, the excommunication which befell its violators was reserved to the Holy See. As in the case of Papal privileges, so now all nuns who permitted entry in recognition of such unwarranted permission were equally and similarly excommunicated.[66]

Thus Gregory only reaffirmed in a more salutary and forcible manner what Boniface VIII and the Council of Trent had enacted before him. It was not the permission which was to be considered, but rather the cause which justified its grant.[67] The Sacred Congregation of the Council declared that this Constitution and the enactment of the Council of Trent did not embrace doctors, surgeons, millers and other such necessary persons. The bishop could, without worry, allow their entry.[68]

The first word of the Constitution *"Dubiis"* issued by Gregory XIII on December 23, 1581, furnishes an insight into its purpose.[69] Many doubts and anxieties had arisen concerning not only his own previous Constitution *"Ubi gratiae,"* but also regarding the enactments of Pope Pius V and the decrees of the Council of Trent. Since those decrees were pointed more specifically to the requisite of the causes necessary for externs to enter the monastery, it was queried whether the prohibition embraced also those whose prerogative it was to concede that permission. Grave circumstances attended these doubts, especially with regard to the nuns, for under severe penalties they had been warned not to grant entrance except in cases of necessity.[70]

Settling decisively these questions, Gregory XIII decreed that

[66] Const. *"Ubi gratiae,"* § 4—*Fontes,* n. 147.

[67] S. C. C.—Pallottini, s. v. "Monasteria Monialium," § II, n. 88; Bonacina, *De Clausura,* q. IV, p. IV, n. 19; Suarez, *De religione,* tract. VIII, lib. I, cap. X, n. 10.

[68] May, 1585—Pallottini, *ibid.,* n. 90; Feb., 1586—Pallottini, *ibid.,* n. 91.

[69] *Fontes,* n. 148.

[70] Const. *"Dubiis"*: ". . . a nonnullis dubitatum fuisse sciamus circa personas, quae alterius ad id licentia non indigent, sed sui auctoritate officii nituntur, an liceat eis pro libito suae voluntatis huiusmodi septa ingredi, vel potius servare debeant ipsi quoque regulam a Concilio praescriptam. . . ."—*Fontes,* n. 148.

all bishops, cardinals and monastic superiors to whom the care of monasteries had been entrusted and to whom, consequently, had been given the privilege of entering these monasteries, could use their faculties only in cases of necessity. In these cases of necessity all of the above-mentioned superiors were to be accompanied by a small retinue of elderly men and religious persons.[71] If one judge from the many subsequent decisions, then the canonical visitation was indeed interpreted as a necessary case and thus warranted a lawful entry.[72] When doubts arose concerning those who visited the monastery with the bishop, it was declared that no further permission than their very association with the bishop was required.[73]

The position which Gregory XIII adopted in this regard was sanctioned with severe penalties. In his wisdom and experience he knew that even bishops and monastic superiors were wont to disregard, or rather interpret favorably to themselves, the legislation which was issued relative to the cloister. And so punishments befell those bishops who disobeyed his decree. Mitigating somewhat the penalties he had fulminated against other externs, Gregory XIII wished that there be a gradation in the penalties incurred by bishops guilty of these offenses. A first offense was punished with interdict

[71] Const. *"Dubiis,"* § 1: ". . . Declaramus praelatos omnes, tam saeculares, quam regulares, quibus cura et regimen monasteriorum monialium quovis modo incumbit, facultate sibi ex officio attributa ingrediendi monasteria praedicta ita uti posse, si id faciant in casibus necessariis, et a paucis, iisque senioribus, ac religiosis personis comitati. Quocirca . . . serie monemus, ut facultate huiusmodi, qui eam habent, praeterquam in casibus, ut praefertur, necessariis neutiquam utantur . . ."—*Fontes,* n. 148.

[72] S. C. C., *Regien.*, 7 mart. 1608, ad 7—*Fontes,* n. 2372; *Civitatis Regum,* 17 iun. 1617—*Fontes,* n. 2304; 24 sept. 1622—*Fontes,* n. 2434; 17 febr. 1624—*Fontes,* n. 2449; *Regien.* 13 ian. 1624—*Fontes,* n. 2446; *Giennen,* 7 sept. 1625—*Fontes,* n. 2462. These are decisions wherein the stated interpretation was manifested. Cf. also Alexander VII, const. *"Felici,"* 20 oct. 1664—*Fontes,* n. 240. Herein are contained explicit rules for the visitation made by monastic superiors. Personal visitation exclusive of all delegation was required. Cf. P. Mocchegiani, *Iurisprudentia Ecclesiastica* (3 vols., Ad Claras Aquas-Friburgi: Brisgoviae, 1904-1905), I, nn. 234-244.

[73] S. C. C.—Pallottini, s. v. "Monasteria Monialium," § II, nn. 80-81. The retinue was limited to two prudent men in these decisions. Cf. authors and decisions quoted above.

ab ingressu ecclesiae; a repetition of the offense brought suspension from functions of a pontifical character and *a divinis;* any further offense begot *ipso facto* excommunication. Monastic superiors suffered the same fate plus privation of their office and of their ministry.[74]

The question quite naturally arose whether the penalty of excommunication aimed at these incorrigible bishops and monastic superiors was equally reserved to the Holy See. The reason for this perplexity derived from the fact that the Constitution "*Dubiis*" was issued to settle the doubts which resulted from the interpretation of the earlier Constitution "*Ubi gratiae.*" Since it seems, then, that the later of these two Constitutions was simply promulgated in the character of a declaratory interpretation, its scope, its extent, and its legal force were apparently to be regarded as the equivalent of what it was meant to interpret. Consequently, as the Constitution "*Dubiis*" seems to imply, if the bishops and regulars were included in the Constitution "*Ubi gratiae,*" then the penalty which they incurred had to be considered as reserved to the Holy See, for as Fagnanus argues: "qualitates omnes, quae insunt legi declaratae, censentur inesse illius declarationi. . . ."[75]

But in that section of his Constitution "*Dubiis*" Gregory XIII did not intend to furnish merely a declarative statement. Since he employed the words "*statuimus*" and "*decernimus,*" he meant not to declare a pre-existing obligation, but rather to impose a new one. In view of this fact, then, and in consideration also of the lack of any expressed reservation in the Constitution "*Dubiis,*" the excommunication incurred by bishops and monastic superiors could be absolved by inferiors.[76]

Whether monastic superiors incurred excommunication for the initial offense or only upon a twofold repetition of it is not sufficiently evident from the wording of the Constitution. While he himself inclined to the opinion that they incurred the excommuni-

[74] Const. "*Dubiis,*" § 2—*Fontes,* n. 148. Cf. also S. C. C.—Pallottini, s. v. "Monasteria Monialium," § II, nn. 37, 42.

[75] *Commentaria,* lib. V, *de sent. excomm.,* c. XXIX, *Nuper,* n. 37.

[76] Cf. Fagnanus, *ibid.,* n. 38; Bonacina, *De Clausura,* q. VI, p. VI, n. 13; Ferraris, *Bibliotheca,* s. v. "Moniales," art. III, n. 67.

cation immediately upon a single visit, Bonacina nevertheless respected the opposite opinion as probable.[77]

Bishops who were outside of their diocese were not permitted to enter the cloisters of women.[78] In his own diocese, however, the bishop was permitted to visit a monastery though it was subject to another bishop.[79]

In the course of the following years the generosity of the Popes inclined them to listen and accede to lay women's requests for less rigidity in the law which governed the monastic cloister, and in consequence there was conceded a greater number of permissions for entering the monasteries of nuns. The result of abuse which followed upon these grants once again made it necessary to effect their revocation. This revocation was issued by Pope Paul V (1605-1621) on July 10, 1612 in his Constitution "*Monialium.*" [80] The punishments contained in this Constitution were the same as those which had been enacted in the Constitution "*Ubi gratiae*" of Pope Gregory XIII. Excommunication reserved to the Holy See befell all those women who persisted in invoking the privileges which had been revoked. The same punishment was incurred by those abbesses and other superiors who introduced or admitted them. Pope Paul V added that the punishment applied also to those superiors who, though they had not admitted the women, allowed them to remain in the monastery.[81]

In his Constitution "*Felici,*" Pope Alexander VII (1655-1667) determined specifically the conditions and the time pertinent to the visitation of convents by regular prelates.[82]

Pope Alexander explained precisely that no regular superior was authorized to enter the cloister of nuns except for the local visitation. This could be done only once a year and, if it was fulfilled

[77] *De Clausura, ibid.*, n. 11.

[78] S. C. C., *Ianuen*, 10 maii 1631—*Fontes*, n. 2531.

[79] S. C. C.—Pallottini, s. v. "Monasteria Monialium," § II, n. 49.

[80] *Fontes*, n. 197.

[81] Const. "*Monialium,*" §§ 2-3—*Fontes*, n. 197; Ferraris, *Bibliotheca*, s. v. "Moniales," art. III, n. 49. Herein Ferraris asserts that this Constitution likewise extended to those who entered the cloister on their own authority.

[82] 20 oct. 1664—*Fontes*, n. 240.

by one superior, it could not be repeated by another. Provision was made, however, for unexpected and urgent necessities which could arise to require more than one visitation. But since even exempt monasteries were entrusted chiefly to the care of bishops by the Council of Trent, it was required that they accompany the regular superior personally or by special delegate on all such urgent occasions. In requiring that the visitations conducted by the general superior be always fulfilled personally, Pope Alexander VII conceded to him the privilege of a retinue composed of two fellow religious. All other visitors were permitted only one companion, and at all times the designated companion was never to wander from the sight of the visitor. Moreover, during the entire time of the visitation, four nuns were to be constantly associated with the visitation tour. The visitation had to be made during the day time. All personal visitations were to be made, of course, at the grate.

The sanction attached to this Constitution forbade under pain of excommunication, deprivation of office and future incapacity to attain other offices, any violation of its enactments, whether by commission or omission. Moreover, the bishop was likewise authorized to inflict the additional punishments which he thought necessary.

This Constitution was issued for Italy and its adjacent islands, as Alexander VII noted in the decree itself. Bouix [83] cites Ferraris [84] as being of the opinion that this Constitution possessed the force of common law. The foundation for the arguments drawn by Bouix rests upon the consideration that Ferraris made no mention of any limiting clauses as being placed by Pope Alexander VII. Though it is entirely possible that Ferraris based his conclusion on a subsequent extension of this Constitution as issued by some later Pontiff, he failed to mention this fact, and such an enactment was wholly unknown to Bouix. Prescinding from the possibility of such an extension, regular superiors throughout the remaining countries of the world were necessarily bound by the enactment of Pope Gregory XIII in his Constitution *"Dubiis."* [85]

[83] *Tractatus de Iure Regularium* (2. ed., 2 vols., Bruxellis: 1867), II, pars 5, sec. V, cap. I, q. VI.

[84] *Bibliotheca,* s. v. "Moniales," art. III, nn. 73-78.

[85] Bouix, *loc. cit.*

The history of papal Constitutions relative to the cloister has been also the history of privileges which were abused. The reception of the Constitution "*Salutare*" of Benedict XIV was just another proof of this sad fact.[86] While it is true that in this Constitution distinct mention was made of nuns who had in some manner unjustly acquired permission to leave the cloister, the tenor of this papal document was directed against the more abundant abuses which had arisen from entry by externs into the monasteries of nuns. Far from enacting new legislation, Benedict XIV simply renewed all the former papal Constitutions and declared not only that they had to be observed, but insisted that the failure to do so would bring the penalties of all the severe sanctions contained in them.

Excepting the proper faculty inherent in the authority possessed by bishops and monastic superiors to be used for their entering of monasteries in necessary cases only, Benedict XIV declared null and void all other faculties for dispensing in this regard. An illegal persistence in the use of the voided faculties, either for one's self or for another, connoted not only that the permission was null and void, but likewise that the one who granted as well as the one who used it incurred an excommunication reserved to the Holy See.[87]

One is perhaps inclined to hazard the guess that ultimately the desired results were effected by all this strict legislation. Yet, within a few years Pope Benedict XIV felt constrained to legislate against the new arts and devices which were then being practiced to afford entry into the monasteries of women. Certainly that which was prohibited could not have been minus all beguiling attraction, otherwise it becomes difficult to comprehend the lingering unwillingness to comply with the sundry prohibitive enactments.[88]

Grave abuses had arisen through the admittance of women servants into the monastery. Moreover, laxity had so infected the pristine fervor of the nuns, that they felt no shame in openly speaking with persons of both sexes without observing the strict rules of the

[86] 3 ian. 1742—*Fontes*, n. 323.

[87] Const. "*Salutare*," §§ 2, 4—*Fontes*, n. 323.

[88] Const. "*Per binas*," 24 ian. 1747—*Fontes*, n. 375. This Constitution was sent to a bishop in Portugal.

grate. Some women, indeed, had even entered into the cloister. Once again, then, Pope Benedict XIV renewed all the former legislation, not only of the Popes, but likewise of the various Roman Congregations.

Establishing rigid rules to govern the admittance into the monastery of servants and of girls for schooling, Pope Benedict XIV ordered that only an Apostolic indult given for each particular occasion could permit this. Any violation of these precepts implied the incurring of censures not only for the nuns but also for those whom they permitted to enter. The faculty to absolve from these censures, along with the faculty of subdelegating others, was delegated to the bishop.

C. *Visiting Monasteries of Nuns*

Much consideration has already been given to the punitive legislation occasioned by the practice of visiting the monasteries of women, as distinct from the entering into the cloister.[89] Renewing the Constitution "*Periculoso*" of Pope Boniface VIII, both the Council of Trent in its decrees and Pope St. Pius V in his Constitution "*Circa pastoralis* [90] did not make any explicit mention of that particular phase of cloistral violation.[91] The Council of Trent did, however, establish the bishop as the custodian of all monasteries, and empowered him to punish with censures and other penalties those who did not observe the strict regulation of the cloister. One of the elements involved was what the enactments and authors refer to as "*accessus.*" What is meant by this term must necessarily be clarified if one is to have a lucid understanding of the legislation. The use of this word is not meant to convey the notion of visiting or of going

[89] Cf. c. 8, X, *de vita et honestate clericorum*, III, 1; c. un., *de statu regularium*, III, 16, in VI°.

[90] 29 maii 1566—*Fontes*, n. 112.

[91] Suarez, *De religione*, tract. VIII, lib. I, cap. X, n. 26; Schmalzgrueber, *Ius Ecclesiasticum*, lib. III, tit. XXXV, n. 128; Piatus, *Praelectiones*, I, 389, note 6; Navarrus held the opposite opinion with which Suarez differed sharply. —*Comment. IV, De regularibus*, n. 61.

to the monastery considered as a material structure, but rather of visiting the monastery and there speaking with the nuns.[92]

1. Legislation Regarding Regulars

With the approbation of Pope Sixtus V (1585-1590) the Congregation of Bishops and Regulars issued a decree which absolutely forbade all Regulars of any Order to visit convents and there speak with any of its inhabitants, without having first received special permission from that Congregation. From that decree were exempted the superiors who had the care of the convent, canonical visitors, ordinary and extraordinary confessors. Disobedience to the decree implied the privation of all offices, active and passive electoral rights in the community, and also other penalties which the Sacred Congregation desired to impose.[93] On July 7, 1606, the Sacred Congregation of the Council affirmed that, apart from the above mentioned penalties, any regulars who visited convents without permission were guilty of mortal sin.[94]

It was not required that the visits to the convent be multiplied before the punishments were incurred. One visit sufficed. No distinction was made in the decision of the Sacred Congregation of Bishops and Regulars. This law, then, was more severe than that which was enacted in the Decretals.[95]

[92] "Accessus ad monasteria monialium non sumitur materialiter, id est, intelligitur et sumitur aditus, non quidem simpliciter ad monasteria monialium materialiter, seu pro muris, et parietibus sumpta, sed aditus et accessus ad ipsas moniales causa illas visitandae, aut alloquendi . . ."—Ferraris, s. v. "Moniales," art. IV, n. 3. Cf. Fagnanus, *Commentaria*, lib. V, *De privilegiis*, c. XXVI, *Quarto;* Bonacina, *De Clausura*, q. III, p. I, n. 3; Bouix, *Tractatus de Iure Regularium*, II, pars 6, sec. V, cap. XIII, § IV, q. 1; Suarez, *De religione*, tract. VIII, lib. I, cap. X, n. 25.

[93] 7 maii 1590—Quaranta, *Summa Bullarii*, p. 451; Ferraris, *Bibliotheca*, s. v. "Moniales," art. IV, n. 14; Bizzari, *Collectanea*, p. 24; Bonacina, *De Clausura*, q. III, p. IV, n. 3.

[94] Piatus, *Praelectiones*, I, 391, q. 3; cf. Bonacina, *De Clausura*, q. III, p. IV, n. 4.

[95] Cf. c. 8, X, *de vita et honestate clericorum*, III, 1; c. un., *de statu regularium*, III, 16, in VI°; Mocchegiani, *Iurisprudentia Ecclesiastica*, I, n. 430; St. Alphonsus, *Theologia Moralis* (10 vols., Mechliniae: 1852), lib. VII, n. 235.

In his Constitution "*Inscrutabile,*" Pope Gregory XV (1621-1623) explained and amplified the power and authority which the Council of Trent had given to bishops.[96] This Constitution explicitly and plainly stated that a bishop could punish regulars who violated the cloister, even of convents subject to them. Experience had manifested, stated Fagnanus, that one of the problems confronting bishops who were given the obligation of preserving intact the cloister was that of preventing regulars from visiting those convents and there speaking with the nuns. It would have been absurd to think that bishops, being obliged to preserve inviolate the cloister, could not punish those who hindered the fulfillment of that obligation.[97]

The former decree of the Sacred Congregation of Bishops and Regulars was modified somewhat by Pope Urban VIII (1623-1644) in another decree of the same Congregation. Thus, four times a year the bishop was empowered to grant to regulars permission to visit nuns related by blood in the first and second degree. However, they were not allowed to visit on feast days, during Advent, Lent, or on Sundays, Saturdays and vigils.[98]

By authority, then, of the Sacred Congregation of Bishops and Regulars, this concession was given to bishops only in the stated cases. They were warned of this limitation, and told that permission granted to others and at different times would constitute the bishops as transgressors of the law of the Pope and the Sacred Congregation. Moreover, regulars were again warned to obtain permission, and, if they failed, they were subject to even more severe penalties.[99]

On June 26, 1627, the Sacred Congregation of the Council affirmed that the bishop could punish with the sentence of excommunication reserved to himself those regulars who violated the cloister

[96] 5 febr. 1622—*Fontes,* n. 199; Benedict XIV, *De Synodo Dioecesana,* lib. IX, cap. 15, n. 6.

[97] *Commentaria,* lib. V, *De privilegiis,* c. XXVI, *Quarto,* n. 11; cf. Bonacina, *De Clausura,* q. III, p. IV, n. 8; St. Alphonsus, *Theologia Moralis,* lib. VII, n. 241.

[98] 20 nov. 1623—Bizzarri, *Collectanea,* p. 24; Bonacina, *De Clausura,* p. III, p. IV, n. 4.

[99] Bonacina, *ibid.,* n. 4.

by visiting it and speaking with the nuns. This decree was repeated by the Sacred Congregation in 1658.[100] The prohibition embraced even conversations with abbesses and prioresses.[101]

St. Alphonsus did not admit this opinion. He dismissed the Constitution of Pope Alexander VII as applying only in Rome. According to him, this Pontiff did not wish to include others. However, St. Alphonsus made no mention of the decision of the Congregation of the Council.[102]

Gradually, however, casuistry came to the fore and regulars affirmed that visits made to convents for a reasonable cause and an honest motive were not comprehended in the former legislation. Some, in fact, arguing from the length of time in one day, concluded that a few moments' conversation with a nun constituted slightness of matter, and so was to be dismissed without further thought. Despite the fact that Pope Sixtus V (1585-1590), in confirming the decree of the Sacred Congregation of Bishops and Regulars, had forbidden regulars to delay for one moment to hold conversations with nuns after the completion of the divine services, some regulars at this later period considered such a procedure perfectly licit.[103]

Needless to say, timely legislation was imperative if such quibbling was to be stopped. This was forthcoming in three decisions which were issued by the Sacred Congregation of the Council. The first decision was directed at those whose sophistry condoned brief conversation with nuns and others residing within the cloister. The Congregation asserted that not only did they commit a mortal sin, but likewise they could be punished by the bishop as a delegate of the Holy See, even with the penalty of excommunication. The pen-

[100] *Auximana*, 26 ian. 1658—*Fontes*, n. 2753. The decision of 1627 is not contained in the *Fontes* except by way of mention in the decision of 1658. A like decision was issued in 1656 on May 6—*Fontes*, n. 2748. Cf. S. C. C., 27 maii 1634—*Analecta Juris Pontificii*, XXVII (1887-1888), 837; S. C. C., 10 ian, 1637, 7 aug. 1638—*ibid.*, p. 838; 12 aug. 1645—*ibid.*, p. 839; 16 sept. 1645 —*ibid.*, p. 840; 8 aug. 1654—*ibid.*, p. 841.

[101] Alexander VII, Const. "*Sacrosancti*," 30 mar. 1658, § 6—*Bull. Rom.*, XVI, 341; S. C. C., 14 nov. 1654—*Analecta Juris Pontificii*, *loc. cit.*, Ferraris, *Bibliotheca*, s. v. "Moniales," art. IV, n. 31.

[102] *Theologia Moralis*, lib. VII, n. 238.

[103] Cf. Benedict XIV, *De Synodo Dioecesana*, lib. IX, cap. XV, n. VII.

alties of deprivation of office and of the right to vote could also be enforced by the bishop.[104]

Even a reasonable cause and an honest motive could not excuse regulars from mortal sin when, having no permission, they conversed with nuns.[105] Finally, the Sacred Congregation of the Council discountenanced the practice of some preachers who after their sermons delayed to speak with the nuns, even concerning spiritual matters. Such regulars were declared to incur mortal sin and the various censures and penalties attached to such forbidden conversations.[106]

In his Constitution "*Romanus Pontifex,*" Pope Clement XII (1730-1740) revoked all permissions which had been given orally, or in writing, by any Pontiff, Cardinal or other official, and which allowed regulars to visit monasteries and there converse with nuns or other residents within the convent. This applied even in the case wherein a family relationship existed, unless special permission was previously obtained on each occasion. Anyone who presumed to use the revoked privileges suffered excommunication, deprivation of office, of dignities and of benefices, plus the incapacitation to hear confessions or to attain other offices and dignities.[107]

In its decision of November 26, 1672, the Sacred Congregation of the Council declared, in answer to the question whether regulars speaking to nuns without permission of the bishop were guilty of mortal sin, that when no permission had been obtained, sin was incurred.[108] Thus, it may seem that the former decisions of the Sacred Congregation of Bishops and Regulars which required the obtaining of its own permission except in certain stipulated cases, were abrogated. But strongly opposed to this interpretation are the *Animad-*

[104] S. C. C., 11 maii 1669—Ferraris, *Bibliotheca,* s. v. "Monials," art. IV, n. 17; cf.—*Fontes,* n. 1918, *Animadversiones;* St. Alphonsus, *Theologia Moralis,* lib. VII, n. 236.

[105] S. C. C., 26 nov. 1672—Ferraris, *ibid.,* n. 19; cf. also—*Fontes,* n. 1918, *Animadversiones.*

[106] S. C. C., 21 maii 1678—Ferraris, *Bibliotheca,* s. v. "Moniales," art. IV, nn. 20, 21.

[107] 12 feb. 1732, § 13—*Bull. Rom.,* XXIII, 314; Ferraris, *ibid.,* n. 21.

[108] Ferraris, *ibid.,* n. 19.

versiones appended to a decision of the Sacred Congregation of Bishops and Regulars cited in the *Fontes.* This opposition is based on the fact that the decision of the Sacred Congregation of the Council was not given in the name of the Pontiff, and contained no abrogation of the decrees approved by Popes Sixtus V and Urban VIII. It is recalled, furthermore, that Pope Clement XII, while revoking all privileges, left intact the right to obtain permission from the proper superior. But that superior was the bishop solely in the case wherein a close relationship existed between the regular and the nun. Moreover, though the decision was rendered affirmatively by the Sacred Congregation of the Council, it did not explicitly state that the permission of the bishop was sufficient.[109]

2. Legislation Regarding Clerics and Laity

The legislation which forbade the visiting of convents to clerics and lay persons was not so restrictive as that which pertained to regulars. Whereas the latter were prohibited even one visit, the enactments which appeared in the *Decretals* of Gregory IX (1227-1241) and in the *Liber Sextus* of Boniface VIII (1294-1303) forbade only frequent visits, undertaken without a just and reasonable cause, by those who were not regulars. Moreover, the warning of the bishop was a prerequisite for the imposing of excommunication upon laymen who persisted in their social tendencies.[110]

Later authors and commentators reflected the interpretation of their own period in relation to that legislation. Suarez initiated the discussion with the assurance that the Gregorian legislation certainly had not been derogated by custom.[111] Endeavoring to deter-

[109] S. C. Ep. et Reg., *Neapolitana,* 6 dec. 1838—*Fontes,* n. 1918. St. Alphonsus was of the opinion that the permission of the bishop sufficed. It was his mind that Pope Benedict XIV in the Encyclical Letter *"Gravissimo"* had required only the permission of the bishop. Other decrees, he stated, had fallen into desuetude—*Theologia Moralis,* lib. VII, n. 232; cf. ep. encycl. *"Gravissimo,"* 31 oct. 1749—*Fontes,* n. 401.

[110] C. 8, X, *de vita et honestate clericorum,* III, 1; c. un., *de statu regularium,* III, 16, in VI°

[111] *De religione,* tract. VIII, lib. I, cap. X, n. 27.

mine what constituted frequency in this matter, some authors regarded the judgment of prudent men as the proper criterion.[112] Other authors estimated that three visits within three consecutive days, two visits on one day, or four visits in a week, were sufficient to be comprehended in the meaning of the word "*frequentare.*"[113] While it is true that the penalties were incurred after the warning of the bishop and upon continued persistence, yet, since a reasonable and manifest cause was demanded, a grave sin attended every arbitrary visiting of convents.[114] Schmalzgrueber, on the contrary, concluded that since the early legislation had not been renewed by the Council of Trent nor by Pope Pius V (1566-1572), and by non-use had been abrogated, it was no sin to frequent the monasteries of women, excluding always scandal and evil motives.[115]

However, such unwarranted visits constituted cases which the ordinary could reserve to himself.[116] Parents,[117] children of those within the cloister,[118] brothers and sisters,[119] and those related by blood in the first and second degree,[120] were allowed to visit nuns without having first obtained permission. The reason for these exceptions rested on the presumption that danger and scandal were not likely to emerge from such visits.[121]

112 A. Barbosa, *Collectanea doctorum tam veterum quam recentiorum in ius pontificum universum* (Lugduni: 1669), lib. III, tit. I, cap. VIII, *monasteria,* n. 8; Navarrus, *Comment. IV, De regularibus,* n. 61; It does seem, however, from the examples cited by these authors, that they regarded as admissible the opinions which reflected other enumerations and calculations.

113 Cf. Bonacina, *De Clausura,* q. III, p. II, n. 4; E. Pirhing, *Ius Canonicum Novo Methodo Explicatum* (5 vols., in 4, Dilingae: 1674-1678), lib. III, tit. I, n. 3.

114 Bonacina, *op. cit.,* q. III, p. III, n. 1; Navarrus, *Comment. IV, De regularibus,* n. 61; Ferraris, *Bibliotheca,* s. v. "Moniales," art. IV, n. 4.

115 *Ius Ecclesiasticum,* lib. III, tit. XXXV, n. 128.

116 S. C. Ep. et Reg., 26 oct. 1604—Ferraris, *ibid.,* n. 5.

117 S. C. Ep. et Reg., 15 ian. 1616—Ferraris, *ibid.,* n. 8.

118 S. C. Ep. et Reg., 15 mar. 1619—Ferraris, *ibid.,* n. 9.

119 S. C. Ep. et Reg., 20 sept. 1593—Ferraris, *ibid.,* n. 10.

120 S. C. Ep. et Reg., 18 ian. 1618—Ferraris, *ibid.,* n. 11.

121 Bonacina, *De Clausura,* q. III, p. V, n. 9.

In his Constitution *"Inscrutabili,"* Pope Gregory XV (1621-1623) stated that bishops could legislate punishments against those seculars who violated, in any way, the monastery of nuns.[122] The terminology which he employed was universal enough to include even the visiting of monasteries of women. And certainly this was the mind of the Sacred Congregation of the Council when it declared that bishops could prohibit visits under penalty of excommunication.[123]

In his Encyclical Letter *"Gravissimo,"* Pope Benedict XIV (1740-1758) strongly legislated against bishops and other prelates who had freely visited the monasteries of nuns outside of their own dioceses. In stating this prohibition, Pope Benedict pointed to a previous decree of the Sacred Congregation of the Council which long before had ruled otherwise.[124] Since certain officials of civil life likewise were in need of correction in this matter, Benedict XIV renewed all previous legislation pertinent to the question and demanded that it be observed.

D. *Exemptions Conceded to Royalty*

The language employed by Pope Boniface VIII, in the Council of Trent and in the various Constitutions of the Pontiffs regarding exclusion from the cloister, seems to have been so comprehensive that it admitted of no exception or exemption. Such, however, was not the opinion of the authors who concluded that these rigid prohibitions were not universally comprehensive.

1. Monasteries of Monks

Endeavoring to determine whether the prerogatives of queens, of empresses, and of their daughters embraced even the faculty of en-

[122] 5 febr. 1622—*Fontes,* n. 199.

[123] 26 iun. 1627; *Auximana,* 26 ian. 1658—*Fontes,* n. 2573; Ferraris, *ibid.,* nn. 6, 29, 30.

[124] 31 oct. 1749—*Fontes,* n. 401; S. C. C., 20 mart. 1619—Ferraris, *Bibliotheca,* s. v. "Moniales," art. IV, n. 34.

tering within the monasteries of men, despite rigid prohibition, Suarez drew his conclusion of exemption from the terminology employed by Popes Pius V in the Constitution *"Regularium"* and Gregory XIII in the Constitution *"Ubi gratiae."* [125]

Basing his argumentation upon the classification invoked by Pope Pius V to designate the women who could no longer avail themselves of previously granted privileges, Suarez explained that this classification achieved its greatest comprehensiveness with the inclusion of countesses, marchionesses, and duchesses in this list. Consequently, such women who were of a higher social standing in view of a superior rank among the nobility were not meant to be included in this list. Since Pope Gregory XIII, however, extended the application of this list, even though he used the same classification, Suarez at first demurred at accepting the same interpretation for the enactment of Gregory which thus seemed to include even queens and empresses. Upon continued thought and study, Suarez nevertheless concluded that the two Pontiffs professed identical intentions in their legislation. In support of his ultimate conclusion Suarez appealed to the Rule of Law which, when formulated by way of its positive import, indicates that in a general concession there are comprehended also those items which anyone would in all likelihood be willing to bestow by way of particular concession.[126]

Bonacina employed the same kind of reasoning when he stated that empresses, queens and their daughters were not comprehended in the law which prohibited women from entering the monasteries of men. He admitted their exemption from this law even then when they had never possessed any specific privileges which made it lawful for them to enter the monasteries of men.[127]

In his Constitution *"Regularis disciplinae,"* which derogated all the current privileges that permitted entry into the monasteries

[125] *De religione,* tract. VIII, lib. I, cap. VII, n. 5.

[126] Cf. Reg. 81, R. J., in VI°: "In generali concessione non veniunt ea, quae quis non esset verisimiliter in specie concessurus."

[127] *De Clausura,* q. V, p. II, n. 5; cf. Ferraris, *Bibliotheca,* s. v. "Conventus," art. III, n. 22; Schmalzgrueber, *Ius Ecclesiasticum,* lib. III, tit. XXXV, n. 130; Mocchegiani, *Iurisprudentia Ecclesiastica,* I, n. 335.

of men, Pope Benedict XIV (1740-1758) explicitly stated that the privileges possessed by noble women who were the descendants of founders and benefactors of the monastery, as well as the privileges enjoyed by women related by blood or affinity to the rulers of the particular territory wherein the monastery was situated, were not abrogated. However, it was necessary that these privileges were confirmed by an Apostolic Letter, and that prior to the use of these privileges this letter had to be shown to the ordinary of that territory. The use of the privileges was confined with the fulfillment of religious motives.[128]

2. Monasteries of Nuns

In relation to the monasteries of nuns similar exemptions prevailed. Thus, kings and emperors together with their families and retinue were generally conceded the privilege of entering into the monasteries of nuns.[129].

The same process of reasoning was employed by the authors in exempting royalty in this situation as was utilized by them with reference to the permissible entering of the monasteries of men. Reiffenstuel extended this exemption to the electors and princes of the Roman Empire, since they likewise enjoyed some of the prerogatives proper to kings and emperors.[130] Custom, it seems, was the best criterion for determining what number of persons could allowably compose the retinue.[131]

Article III. The Constitution *Apostolicae Sedis*

The final papal penal legislation relative to the violation of the cloister which was issued before the promulgation of the Code of

[128] 3 ian. 1742, § 8—*Bullarium Benedicti XIV* (3 vols. in 4, Prati, 1845-1847), I, 128.

[129] Cf. Ferraris, *Bibliotheca*, s. v. "Moniales," art. III, n. 53; Reiffenstuel, *Jus Canonicum*, lib. III, tit. XXXV, n. 42. Bonacina (*De Clausura*, q. IV, p. I, n. 4) admitted that this permission was at least probably extant. Cf. also Mocchegiani, *ibid.*, n. 371.

[130] *Jus Canonicum*, lib. III, tit. XXXV, n. 49.

[131] Reiffenstuel, *ibid.*, nn. 45-48.

Canon Law was enacted by Pope Pius IX (1846-1878) on October 12, 1869. This legislation was almost the same as that which is now contained in the Code. Excommunication reserved *simpliciter* to the Holy See was inflicted upon women who violated the enclosure of regulars, as also upon the superiors and others who admitted them. Similar excommunication befell anyone who violated the cloister of nuns by entering it without having first received the proper permission. This applied equally to the nuns who introduced or admitted within their cloister persons who did not possess the proper permission. Adhering to the Constitution "*Decori*" and its specific enumeration of the instances in which a nun was allowed to leave the cloister, Pope Pius IX declared that any violation of that enactment likewise resulted in excommunication reserved to the Holy See.[132]

This Constitution of Pope Pius IX abrogated all former *latae sententiae* censures which it did not explicitly mention. Those censures which were mentioned drew their binding force, not from the previous legislation, but from the Constitution itself. Thus the former vindictive penalties which involved deprivation of offices and dignities, together with the incapacitation to attain others, were not abrogated by this Constitution, but continued in force.

Historical Summary

The outstanding conclusion drawn from this historical conspectus is the revelation of the struggle encountered by the Church in firmly establishing and maintaining the inviolability of the cloister. The constant and unflinching solicitude of the Church met dogged opposition from the belittling appraisal of the true monastic spirit, from stubbornness in the face of authority, and from adherence to worldliness, even on the part of those whom she endeavored to aid and protect. Born of the violations committed by monks and nuns themselves, this legislation grew in severity and achieved universal application only in so much as persistent disobedience demanded an effective countercheck. Never was there portrayed in the pertinent ecclesiastical legislation, drastic though it was, any other motive than that of kindly and merciful protection. With characteristic

[132] Const. "*Apostolicae Sedis*," § II, nn. 6, 7—*Fontes*, n. 522.

perspicacity the Church sensed spiritual dangers and potential moral ruin when monks and nuns were still heedless of the harm which impended for them.

But it was not only from and against themselves that the Church desired to protect the followers of monastic life. Though they had left the world behind, yet, strangely enough, the world in the person of some over-curious men and women persisted in pursuing into the cloister itself the adherents of monastic life. From this source, also, flowed dangers which necessarily had to be counteracted. Always with the purpose of protecting and preserving the priceless virtue of chastity, the legislation was directed most vehemently against the free and unrestricted access to monasteries by those of the other sex. Though both men and women were excluded from the monasteries of nuns, there has never been a universal law which prohibited under penalty the entry of men into the cloister of regulars.

In relation to the monasteries of women the Constitution "*Periculoso*" of Pope Boniface VIII stands out in history as the true turning point in the severity of cloistral legislation. It is true that before that time some conciliar legislation enacted rigid restraints, but the tide of severe legislation rose greatly under the impetus of Pope Boniface VIII, who himself, however, did not fulminate any penalties. The climax of the law's severity as well as its comprehensiveness in the framework of the Church's universal legislation was reached during the second half of the sixteenth century, through the decrees of the Council of Trent and the sundry enactments of Popes Pius V and Gregory XIII. Subsequent legislation was content mainly to reaffirm and renew what had gone before.

In relation to the monasteries of men the legislation was generally much more lenient. This greater leniency was reflected not only in the law which governed the visiting, the admission and the entry of outsiders into the monastery, but also in the legal norms which regulated the departure or egress of the monks from the monastery. Pope Pius V established the legislation which universally forbade the entry of women into the cloisters of the monasteries of the monks. Fundamentally, the later laws reflected the substantial repetition of his enactments. With reference to the matter of departure or egress from the monasteries of monks the law in the

Church, whether that law was of a universal or merely of a particular character, was never of an extremely rigorous or severely rigid tenor. The due permission for monks to absent themselves from the confines of the monastic enclosure was made available through their various monastic and ecclesiastical superiors for any righteous and reasonable cause.

Part Two

Canonical Commentary

CHAPTER IV

SCOPE AND CONFINES OF THE CLOISTER

A correct concept of the cloister and of its laws will necessitate a proper and lucid understanding of the terms usually employed not only by the Code itself, but also by authors who comment upon its enactments.

The *papal* cloister is that which is established by the Code for religious communities in which solemn vows are taken. It is enforced by canonical sanctions explicitly stated in the Code.[1] The *episcopal* or *common* cloister is that which is established by common law for religious congregations of simple vows. Its observance can be sanctioned with episcopal censures.[2] The statutory cloister is that which is prescribed by the rules and constitutions of the indi-

[1] Cf. canons 597, § 1; 2342; T. Schaefer, *De Religiosis ad Normam Codicis Iuris Canonici* (3. ed., Roma: S. A. L. E. R., 1940), n. 347. Hereafter this work will be cited *De Religiosis*. G. Cocchi, *Commentarium in Codicem Iuris Canonici ad Usum Scholarum* (8 vols., Vol. IV, *De Religiosis*, 3. ed., Taurinorum Augustae: Marietti, 1932), IV, n. 97. Hereafter cited as *Commentarium*. Vermeersch-Creusen, *Epitome Iuris Canonici cum Commentariis ad Scholas et ad usum Privatum* (3 vols., Vol. I, 6. ed., Mechliniae et Romae: Dessain, 1937), I, n. 753. Hereafter cited *Epitome*. M. Coronata, *Institutiones Iuris Canonici ad Usum Utriusque Cleri et Scholarum* (5 vols., Vol. I, 2. ed., Taurini [Italia]: Marietti, 1939), n. 610. Hereafter cited *Institutiones*. L. Fanfani, *De Iure Religiosorum ad Normam Codicis Iuris Canonici* (2. ed., Taurini-Romae: Marietti, 1925), n. 303, B. Hereafter cited *De Iure Religiosorum*. G. Oesterle, *Praelectiones Iuris Canonici*, Vol. I (Romae: In Collegio S. Anselmi, 1931), p. 336. C. Berutti, *Institutiones Iuris Canonici* (6 vols., Vol. III, *De Religiosis*, Taurini-Romae: Marietti, 1936), III, n. 113. Hereafter cited *Institutiones*. U. Beste, *Introductio in Codicem* (Collegeville, Minn.: St. John's Abbey, 1938), p. 407. P. Bastien, *Directoire Canonique a L'Usage des Congregations a Voeux Simples* (3. ed., Bruges: Beyaert, 1923), n. 265. Hereafter cited *Directoire Canonique*.

[2] Cf. canon 604, § 1; cf. also the authors cited above.

vidual communities.[3] As its meaning implies, the *passive* cloister relates to the forbidden entry of outsiders or externs; the *active* cloister refers to the prohibited egress of those who dwell within the cloistered house.

Article I. Papal Cloister

A. *Cloister of Regulars*

Canon 597, § 1, legislates that the papal cloister must be observed in houses of regulars which have been canonically established, even though they be not formal. A "formal" house is one inhabited by six professed religious, four of whom, if the house be one of a clerical Institute, are priests.[4] Regulars are members of a religious Order in which solemn vows are taken. However, to constitute them as regulars, it is not necessary that all the members pronounce solemn vows.[5] Canonical establishment of a house must always precede the enforcement of papal cloister. This establishment is effected by the issuance of a decree by the proper religious superior coupled with the written consent of the local ordinary and the approval of the Holy See.[6]

Since the Code does not require a formal house and, moreover, does not exact any specific number for the erection of a non-formal religious house, the question presents itself concerning the number of regulars which is required before the cloistral laws will begin to function. It may be concluded from the enactments of the Code that each religious house is a collegiate moral person [7] and each collegi-

[3] Cf. authors cited above.

[4] Cf. canons 597, § 1; 488, 5°.

[5] Cf. canon 488, 2°, 7°; A. Larraona, "Commentarium Codicis"—*Commentarium pro Religiosis* (Romae: 1920—), II (1921), 276. Hereafter cited *CpR*. "Commentarium Codicis"—*CpR*, IV (1923), 11; Schaefer, *De Religiosis*, n. 41; n. 46, c. It is inconsequential that other names be given to regulars, *e. g.*, Canon Regulars, Monks. These are but species of the generic term. Cf. canon 491, § 1; Larraona, "Commentarium Codicis"—*CpR*, IV (1923), 11, note 242.

[6] Cf. canon 497, § 1; Schaefer, *op. cit.*, n. 80.

[7] Cf. canons 531; 536, § 1; Vermeersch, "De Persona Morali"—*Periodica de Re Canonica et Morali praesertim Religiosis et Missionariis* (Brugis: 1905—), X (1922), (34). Hereafter this periodical will be cited *Periodica*. Larraona, "Commentarium Codicis"—*CpR*, III (1922), 48.

ate moral person must consist at least of three physical persons.[8] It appears, then, that a religious house inhabited by less than three members does not possess canonical erection and, consequently, has no papal cloister.[9] Vermeersch, however, was of the opinion that a non-collegiate personality could be attributed to a religious house erected with the approval of the Holy See and inhabited by only two religious.[10]

Two decrees were issued by the Sacred Congregation for the Propagation of the Faith pertinent to the cloister maintained by missionaries in China. By virtue of these decrees those mission houses in which only two or three regulars of the Latin rite habitually resided were subject to the cloistral laws. The decrees did permit, however, that women be allowed entry into the inner oratories, the churches and other places for assistance at Mass, confession and other sacred functions.[11] Do those decrees still possess canonical value and sanction? The opinion expressed in *Periodica*[12] and adopted by Schaefer[13] answers this question in the negative. In missionary countries regulars occupy some houses as quasi-pastors and curates in dependence either on the vicar or prefect apostolic, or the bishop. Since such houses are not primarily *"domus regulares,"* but rather the rectories within the quasi-parishes which are entrusted to regulars, no apostolic approval is needed for their erection.[14] If a canonically established house of regulars embraced in its concept any legitimately existing house in which regulars live, then the above mentioned decrees would imply but an application of the rule expressed in canon 597, and, consequently, would still remain in force. If, on the other hand, a canonically established

[8] Canon 100, § 2.

[9] Larraona, *loc. cit.*; Coronata, *Institutiones*, nn. 523, 611, a.

[10] "De Persona Morali"—*Periodica*, X (1922), (34)-(35).

[11] 26 aug. 1780—*Fontes*, n. 4582; 5 mart. 1787—*Fontes*, n. 4614.

[12] "De Beneplacito Apostolico et Clausura in Missionibus"—*Periodica*, XII (1924), (1)-(3).

[13] *De Religiosis*, n. 348, 3; cf. Coronata, *Institutiones*, n. 611, p. 795, note 6.

[14] Canon 497, § 1; *Periodica*, *loc. cit.*

house is exclusively one which has been erected with apostolic approval along with the consent of the local ordinary—and it has been shown that such is the case,—then those decrees extend beyond the enactments of the Code and, consequently, are suppressed.[15]

Basing his argumentation upon the fact that canon 597 refers only to the solemnities required by canon 497, the writer in *Periodica* concludes that those decrees no longer possess any canonical force which necessitates the papal cloister in those houses in which regulars reside as quasi-pastors.[16] Coronata notes, however, that a religious parish generally presupposes a canonically constituted religious house to which the parish is united *"pleno iure."* Such houses would certainly be bound by the laws of cloister.[17]

It is not required that the regulars possess a civil deed attesting to their ownership of the religious house. If the assurance of abiding living facilities is guaranteed, then a sufficient fulfillment of the requirements in this regard is present.[18] Indeed, even those houses which serve regulars who work in parishes must be canonically erected, for this is not an arbitrary matter which is left simply to the good judgment of the religious. Unless a serious reason offer an excuse (necessity of dispersion, etc.), all houses destined for stability of life on the part of regulars must be canonically established.[19] The requirement of residence in fixed and permanent houses does not, however, necessarily exclude the existence of vacation homes destined for the purpose of recreation during the summer months, or of rest homes erected to afford a place of recuperation after illness. Such places are not generally erected canonically, and for that reason are not subject to the observance of papal cloister. The oppo-

[15] Cf. canon 6, 6°; "De Beneplacito Apostolico et Clausura in Missionibus" —*Periodica*, XII (1924), (1)-(3).

[16] *Periodica, loc. cit.*

[17] *Institutiones*, n. 611, p. 795, note 6.

[18] Vermeersch-Creusen, *Epitome*, I, n. 754, a; Berutti, *Institutiones*, III, n. 113, II; Coronata, *Institutiones*, n. 611, a.

[19] Vermeersch-Creusen, *loc. cit.*; "De Domibus filiabus apud religiosos"—*Periodica*, XVII (1928), 89*; G. Vromant, *Ius Missionariorum de Personis* (2. ed., Louvain: Museum Lessianum, 1935), n. 381. This work is henceforth cited *De Personis.*

site would, of course, be true if such houses were erected with the intention of providing permanent habitation.[20]

There can be no doubt that the force of the verb *"servetur"* as employed by canon 597, § 1, imposes a strict command to establish and maintain the cloistral limits. Aside from the fact that this regulation is coupled with severe sanctions, which would never be invoked by law if the observance of the cloister were the consequence of a mere recommendation, the binding force of the rule which is contained in this canon may likewise be derived from the strictness of the old law upon which it is founded.[21]

The restrictive legal force of the papal cloister affects all the parts of the house which are used exclusively by the regulars. In this regard there has been practically no change from the rule as expressed in the former law. Thus the cloister of necessity includes the rooms and dormitories of the religious, the refectory, the recreation room, the private oratories, the offices, in a word, all those places which one cannot declare as being outside of the cloister without presupposing a radical change in the arrangement of the everyday living quarters of the residents of the house.[22] A newly constructed house, ready in every way for habitation but as yet still unoccupied, does not possess the cloister. The same can generally be said of a house not yet fully completed as well as of one recently acquired but not yet inhabited. To determine the time when the

[20] Vermeersch-Creusen, *loc. cit.*; Coronata, *loc. cit.*; Fanfani, *De Iure Religiosorum*, n. 307, A; Schaefer, *De Religiosis*, n. 348, 3; Cocchi, *Commentarium*, IV, n. 98, a; F. Claeys-Bouuaert-G. Simenon, *Manuale Iuris Canonici ad Usum Seminariorum*, 3 vols. (Vol. I, 3. ed., Gandae et Leodii: 1930-1931), I, n. 666. Hereafter cited Claeys-Bouuaert, *Manuale*. Beste, *Introductio in Codicem*, p. 406; J. Pejska, *Ius Canonicum Religiosorum* (3. ed., Friburgi Brisgoviae: Herder, 1927), p. 152. Hereafter cited *Ius Canonicum*.

[21] Petrus Doink, "Pastoral-Fälle"—*Theologisch-praktische Quartalschrift* (Linz: 1832—), LXXVII (1924), 119-121. Hereafter cited *ThPrQs*. Cf. also canon 6, 4°.

[22] Canon 597, § 2; Bonacina, *De Clausura*, q. V, p. I, n. 1; Ferraris, *Bibliotheca*, s. v. "Conventus," art. III, n. 9; Reiffenstuel, *Jus Canonicum*, lib. III, tit. XXXV, n. 26; Mocchegiani, *Iurisprudentia Ecclesiastica*, I, n. 319; Coronata, *op. cit.*, n. 611, b; T. Gerster a Zeil, *Ius Religiosorum in Compendium Redactum pro Iuvenibus Religiosis* (Taurini [Italia]: Marietti, 1935), p. 186. Hereafter cited *Ius Religiosorum*.

cloistral laws begin to exercise their force in such houses is the right and duty of the major superiors or general chapters.[23]

Once the house is inhabited by regulars, however, the law of the cloister commences. A subsequent temporary absence of all the religious from that house does not imply a relaxation of the law so as to permit entry to women. It is quite true that the end of the law, which is the protection of the inhabitants of the house, is not involved on such occasions. But such a fact is only accidental in reference to the law. The law establishes certain limits beyond which no woman may go without the proper dispensation or permission. It is the violation of the law as such, and not simply the transgression of its purpose, which primarily and always must be avoided.[24]

The normal course of a healthy existence demands the benefits which can come only from time spent out of doors. In this matter the life of the regulars is no exception to the general rule. And so it is that the seclusion and protection which are enjoyed by the material house should be extended to the grounds which surround the house and which are used by the religious for the purposes of recreation, health, agriculture and other such ends. With this in mind the legislator of the Code has stated that the law of the cloister embraces all the gardens and tree shaded parks the access to which is reserved to the religious.[25] The language employed by the Code can give rise to some practical questions. As it states, the grounds enjoying the cloistral protection are those which are reserved for the access of the religious. Does this mean that they must be absolutely contiguous to the house itself? Will it be necessary that the only entrance to those grounds be from the cloistered house? May other

[23] S. C. Ep. et Reg., *Capuccinorum,* 18 apr. 1605, ad I—*Fontes,* n. 1634; Schaefer, *De Religiosis,* n. 348, 3; Fanfani, *De Iure Religiosorum,* n. 307, A; Vermeersch-Creusen, *Epitome,* I, n. 754, a; Oesterle, *Praelectiones Iuris Canonici,* I, p. 336; Berutti, *Institutiones,* III, n. 113, II; Beste, *Introductio in Codicem,* p. 406; Gerster a Zeil, *Ius Religiosorum,* p. 185.

[24] Cf. canon 21; Bonacina, *De Clausura,* q. V, p. II, n. 7; Schaaf, *The Cloister,* pp. 59-60.

[25] Canon 597, § 2: ". . . cum hortis et viridariis accessui religiosorum reservatis. . . ."

entrances be allowed? May the only entrance to these grounds proceed from a place which is outside of the cloistral limits, *e. g.*, from a street?

It seems certain that in answer to the first question the grounds must be adjacent to the house of the religious. If this were not so, then the use of the grounds by the religious would necessitate an egress from the cloister, a passage through uncloistered places, and then an entry within the cloistered grounds. But such a case or situation was considered as not falling within the concept of the cloister both in the former law and among the pre-code authors.[26]

The fact that other entrances lead into the cloistered grounds from a position beyond the cloister's limits implies no contradiction to the notion of cloistered grounds or of their contiguity to the house.[27] Access to the grounds can still be reserved to the religious even in circumstances such as these. The obvious and most certain manner of reserving grounds to the religious is to establish an entrance to them solely from the cloistered house itself. When, however, other entrances are present, the necessary reservation will proceed from a formal prohibition, issued by the proper superior, which forbids entrance to all other persons.[28] But none of the gardens, fields, woods and orchards to which the religious do not have free canonical access can be considered as forming part of the cloister.[29]

If a situation is assumed wherein the *only* entrance to the clois-

[26] ". . . hortos religiosorum monasterio contiguos subjectos esse clausurae. . . ." Bonacina, *De Clausura*, q. V, p. I, n. 6; ". . . Viridaria, seu Horti et Prata cum Conventu et Claustra conjuncta nomine Clausurae, ita ut mulieres ipsa ingredientes excommunicationem incurrant: Sacra Congreg. Episcoporum et Regularium *in una Dominic.* 24 apr. 1582, in Laudensi, 13 septemb. 1583 et in Arben. 3 junii 1606"—Ferraris, *Bibliotheca*, s. v. "Conventus," art. III, n. 10; J. Pennacchi, *Commentaria in Constitutionem "Apostolicae Sedis"* (2 vols., Romae: 1883), I, 775. Hereafter cited as *Commentaria.*

[27] Schaefer, *De Religiosis*, n. 348, 2, note 205; Berutti, *Institutiones*, III, n. 113, III; Schaaf, *The Cloister*, p. 63.

[28] Vermeersch-Creusen, *Epitome*, I, n. 754, b; Fanfani, *De Iure Religiosorum*, n. 307, A.

[29] Wernz-Vidal, *Ius Canonicum ad Codicis Normam Exactum* (7 vols. in 8, Romae: apud Aedes Universitatis Gregorianae, 1927-1938), III, (*De Religiosis*), n. 374, II, note 6. Hereafter cited as *Ius Canonicum.*

tral grounds is from a place outside of the cloister, can it still be canonically maintained that these grounds form part of the enclosure? From a purely physical aspect it can, of course, be said that the grounds, even in that arrangement, are adjacent to the house. If one judge, however, from the concept expressed in the canon, then that contention seems hardly supportable. An arrangement such as that would, as it was said above, necessitate egress from the cloistered limits of the monastery before entry could be gained into the grounds. And certainly it does not seem admissible to hold that the law intended to comprehend even that situation wherein religious would be required to obtain a permission to leave the cloister each time they were to enjoy the use of such grounds.[80] Moreover, in the case of *nuns*, excommunication would attach as a penalty to every unauthorized effort on their part to enjoy the use of their grounds without the requisite papal permission.[81] It is this necessity of permission that Berutti necessarily implies when he speaks of the case in which grounds can be considered reserved to the religious even when the sole entrance to them is placed outside of the cloister.[82] The common law, as expressed in canon 597, § 2, permits religious to go any place within the limits of the enclosure. The only reasonable conclusion, then, is that, since free access may also be had to the cloistral grounds, these should form one continuous and integral part of the cloister.

The entire concept, both of the grounds contiguous to the house of religious and of the entrances leading to these grounds, has always implied that some form of wall encloses the grounds. It is difficult to conceive of a cloister, or any type of enclosure, which is without physical limits and boundaries. Yet there is no direct mention in the Code of any such barriers. At the most, the presence of a barrier is simply implied in canon 597, § 2, which employs the words

[80] Cf. Wernz-Vidal, *loc. cit.*; Schaaf, *op. cit.*, p. 65.

[81] Cf. canon 2342, 3°.

[82] "Horti et viridaria, domui regularium adnexa, religiosorum accessui reservata dicuntur si ad ea ingressus non pateat nisi a claustris monasterii, *vel*, si alius quoque vel *unicus aditus ad ea adsit extra clausuram*, idem in commodum dumtaxat religiosorum destinetur et ceteris praecludatur"—*Institutiones*, III, n. 113, III.

"accessui . . . reservatis." The generally accepted and normal manner of establishing this reservation for the benefit of some to the exclusion of others is by means of a barrier. This fact is evident to all from everyday experience. Yet, though the necessity of a barrier may be deduced from the canons pertinent to the cloister, there is no direct mention of what that barrier should be.[33]

The pre-Code law and its commentators always conceived of and wrote of barriers around the cloister as Jombart shows in his discussion of this problem.[34] Thus the Council of Trent forbade entry within the enclosure (*septa*) of monasteries.[35] Authors used this identical or at least a similar expression when they discussed the notion and limits of the cloister.[36] There was, however, no universal use of one specific word to designate the particular material barrier or structure which was to provide the necessary protection to the monastery both from within and from without. The words *"septa"* and *"murus"* were most frequently employed. In fact, Reiffenstuel used three different terms which he apparently considered to be interchangeable.[37] The Code refrains from employing any terminology to explain the concept. Jombart offers as a reason for the nonuse of the word *"septa"* by the Code the obscurity which this word possessed in the former law.[38]

The concept of enclosure with reference to the cloistral grounds will be, it seems, sufficiently preserved if a closed board fence, a

[33] Canon 602 does require a barrier around the cloister of *nuns.* This barrier must be of such a nature that the persons outside of it cannot look in and that the persons inside of it cannot look out.

[34] "Questio de clausura materiali regularium"—*Periodica,* XVI (1927), 48*-52*.

[35] ". . . Ingredi autem intra septa monasterii nemini liceat. . . ."—Sess. XXV, *de regularibus,* c. 5; cf. Benedictus XIV, Const. *"Regularibus disciplinae,"* 3 ian. 1742—*Fontes,* n. 322.

[36] Suarez, *De religione,* tract. VIII, lib. I, cap. X, n. 8; Ferraris, *Bibliotheca,* s. v. "Conventus," art. III, n. 9; Bonacina, *De Clausura,* q. IV, p. I, n. 1.

[37] ". . . clausura monasterii est totum illud spatium, quod ambitur et clauditur *muris, parietibus* seu *septis* monasterii. . . ."—*Jus Canonicum,* lib. III, tit. XXXV, n. 26.

[38] "Questio de clausura materiali regularium"—*Periodica,* XVI (1927), 50*.

thick hedge,[39] or a stone wall is employed to determine and establish the cloistral boundaries. These are the commonly accepted means in use today among all persons who wish to protect their property against outside approach. And their use is found to be effective. Granted that the normal safeguards and precautions are employed, the possibility of the use of force and fraud by some persons to gain entry or egress need not necessarily be given serious consideration. Persons whose intent looks to the use of force and fraud will generally find means to surmount the obstacles raised by any normal barriers.[40] Though the Code does not demand that the grounds of the houses of regulars be hidden from the public gaze, yet an atmosphere which is more conducive to privacy and seclusion would be created if by some effective means the grounds were protected against all public view.

Exempted from the law of enclosure is the public oratory attached to the monastery.[41] It needs only to be mentioned here that the direct entrance which leads to this oratory must always be placed outside of the limits of the cloister.[42] The requirement is stated in canon 597, § 2, that this place of worship must be one of public character. Berutti [43] and Blat [44] maintain that a semi-public oratory is comprised within the meaning of this canon.

By reason of its contiguity to the church or oratory, the sacristy likewise enjoys immunity from the cloistral limits.[45] This condition is absolutely certain to obtain when the only door which leads to the sacristy opens from the church. The words of the Code [46]

[39] Jombart, *op. cit.*, 51*.

[40] F. Wernz, *Ius Decretalium ad usum Praelectionum in Scholis Textus Canonici sive Iuris Decretalium,* 6 vols. in 7 (Vols. I-III, 2. ed., Romae, Vols. IV-VII, Prati: 1905-1914), III, n. 658, II. Hereafter cited *Ius Decretalium.*

[41] Canon 597, § 2.

[42] Berutti, *Institutiones,* III, n. 113, III.

[43] *Loc. cit.*

[44] *Commentarium,* II, n. 525.

[45] I. Chelodi, *Ius de Personis iuxta Codicem Iuris Canonici* (ed. altera a Sac. Ernesto Bertagnolli recognita et aucta, Tridenti: Libr. Edit. Tridentum, 1927), n. 277, p. 463, note 1. Hereafter cited as *Ius de Personis.*

[46] Canon 597, § 2: ". . . excluso, praeter publicum templum cum continente sacrario. . . ."

are then fulfilled in their most obvious meaning. Before the promulgation of the Code much discussion centered about the exclusion from the cloister of a sacristy which possessed two doors: one leading from the church, the other from the cloistered precincts of the monastery.[47] While citing decisions of the Sacred Congregation of Bishops and Regulars which declared that such a sacristy was included within the cloister, the authors nevertheless indicated that the universal practice and custom deviated somewhat from this interpretation.[48] This more common opinion and universal practice was incorporated into the Code. The sacristy can be considered as contiguous to the church despite the presence of other doors leading to it from the cloistered house.[49]

Though no mention of the choir is contained in the canons which refer to the cloister, the choir can be considered immune from clois-

[47] Cf. *supra*, p. 55, note 24.

[48] ". . . in praxi tamen non condemnarem illos religiosos, apud quos receptum est, ut foeminas in sacristiam causa confessiones audiendi, aut alia de causa admittant, quia non omnino perspicuum est Sacristiam sub monasterii nomine comprehendi. . . ."—Bonacina, *De Clausura*, q. V, p. I, n. 4; ". . . Sed praxis fere ubique videtur in contrarium. . . ."—Ferraris, *Bibliotheca*, s. v. "Conventus," art. III, n. 15; ". . . Romae enim plurimae sunt sacristiae in ecclesiis regularium habentes duplicem huiusmodi ingressum, in quibus nulla observatur clausura relate ad mulieres, quamvis positae sint extra ipsa ecclesiarum moenia, et infra monasteriorum septa. Idipsum autem contingere scimus etiam extra Romam. Quid ergo dicendum? Ni fallimus clausura pro sacristiis huiusmodi in desuetudinem abiit; et cum in eis non observetur, vidente et sciente ipso Romano Pontifice, non sunt de excommunicatione damnandi neque admittentes, neque introeuntes in illas. Etenim, ratione vere probabili ab excommunicatione excusantur. . . ."—Pennacchi, *Commentaria*, I, 777; Mocchegiani, *Iurisprudentia Ecclesiastica*, I, nn. 322-323; Reiffenstuel, *Jus Canonicum*, lib. III, tit. XXXV, n. 27; Hollweck, *Die kirchlichen Strafgesetze*, § 152, note 3; Bachofen held rigidly to the opposite opinion—*Compendium Juris Regularium* (New York, Cincinnati, Chicago: 1903), p. 152.

[49] "Controversia de sacristia, quae ante Codicem movebatur, supprimitur distinctione quae communiore opinione admittebatur: prout publicam ecclesiam continuat vel ab ea separatur, sacristia est extra vel intra clausuram"—Vermeersch-Creusen, *Epitome*, I, n. 754, b. "Si quid severius in aliqua religione statutum fuerit circa sacrarium, id servari poterit, at severior praxis vel legislatio non facit ut ultra limites a Codice statutos extendatur de iure clausura. . . ." Coronata, *Institutiones*, n. 611, b, note 4. Cf. Schaaf, *The Cloister*, p. 67.

tral observance, for it forms a part of the oratory or church. This was the interpretation of the old authors and has been continued by the commentators of the Code. With reference to the choir there must be invoked a distinction which is identical with the one that pertains to the sacristy. If the choir's sole approach leads from the cloistered precincts of the monastery, then the choir must likewise be considered as reserved exclusively for the regulars and consequently constitutes part of the cloistral limits.[50]

Thus the church, sacristy, and choir occupy a unique status in regard to the cloister laws. Being exempted from the cloistral limits, they may be entered by women. And yet, as regards the regulars themselves, a free access to these places is permitted, for in this respect they are not considered to be beyond the cloister.[51]

The Code recognizes the probability that guest-houses will oftentimes be required in connection with religious houses. Consequently, provision is made for them. In this matter there is a twofold possibility. The guest-house can be a separate building, or it can occupy a part of the house in which the regulars reside. In either case it must be placed outside the confines of the cloister.[52] If a section of the house has been reserved for guests, then it should so be situated as not to interrupt in any way the continuity of the cloistral boundaries.[53] This may easily be effected by designating a corner or wing of the building as the guest-house. Much of this planning will be left to the discretion of those superiors whose duty it is to establish the cloistral boundaries. It must always be kept in mind that the obligation of preserving inviolate the cloistral regulations is a primary consideration. First things come first. The provision of a guest-house is dictated only by charity and courtesy, and must be

[50] Bonacina, *De Clausura,* q. V, p. I, n. 3; Pennacchi, *Commentaria,* I, 776; Mocchegiani, *Iurisprudentia Ecclesiastica,* I, n. 326. The last mentioned of these authors notes that he has seen many choirs to which entrance is available only from the cloistered precincts of the monastery. Cf. also Coronata, *Institutiones,* n. 611, b; Schaefer, *De Religiosis,* n. 348, 3; Goyeneche, "Consultationes"—*CpR,* XVI (1935), 435-438.

[51] Pejska, *Ius Canonicum,* p. 152.

[52] Canon 597, § 2.

[53] Vermeersch-Creusen, *Epitome,* I, n. 754, b.

given consideration only after the primary obligations have been fulfilled. Superiors should always be guided by the thought that first and foremost the religious house is for the religious. This is the mind of the Code. Its law seeks to ensure the prevention of untold harm, not only to individuals in the community, but to the entire religious spirit and atmosphere as well.

Vermeersch [54] and Vromant [55] permit superiors to separate a corridor from the enclosure in order to provide a passageway through which guests may pass to reach their section of the house. Desiring apparently to follow the opinion of Vermeersch, whom he cites, Coronata becomes so yielding in his opinion that, if it be pressed to its natural conclusion, he appears to permit what must be regarded as a violation of the cloister. He holds the position that the church, guest-house and parlor are excluded from the cloistral boundaries, even when access to them necessitates passage through a corridor which is subject to the cloistral laws. The present writer cannot agree with him that such an arrangement is to be avoided simply *in the measure and to the extent in which it is possible to do this.* The prohibition is not to be formulated in this contingent manner; it stands as something absolute, for any transgression against it of necessity involves a violation of the cloister.[56]

The normal course of social and business life will dictate that each monastery provide a parlor in which the admissible visitors may be met for the purposes of discussion, of advice, and even of the properly suited entertainment. Though the Code confines its terminology to the singular, it does not seem that only one such parlor is permitted. The demands of courtesy and the need of privacy will often require more than one such room. The number will depend largely upon the size of the house and the frequency of the visits.

[54] *Epitome,* I, n. 754, b.

[55] *De Personis,* n. 384, II.

[56] "Excluduntur omnino a clausura ecclesia, hospitium pro advenis et collocutorium; quae sunt exclusa *etsi ad ea adeunda forte per atrium clausurae subiectum transeundum sit,* quod tamen vitandum est, *quantum fieri potest. . . .*" *Institutiones,* n. 611, b; Schaefer explicitly states that the entrance to the guest-house and to the parlor must not be made approachable by means of a corridor which is subject to the cloister laws—*De Religiosis,* n. 348, 2.

Always, however, every reasonable effort must be made to situate the parlors as near to the outside entrance as possible.[57] Such a procedure will render as remote as possible all dangers of cloistral violation. The designation of such parlors postulates once again prudence and sound, practical, canonical judgment on the part of the superiors. The phrase, "*quantum fieri potest,*" as employed in canon 597, § 2, has primary reference to houses already constructed. In designing new houses, superiors would do well always to situate the parlors immediately within the outside doors.

Canon 597, § 3, ordains that the limits of the cloister be plainly indicated. It seems that no strict obligation of employing a sign to fulfill this purpose can be deduced from this canon. While admitting that perhaps the best manner in which to indicate the boundaries of the cloister consists in the use of a definite sign or notice, Vermeersch maintains that this precept can be fulfilled in other ways. Whereas in canon 836, with reference to the prospective reception of Mass stipends at churches where such offerings are left in great number, the legislator has designated the use of some external sign to assure the faithful regarding the celebration of the ordered Masses either there or elsewhere, such a method of warning and notification is not commanded in canon 597, § 3.[58] Vermeersch is not alone in this opinion.[59]

There are other authors who content themselves simply with stating that the use of an external sign is the manner in which the proper indication shall be given. The question of the necessity of employing such a sign is not considered by them.[60]

[57] Canon 597, § 2; Vermeersch-Creusen, *Epitome,* I, n. 754, b.

[58] *Epitome,* I, n. 754, c.

[59] Cf. Coronata, *Institutiones,* n. 611, b, note 6; Schaefer, *De Religiosis,* n. 348, 2, note 207; Gerster a Zeil, *Ius Religiosorum,* p. 186; Beste, *Introductio in Codicem,* p. 407.

[60] Cocchi, *Commentarium,* IV, n. 98, C; Berutti, *Institutiones,* III, n. 113, IV; Blat, *Commentarium,* II, n. 525; Vromant, *De Personis,* n. 384, II; E. Eichmann, *Lehrbuch des Kirchenrechts auf Grund des Codex Iuris Canonici für Studierende* (2. ed., Paderborn: Ferdinand Schöningh, 1926), p. 243. Hereafter cited as *Lehrbuch.* C. Augustine, *A Commentary on the New Code of Canon Law* (8 vols., Vol. III, 5. ed., Herder: St. Louis, Mo., 1938), III, 313. Hereafter cited as *Commentary.*

While it is undoubtedly true that the canon does not specify the use of an external sign, yet it does command that the cloistral limits be clearly indicated. It seems permissible to observe that today persons have become sign conscious. Manifold signs greet the gaze of persons everywhere. Warnings are constantly being posted to prevent entry into certain property which must be protected. Large signs remind one of speed limits which must be observed. All of this is just the normal manner of expressing, at least in this country, laws which must be obeyed. Moreover, persons have come to expect and look for such signs. It is one method by which they come to a knowledge of their obligations. It seems, then, that in a matter of such importance as the preservation of the cloister, similar methods could best be employed. The object to be protected is of far greater price than mere material property. Since the same persons who have become accustomed to expect directive signs in the world are they whose entry into the cloister is forbidden, it seems best that they be notified and warned in the manner to which they are accustomed. The knowledge of the average layman concerning the cloister and its severely sanctioned laws is, at the most, scant. Very often their natural curiosity will lead them astray into precincts of the religious house which are forbidden to them. If they have an obligation to remain out of the cloistered sections of the monastery, there is a concomitant obligation incumbent upon the proper religious superiors, whose duty it is to protect the cloister from violation, to inform them of that duty. While it is not denied that this can be done in many ways, it does seem that one of the most effective methods will be the use of signs expressing the presence of the cloister and the resultant prohibition against admittance to it. Vermeersch [61] and Schaefer [62] consider such signs as "CLOISTER" or "THIS PART RESERVED TO THE RELIGIOUS" as sufficiently expressive signs. Others are content with the simple posting of the word "CLOISTER." [63] Augustine advises the use of the expression, "POSITIVELY NO ADMITTANCE." [64] It may here be suggested

[61] *Epitome*, I, n. 754, c.
[62] *De Religiosis*, n. 348, 2, note 207.
[63] Cocchi, *loc. cit.*; Eichmann, *loc. cit.*; Blat, *loc. cit.*; Coronata, *loc. cit.*
[64] *Loc. cit.*

with Schaaf [65] that, in order to obtain the greatest effectiveness for the posted sign or notice, a combination of these two be employed: "CLOISTER—POSITIVELY NO ADMITTANCE."

In its legislation on the confines of the cloister the Code is more or less general. This must, of necessity, be the case in universal legislation. The more specific regulations concerning the explicit confines of the cloister the Code leaves to the determination of religious superiors. Moreover, the choice of the specific superiors whose duty it will be to perform this task must be regulated by the rules and constitutions of the Order. And the latter in turn must attribute this right only to major superiors [66] or to general chapters.[67] Consequently, all competence in this matter is withdrawn from local superiors, even together with a determinative vote of their council or chapter.[68]

The very nature of a general chapter, and also the infrequency of its meetings, seems practically to dictate that this power be deputed rather to some specifically designated major superiors. Blat believes that the general chapter's competence should be directed especially toward laying down general determinations for the entire Order.[69] It is the opinion of Berutti that the competence in this respect can be considered as proper to the major superiors unless the constitutions expressly state that it is reserved to the general chapter.[70] This rule is wise and practically prudent, for the determination of the limits of individual cloisters postulates a personal knowledge of the architectural design of each separate religious house and of its adjoining grounds. Such a knowledge is more readily available to major superiors.

The determination of the cloistral boundaries must, of course, be effected not arbitrarily, but in accordance with the prescriptions

[65] *The Cloister*, p. 70.

[66] Canon 488, 8°.

[67] Canon 597, § 3.

[68] Berutti, *Institutiones*, III, n. 113, V.

[69] *Commentarium*, II, n. 525.

[70] *Loc. cit.*

of canon 597, § 2.[71] It is necessary that the entire section of the house in which the regulars actually live, together with the contiguous grounds which are reserved for the use of the religious, be enclosed. Any contrary regulations, even though they be motivated by a consideration of the purposes of study or of the fulfillment of the proper ends of the Order, would be a usurpation of powers which the Holy See has reserved to its own competence.[72] On the other hand, superiors must not include within the precincts of the cloister those places which the common law has placed beyond the cloistral area. Coronata mentions only the parlor as being beyond the powers of the superiors to include within the cloister.[73] About this, of course, there can be no doubt. To place it within the cloister would mean that it would cease entirely to be a parlor. May a like statement be made about the sacristy and the choir? The pre-Code authors maintained that these could be placed within the limits of the cloister. But their conclusions were based upon the confusion and indecision which enveloped the law of that time in relation to these two places.[74] It seems, therefore, that inasmuch as the law has since become clear, the authority of those authors ceases any longer to possess a telling force. Prescinding from all particular legislation in this regard, it seems certain that since the common law has placed the sacristy beyond the limits of the cloister, it may not be included by superiors. It is true that the common law today makes no mention of the choir. But the external authority adduced in proof of the fact that it is also exempted from the cloister [75] seems to justify the position that it also enjoys the exempt status which attaches to the sacristy.

The severe sanction which attaches to the law of the cloister be-

[71] Coronata, *Institutiones*, n. 611, b; Schaefer, *De Religiosis*, n. 348, 2, note 208; Fanfani, *De Iure Religiosorum*, n. 307, B; Blat, *Commentarium*, II, n. 525.

[72] Berutti, *Institutiones*, III, n. 113, V; Coronata, *loc. cit.*

[73] *Loc. cit.*

[74] Reiffenstuel, *Jus Canonicum*, lib. III, tit. XXXV, n. 27; Mocchegiani, *Iurisprudentia Ecclesiastica*, I, n. 330; Ojetti, *Synopsis Rerum Moralium et Iuris Pontificii* (3. ed., 3 vols., Romae: 1909-1914), I, n. 1179. Hereafter cited *Synopsis*.

[75] Cf. *supra*, p. 98, note 50.

gets an obligation of extreme care and attention in those whose duty it is to regulate the cloistral limits. For the sake of clarity and for the purpose of obviating all doubts the confines of the cloister should be accurately established.

To competent religious superiors is likewise conceded the privilege of changing the limits of the cloister when a sufficient cause demands an alteration. This change may be made permanently or temporarily. The Code does not distinguish.[76] The legitimate cause which the common law demands must be interpreted as being a serious cause.[77] Gerster a Zeil considers the necessity of undertaking repairs a sufficient reason for a temporary change.[78] Vromant considers it permissible temporarily to place outside of the cloister even a place which is normally used by the regulars, for example, the refectory.[79] Habitually to do this, however, would be equivalent to an abolition of the cloister. The occasion of a great celebration which necessitates the provision of a spacious room for the accommodation of a large group can, so it seems, render this change licit for the duration of a day.

Coronata [80] and Augustine [81] warn against changes being made on the spur of the moment. Such sudden alterations would justify the thought that the motive of avoiding the sanctions of the law was the specific reason for the change. The precincts of the cloister should be fixed and permanent.[82]

The farsightedness, prudence and good judgment of religious superiors are demanded not only in determining the confines of the cloister for the buildings already in existence, but more particularly in preparing for a properly determinable arrangement of the cloister for the buildings which are being constructed. Architectural beauty

[76] Cf. canon 597, § 3; Vermeersch-Creusen, *Epitome*, I, n. 754, e; Schaefer, *De Religiosis*, n. 348, 2; Jombart, *Periodica*, XVI (1927), 51*; Gerster a Zeil, *Ius Religiosorum*, p. 186; D. Prümmer, *Manuale Iuris Canonici* (4. et 5. ed., Friburgi Brisgoviae: Herder, 1927), q. 227, 2.

[77] Vermeersch-Creusen, *loc. cit.*; Gerster a Zeil, *loc. cit.*

[78] *Loc. cit.*

[79] *De Personis*, n. 384, II.

[80] *Institutiones*, n. 611, b.

[81] *Commentary*, III, 312.

[82] Vermeersch-Creusen, *loc. cit.*

and design must always occupy a secondary consideration. The primary purpose of the contemplated house is the provision of a home for religious. And that home demands a proper cloister. It will, therefore, be the duty of superiors not only to acquaint architects with the laws of the Church in this regard but likewise to insist upon their observance. It may happen that the concepts of architects will be directed to designs of beauty rather than to cloistral needs. The two can be compatible. They will be if the proper attention and study is given to the problem.

Canon 599, § 1, provides for a modified and mitigated form of the cloister among regulars. When a house of regulars has annexed to it a house for boarding pupils, or for other works proper to the Institute, a separate part at least of the annexed house should, if possible, be reserved for the habitation of the religious, and remain subject to the law of enclosure.

The situation for which this canon provides may well arise from the foundation of schools, hospitals, retreat houses, asylums and the like. While explicit mention of schools is made by the canon, the sundry ends of different religious communities will justify the presence of the other types of work. Included among the schools will be those buildings or units which are destined for the training of postulants and scholastics (Juniorates).[83]

Coronata [84] and Schaefer [85] maintain that one does not need to lay great stress upon the interpretation which points to merely such works which pertain in a very proper sense to the religious Institute. Any work undertaken with the permission of the Holy See or of the major superiors, so these authors assert, can be understood as a proper work of the Order, even though no mention of this work be contained in the Constitutions or Rule. This opinion, however, appears to permit a latitude which is not warranted by the canon itself. There is a certain definite meaning attached to the words of the canon. And that meaning has the effect of denoting a limitation. Were the opinion of Coronata and Schaefer followed, it seems that

[83] Coronata, *Institutiones*, n. 612, c.

[84] *Loc. cit.*

[85] *De Religiosis*, n. 348, 3, note 213.

the canon would be stripped of all meaning. It is of course true that, if the Holy See grants permission for an Order to undertake a form of work which connotes the application of this canon, then an implicit permission for invoking the favor of the canon would be contained in the grant. Moreover, it is perfectly within the rights of the Holy See to bestow such a permission for the good of the Church. But can the same be said of major superiors? Are they not bound by the dictates of their Constitutions? Adherence to the above opinion would grant them the power to undertake any type of commendable work whatsoever. But this would do violence to Constitutions which were written by the founder of the Order and approved by the Holy See for a specific end.

The ideal arrangement consists in the establishment of separate houses. But this is not demanded by the canon. Even when the school, hospital, etc., are annexed to the religious house, it is not *absolutely* demanded that a separate part of that house be established for the habitation of the regulars. The canon tempers its enactment for the contingency when this will not be possible. If then it is impossible to separate a section of this house and reserve it for the regulars, can it be said that the entire house is free from the law of the cloister? Chelodi does not admit any such freedom for the house. He asserts that the contrary will obtain and that the entire building will be subject to the law of the cloister inasmuch as no monastery of regulars can lawfully exist if it does not properly have a cloister.[86] While not pressing his statement to the same rigid conclusion, Ramos asserts that it is within the power of the major superiors or of the general chapters, according as the Constitutions determine, to place the entire school within the confines of the cloister.[87]

Must not the thought, however, that canon 599, § 1, is here granting a modification of canon 597, § 1, be given its due consideration? This provision for the case wherein some work of religion which is proper to the Institute attaches to the religious house is not absolute.

[86] *Ius de Personis,* n. 277, p. 463, note 4.

[87] "Clausura en los Colegios de Religiosos"—*Ilustracion del Clero,* XXIII (1928), 187. Reference to this article is made from "Excerpta ex ephemeridibus," *Apollinaris* (Romae: 1928—), I, (1928), 313.

It recognizes a just and grave reason as an excuse from the observance of the cloister. Particularly will this be true in buildings which already have been constructed.[88] Since, however, there does exist the obligation of setting aside for cloistral purposes at least a part of the house wherever this is possible, superiors should exert all their efforts when planning new structures to provide for the observance of the canon. The reasons adduced for the practically insurmountable failure to fulfill the requirements of this legislation in an old building will not always possess the same valid claims in relation to a new house.[89]

One cannot admit the opinion of Augustine[90] that, if a part of the house with which some work of religion is connected be set aside by the proper superior, the rigid papal cloister is not demanded by this canon. In the houses of regulars there is only one type of cloister and that is the papal cloister.[91]

While it is true that relative to such houses which have a proper religious work connected with them there does not exist any papal cloister in the parts which have not been set aside for that purpose, nevertheless women are not allowed entry therein. The reason for this inheres in the dictate of prudence.[92] Though the prohibition is rigid, it is not so absolute that exceptions cannot be made. Thus superiors are permitted to grant a relaxation when a righteous cause intervenes. Though the canon seems to favor the granting of permissions only in particular instances, Blat permits superiors to extend a general concession. He requires, however, that this concession be limited by certain conditions. What these conditions are he does not state.[93] In this he is opposed by Vromant.[94]

Among the causes justifying superiors in granting the necessary

[88] Berutti, *Institutiones,* III, n. 114, II; Coronata, *Institutiones,* n. 612, c; Wernz-Vidal, *Ius Canonicum,* III, n. 376; Prümmer, *Manuale Iuris Canonici,* q. 227, 4.

[89] Berutti, *loc. cit.*; Beste, *Introductio in Codicem,* p. 408; Vermeersch-Creusen, *Epitome,* I, n. 755, a.

[90] *Commentary,* III, 315.

[91] Ramos, *loc. cit.*; Beste, *loc. cit.*; Fanfani, *De Iure Religiosorum,* n. 307, A.

[92] Claeys-Bouuaert, *Manuale,* I, n. 666.

[93] *Commentarium,* II, n. 529.

[94] *De Personis,* n. 385, 2.

permissions authors list, for example, the attendance of women at such exercises as the ones connected with graduation,[95] and also the desire on the part of parents to visit their ill sons.[96] In the latter case it seems that the provision of Blat can be justified. Certainly a superior would be acting canonically in permitting a mother to visit her ill son, as often as she liked, but at certain hours.

Unless the constitutions rule otherwise, competence in this regard extends even to the local superior.[97]

Berutti is of the opinion that the houses of regulars may possess certain rooms situated beyond the cloistral boundaries and destined for the daytime teaching of girls and women. The same is true of such parts of the house in which it is necessary for women to perform certain tasks for the good of the community. Such tasks may consist in sewing, in cooking, and in certain other kinds of work which can be best accomplished by women. Into such places, however, no regular may go without the proper permission, for such work-rooms are absolutely outside of the cloister.[98]

B. *Cloister of Nuns*

The rule of canon 597 is applicable also to the convents of nuns.[99] The subsequent commentary on this canon in its relation to nuns necessarily will have to take account of the *Instruction* issued by the Sacred Congregation of Religious on the 6th of February, 1924.[100]

[95] Claeys-Bouuaert, *loc. cit.*

[96] Blat, *loc. cit.*; Claeys-Bouuaert, *loc. cit.*

[97] Fanfani, *De Iure Religiosorum*, n. 307, D; Schaefer, *De Religiosis*, n. 349; Berutti, *Institutiones*, III, n. 114, 2.

[98] Berutti, *ibid.*, Scholion.

[99] "In domibus regularium sive virorum sive mulierum. . . ."

[100] *Acta Apostolicae Sedis* (Romae: 1909—), XVI (1924), 96-101. Future references will cite this decree as *Instructio*. Though this teaching of the Sacred Congregation bears the title *Instructio*, it must be considered as having the obligatory force of a decree. These words are used: ". . . Re igitur mature perpensi, Sacra Congregatio ea quae sequuntur, circa legem Clausurae Papalis, servanda decrevit. . . ." Again: ". . . Sanctitas Sua praesertim Instructionem approbavit et ab omnibus servari mandavit. . . ." Cf. Maroto, "Annotationes"—*CpR*, V (1924), 140-141; "Annotationes"—*Periodica*, XIII (1925), 63-68; Schaefer, *De Religiosis*, n. 362; Blat, *Commentarium*, II, n. 530.

By common law the papal cloister prevails only in canonically constituted houses of nuns. Nuns are women who profess solemn vows.[101] There can be no discussion concerning the requisite number of nuns who must be present before the cloistral law exerts its effect. This rigid law will prevail regardless of paucity in the numbers of nuns attached to any given monastery.[102]

Possessing equal application with the cloister in monasteries of regulars with regard to the exemptions permitted by the canons, the convent cloister does not comprise within its limits the church, sacristy, parlor and guest-house. It must be noted here, however, that unlike regulars the nuns are absolutely forbidden all entry into the church and sacristy without the proper permission. The cloistral design in the convents of nuns will assume a different pattern than that found in the monasteries of regulars. The arrangement as it must exist today can best be learned from the detailed *Instruction* of the Sacred Congregation.[103]

Canon 602 ordains that the monasteries of nuns be so sheltered that, as much as possible, no nun can see anyone on the outside or be seen by anyone from the outside. The manner in which this obligation will be carried out is explained by the *Instruction*. Thus, all windows which face a street or some adjacent house, or which are conducive to any communication with those who are outside, must be constructed of opaque glass or be protected by shutters.[104] It appears that Venetian blinds could well fulfill these requirements. Windows made of opaque glass at the bottom and of plain glass at

[101] Cf. canon 488, 7°. This does not include the houses of nuns in those places where, by indult of the Holy See, simple vows only are professed by them. Cf. S. C. Ep. et Reg., *Parisien.*, 1 aug. 1839, ad 2—*Fontes*, n. 1923; *Americana Votorum*, 1 sept. 1864—*Acta Sanctae Sedis* (41 vols., Romae: 1865-1908), I (1865-1866), 708-739; *P. C. I.*, 1 mart. 1921, ad III—*AAS*, XIII, 177. By this response, the only houses in this country in which it was permitted to profess solemn vows were the convents of the Visitation Nuns at Georgetown, Baltimore, Mobile and St. Louis. The number of houses in which the making of a solemn profession is being granted is, however, on the increase at the present time.

[102] *Instructio*, II, b.

[103] Canon 601, § 1; *Instructio*, II, 6°.

[104] *Instructio*, II, 1°.

the top could be further screened by means of Venetian blinds. While allowing sunshine and fresh air to flood a room, such blinds will at the same time serve to prevent all looking into or out from the cloister. Again, wind-breaking shutters could profitably and canonically be used under the bottom of the windows when they are opened. These shutters are so fashioned that it is practically impossible to see through them. It will be noted that the obligation entailed herein to prevent the looking into or out from the cloister is not absolute but contingent upon the location of the convent and the corresponding degree of ease or difficulty attending any effort to gaze into or look out from the cloister.

With reference to the contiguous grounds this legislation on the prevention of reciprocal vision between the inside and outside of the cloister will much more easily be fulfilled in convents which are located in less populated districts. To carry out these prescriptions, however, will be far more difficult when a convent is situated in a modern city. Because such circumstances do exist, it cannot be canonically stated that the grounds which are adjacent to the convent and which are reserved for the use of the nuns should not be used by them. Both the Code and the *Instruction* modify their legislation with the reasonable clause, "*quoad fieri potest.*" [105] Consequently the bishop would, it appears, act contrary to canonical principles were he to exclude the grounds from the limits of the cloister because of reasons such as these. Perhaps it may be stated that the nuns have it in their power to fulfill at least a part of this law. This they could do by refraining entirely from looking beyond the limits of the grounds when they are using them. But even this is to demand more than does the law. The clause inserted into the law implies reasonable effort. Thus to demand of nuns that they constantly keep their heads bowed when they are walking in the grounds is to place a condition which vitiates the very purpose of the grounds —relaxation and recreation. However, studious and protracted gazing beyond the garden shelter would betray an unwillingness to abide by the spirit of the law.

[105] Vermeersch-Creusen, *Epitome,* I, n. 754, d; "Annotationes"—*Periodica,* XIII (1925), 66; Creusen, Garesché, Ellis, *Religious Men and Women in the Code* (3. ed., Bruce Publishing Co.: Milwaukee, 1940), n. 286.

Neither the canon nor the *Instruction* state what type of obstruction should surround the monastery grounds. In answer to the question whether a wall should be employed to encircle the grounds, it seems that since the material obstruction has not been specifically defined, anything suitably fulfilling the requirement of the law will suffice.[106] Vermeersch is quoted by Jombart as stating that even a thick hedge would be sufficient.[107] It does seem, however, that a closed board fence would better fulfill the purpose. Stone or brick walls, too, can readily be constructed at not too great an expense. Far from being unreasonable or constituting a hindrance to the freedom of these nuns who live within the strict enclosure, the cloistral regulations assure the nuns of that greater freedom from the world and from its dangers which they desire to flee.[108]

If the choir is sheltered by grates through which the nuns may view the altar, these grates should so be arranged that the faithful cannot see the nuns from the position which is reserved for the faithful in the church.[109] The construction of the grates will be one of the requirements about which the bishop should inform architects who plan the building of a convent. The altar alone should be made visible for the nuns. And the altar will always be beyond the space reserved for the faithful.

Under ordinary circumstances the confessor is bound to observe the laws of the cloister. Consequently the confessional must always be arranged in such a manner that it will permit the confessor to remain outside of the cloister and the penitents within the cloister.[110] Once again the law demands foresight and knowledge in those whose duty it will be to plan the building arrangement of the convent. Obviously the law implies that the confessor's approach to the confessional will be by an avenue which likewise lies beyond the cloistral limits. The confessional must always be canonically accessible both to the nuns and to the confessor. An opening in the

106 "Annotationes"—*Periodica,* XIII (1925), 66.

107 "Questio de clausura materiali regularium"—*Periodica,* XVI (1927), 51*.

108 Cf. E. J., "Cloture et Rigorisme"—*Revue des Communautés Religieuses* (Louvain, 1925—), XIV (1938), 83-86.

109 *Instructio,* II, 2°.

110 *Instructio,* II, 3°.

wall of the church, of the sacristy or of the choir would canonically fulfill the purpose of the legislation.

During the reception of Holy Communion the nuns must be hidden from all possible sight on the part of the faithful who may be in the church. This requirement may be attained by the use of a curtain or of a door.[111] If the choir is situated some distance from the place in which the nuns will receive Holy Communion, their approach for the reception of the Sacrament must always be by an avenue which not only lies within the cloistral limits but also beyond the view of the persons in the church.

Entire exclusion of the nuns from external communications obviously cannot be had. The necessities of life must come to the convent from the outside world. And always this must be done without any shadow of cloistral violation. It is decreed, then, that at the door of the monastery, in the sacristy, and wherever else there be a demand a turnplate shall be established as the means for passing in and out the necessary objects. A small opening may be contained in the turnplate so that the objects deposited in it may be seen.[112] If the Constitutions permit, this rotary structure may be situated even in the parlor.[113] It is proper to note here that the *Instruction* states that the opening in the turnplate shall serve the purpose of seeing these objects which are placed upon it. Evidently, then, turnplates which are built into the garden walls must be so arranged that outsiders will not be able to look into the grounds through the opening. Moreover, this revolving structure should, at every angle of its turn, prevent all possible looking out from and into the gardens.

The aperture which opens from the cloister into the parlor must be designed with two grates about eight inches apart and so inserted into the wall that they cannot be opened.[114] Nothing is said in the *Instruction* pertinent to the size of this aperture, the material of its grates or the size of the perforations in the grates. Must they be covered with a veil? Or at least must the nun who approaches the

[111] *Instructio*, II, 4°.
[112] *Instructio*, II, 5°.
[113] *Instructio*, V.
[114] *Loc. cit.*

parlor be veiled? It seems that these particular regulations must be determined by the Constitutions of the individual Communities.[115]

A noteworthy change in the confines of the cloistral limits has been introduced by the *Instruction*. Formerly the roof was declared to be beyond the cloistral boundaries.[116] The *Instruction* now declares that, if an ambulatory has been built upon the roof, this may be used by the nuns provided that the roof is sufficiently protected on all sides with a grill.[117]

The right and duty of establishing and changing the confines of the cloistral boundaries pertains to the competence of the bishop in whose diocese the convent is situated.[118] What has been said concerning this matter in reference to the monasteries of regulars will apply equally well here.[119] Though the bishop may not be so interested in and so intimately acquainted with the design of religious houses as are the regular superiors, yet his keen attention and guiding interest are demanded by the Code when there is question of establishing strictly cloistral designs. For this reason the plans of a prospective convent must be referred to the bishop and receive his approval.

Article II. Episcopal Cloister

The reasons adduced for the maintenance of the cloister within the houses of religious who profess solemn vows can be applied with equal validity to the houses of religious who profess simple vows. There is no radical difference in the nature of these two types of vows which would justify the exposure of the simply professed to dangers from which the others are protected. Equally dire results can be the outcome of insufficient protection in all monasteries. It is the same human nature which is clothed in the religious habit, whether that habit connote solemn or simple profession. And the sources whence dangers spring regard not the distinctions of profes-

115 "Annotationes"—*Periodica*, XIII (1925), 67.

116 Cf. S. C. Ep. et Reg., *in Lycien.*, 16 sept. 1609; *in Comen.*, 18 sept. 1609—Ferraris, *Bibliotheca*, s. v., "Moniales," art. III, 11; Mocchegiani, *Iurisprudentia Ecclesiastica*, I, n. 388.

117 *Instructio*, III, 1, c.

118 Canon 597, § 3; Blat, *Commentarium*, II, n. 525.

119 Cf. *supra*, pp. 102-105.

sion. Because of these facts the Church has decreed that a form of cloister be observed in the canonically constituted houses of all religious Congregations, regardlessly whether they be composed of men or of women, and indiscriminately whether they possess diocesan or pontifical approbation.[120] The common law, moreover, lends its special emphasis to the regulations which are contained in the Constitutions of Societies living a common life, but not formally professing the religious vows.[121]

A. *Congregations of Men Religious*

There is no mention in the canons relative to the precincts of this cloister. On the other hand, there has been no derogation of the cloistral concept as expressed in canon 597. It can be concluded, consequently, that the canon intends the pattern and design of that cloister to be followed.[122] Moreover, this conclusion is confirmed by the presence of a like regulation regarding the schools, hospitals, etc., which are joined with a religious house. The same prescriptions must be observed in the houses wherein the members profess simple vows as are demanded with reference to the houses in which the members profess solemn vows.[123] There can be no doubt about the obligation to observe this cloister. Canon 604, § 1, employs the identical verb, "*servetur,*" as used in canon 597, § 1, when it imposes the observance of the cloister.[124]

B. *Congregations of Women Religious*

Canon 604, § 1, in its reference to Congregations of women religious regards primarily those Institutes which always profess simple

[120] Cf. canon 604, § 1.

[121] Canon 679, § 2; Schaefer, *De Religiosis*, n. 608.

[122] Schaefer, *op. cit.*, n. 363, 1; Vermeersch-Creusen, *Epitome,* I, n. 756; Berutti, *Institutiones,* III, n. 118, II; Fanfani, *De Iure Religiosorum*, n. 316, A; J. B. Raus, *Institutiones Canonicae iuxta Novum Codicem Iuris pro Scholis vel ad Usum Privatum Synthetice Redactae* (2. ed., Parisiis: Vitte, 1931), n. 194, 2°. Hereafter cited as *Institutiones Canonicae.* Creusen, Garesché, Ellis, *Religious Men and Women in the Code*, n. 291.

[123] Cf. canon 604, § 2; Vermeersch-Creusen, *loc. cit.*; Blat, *Commentarium,* II, n. 543.

[124] Cf. canons 597, § 1; 604, § 1; Schaefer, *op. cit.*, n. 363, 1.

vows. Its scope, however, embraces likewise the convents of those nuns whose vows normally should be solemn but by virtue of an Apostolic indult are simple.[125] Many such convents are to be found in this country.

The convent of these sisters is not required, of course, to be fashioned along the pattern of the monasteries of nuns. Its design should, however, copy that of the regulars. The modification of the cloister as permitted by canon 599, § 1, pertinent to the case wherein schools, hospitals, etc., which are joined with the religious house, is permitted also in convents of women with simple vows.[126]

[125] Cf. *supra*, p. 109, note 101.

[126] Canon 604, § 2.

CHAPTER V

VIOLATION OF THE CLOISTER OF MALE REGULARS

Section A. Passive Violation

ARTICLE I. EXCLUSION OF WOMEN

A. Extent of Exclusion

HAVING firmly established the law which deals with the cloistral limits and confines, the Code logically legislates concerning those whose presence within the designated boundaries must not be permitted. Canon 598, § 1, states that within the cloister of male regulars women of whatsoever age, class or condition, must not under any pretext be admitted. Prescinding from the exception contained in canon 598, § 2, the prohibition established herein must be considered as possessing universality and finality. It can justly be said to encompass every human being of the female sex.

Canon 598, § 1, deals primarily with the non-admittance of women into the designated enclosure.[1] Although this canon contains no reference to penalties, it must nevertheless be accepted as an authentic norm according to which canon 2342, 2°, is to be interpreted. The present discussion will be confined to an explanation of the various terms which in their application to women are employed in canon 598, § 1. The concept of "admittance" and what it entails will be discussed in conjunction with the interpretation of canon 2342, 2°. It is in that canon that its meaning and consequence will more readily be seen.

The common law of the Church as expressed in canon 598, § 1, prohibits admittance into the cloister of male regulars to women only. Any existing prohibitions which likewise include men will de-

[1] Berutti, *Institutiones*, III, n. 114.

rive, then, only from the specific Constitutions of the Order,[2] or from particular law.[3]

The basis upon which the observance of the strict cloister is founded sufficiently explains this prohibition relative to women. Even a mediocre knowledge of human nature and of its potential frailties will suffice to afford an appreciation and understanding of the dangers and temptations which are hereby being prevented from reaching even an incipient stage of actual existence and manifest reality. To consider this prohibition as a blanket condemnation of the character of all women and of their associations with male regulars within the confines of the cloister is utterly to confuse the problem which is involved. Far from being an outright condemnation of the character of women, or even an implied insinuation which is nurtured by dark suspicion, such a prohibition reflects merely the use of a normal and obvious method for preserving what is good and unsullied from falling a prey to the probable or even possible danger of corruption. It is a matter of commonplace acknowledgment that the greater value of a thing calls for a greater degree of solicitous care in securing its absolute protection.

The non-reception of the Sacrament of Baptism does not avail any woman to exempt her from this rigid exclusion.[4] While it is true that the Church exercises no direct jurisdiction over those who are outside of her pale, in this canon the imposed obligation is one of non-admittance and is therefore meant to attach specifically to those whose duty it is to guard and preserve the cloister. Moreover, the Church has the right to protect her own even when this protection implies obedience to her law on the part of others, for such obedience is in reality nothing more than a manifestation of the dutiful respect which the natural law demands from all alike in relation to the established rights of others.

It has been said above [5] that the direct forerunner of this legisla-

[2] Fanfani, *De Iure Religiosorum,* n. 306, A.

[3] Schaefer, *De Religiosis,* n. 350.

[4] Blat, *Commentarium,* II, n. 527; Schaefer, *loc. cit.*; Cocchi, *Commentarium,* IV, n. 99, note 2; Berutti, *Institutiones,* III, n. 114.

[5] Cf. *supra,* p. 48.

tion was the Bull *"Regularium vitam"* of Pope Eugene IV which was issued in 1436. The prohibition expressed in that enactment embraced women of *all* ages. Ferraris in the eighteenth century cited decisions of the Sacred Congregation of Bishops and Regulars which excluded women of all ages from the cloister of regulars. Though he admitted the validity of these decisions, he also explained that the current practice reflected a divergence from this legislation.[6] Other authors granted the necessity of excluding young girls below the age of seven years from the cloister of regulars, but, nevertheless, excused from censure those who admitted them.[7]

Whatever may have been the prevalent interpretation before the Code, the law is now beyond all discussion. The precise and clear words of canon 598, § 1, prevent all hair-splitting argumentation and recourse to physiological interpretations to prove the contrary. Age is no longer a factor to be considered. The current legislation applies with equal validity to a woman who is approaching senility and to a new-born baby girl.[8] The foundation for this rigid enactment of the Code in reference to infants will be found in the observations of some of the old authors.[9] The presence of mental disorders or even

[6] *Bibliotheca*, s. v. "Conventus," art. III, nn. 19-20.

[7] Cf. Mocchegiani, *Iurisprudentia Ecclesiastica*, I, n. 336; Pennacchi, *Commentaria*, I, 778-779; Hollweck, *Die kirchlichen Strafgesetze*, § 152, note 6; J. D'Annibale, *Summula Theologiae Moralis* (3 vols., 5. ed., Romae, 1908), III, n. 227, note 3.

[8] Vermeersch-Creusen (*Epitome*, I, n. 758) assert that hereby the former controversy is suppressed. Cf. Claeys-Bouuaert, *Manuale*, I, n. 666; Beste, *Introductio in Codicem*, p. 407; Coronata, *Institutiones*, n. 612; Oesterle, *Praelectiones*, p. 336; Berutti, *Institutiones*, III, n. 114; Gerster a Zeil, *Ius Religiosorum*, p. 188; P. Cerato, *Censurae Vigentes ipso facto a Codice Iuris Canonici excerptae* (2. ed., Patavii, 1921), p. 121. Hereafter cited as *Censurae Vigentes*. F. Cappello, *Tractatus Canonico-Moralis de Censuris iuxta Codicem Iuris Canonici* (3. ed., Taurinorum Augustae: Marietti, 1938), n. 322. Hereafter cited as *De Censuris*.

[9] ". . . Finis enim Summorum Pontificum in decernenda clausura fuit, ne Religiosis detur occasio impudicitiae; at haec occasio non omnino cessat in parvulis puellis. . . ." Mocchegiani, *loc cit.;* ". . . hinc si tolerari non debet in monasteriis monialium, ut puellae, licet parvulae, ingrediantur, et egrediantur ad libitum; a fortiori videtur non esse tolerandum in Conventibus et Monasteriis virorum. . . ."—Ferraris, *Bibliotheca*, s. v. "Conventus," art. III, n. 19.

the utter lack of reason in an adult woman can certainly provide no justification for a relaxation of this law.[10]

As a further specific indication of the unbending rigidity of its legislation, the canon employs the phrase "*cuiusvis generis aut conditionis.*" What is the meaning of this phrase? Authors generally agree that the words "*cuiusvis generis*" imply that family relationship which is the consequence of birth.[11] No bonds of blood, then, with the persons residing within the cloister will avail to effect an exemption from this law. The relationship of mother and son is the most intimate in this regard and yet it merits no exemption.[12] If it is true of this which is the closest of human relationships, it is certainly true of all other blood relationships.

The words "*cuiusvis conditionis*" point to the *social* status which is possessed by women. This is the meaning commonly asserted by authors.[13] This concept appears to prescind entirely from all blood relationships with the regulars. Augustine[14] was confused by the English rendition of "*generis*" as "class" in the approved translation issued by the Holy See. "If it (class) is taken to mean birth," he said, "it would refer to nobility; but this seems to be included in *conditio.*" Vermeersch likewise noted the misconception conveyed by that inaccurate translation.[15] But he properly observed that though the translation was approved, it was by no mean an authentic document. He further stated that the notion of "*classis*" was comprehended by the word "*conditio.*" It is quite true, as Schaefer notes,[16] that certain factors connected with a person's birth can constitute a reason for one's position in society. But a social status may

[10] " . . . lex non distinguit ac eadem profecto militat ratio, nempe castitatis tuendae causa. . . ."—Cappello, *De Censuris,* n. 322; cf. Schaefer, *loc. cit.;* Berutti, *loc. cit.;* Cerato, *loc. cit.*

[11] Schaefer, *De Religiosis,* n. 350, note 217; Vermeersch-Creusen, *Epitome,* I, n. 758; Beste, *Introductio in Codicem,* p. 407; Claeys-Bouuaert, *Manuale,* I, n. 666.

[12] Cf. Schaefer, *loc. cit.;* Vermeersch-Creusen, *loc. cit.;* Beste, *loc. cit.*

[13] Cf. Schaefer, *loc. cit.;* Vermeersch-Creusen, *loc. cit.;* Beste, *loc. cit.*

[14] *Commentary,* III, 313.

[15] *Epitome,* I, n. 758.

[16] *De Religiosis,* n. 350.

well be obtained without the intervention of such factors. Thus, the meaning of the canon is that all women are excluded from the cloister regardless of the consanguineous ties (*cuiusvis generis*) which may link them to the regulars, and regardless, likewise, of any noble or exalted status (*cuiusvis conditionis*) which they may hold in the ranks of society.

The reason for the precise language employed by the legislator is, undoubtedly, the fact that many concessions to royalty had been made in former years.[17] Though privileges had been conceded and revoked many times during the course of the development of the cloistral law, the last general revocation was issued by Pope Benedict XIV (1740-1758).[18] Certain privileges, however, were permitted to remain in force. Thus the pontifically approved privileges which had been made available for the noble women of their families by certain founders or by the generous benefactors of a monastery continued in effect and thus accorded to such women the right to enter the monastery. Again, women related by blood or by affinity to the ruling dukes, counts, marquises, etc., could enter those monasteries which were situated within the confines of the territory subject to these members of the nobility, provided always that their privilege was founded upon a legitimate title or custom. It was necessary, also, that all such privileges had been confirmed by Papal brief or bull. It was required, moreover, that an authentic copy of the privilege in question was previously shown to the local ordinary.[19]

May it be said that these privileges, and any others subsequently granted by the Holy See, continue to possess validity? By virtue of canon 4 all the privileges granted by the Holy See which still continue in use and have not been revoked may for the present be legitimately employed, for they remain integral and intact unless they are expressly revoked in the canons of the Code. There does not

[17] Cf. *supra*, pp. 81-83.

[18] Const. "*Regularis Disciplinae*," 3 ian. 1742—*Bullarium Benedicti XIV*, I, 128; cf. Pennacchi, *Commentaria*, I, 774.

[19] Cf. Pennacchi, *loc. cit.*; Mocchegiani, *Iurisprudentia Ecclesiastica*, I, n. 335; St. Alphonsus, *Theologia Moralis*, lib. VII, n. 231.

appear any clause of such express revocation in the canons relative to cloister. Consequently, if the prerequisite conditions of canon 4 are legitimately established and proved, then the existing privileges may justly be used to advantage by those who possess them.[20]

Vermeersch [21] and Schaefer [22] favor the continuance of the privileges accorded by Pope Benedict XIV. It may be asked, however, with Pennacchi [23] whether, despite the validity of these privileges, they may currently be employed? They were granted by Pope Benedict XIV with the prime purpose of permitting entry into the churches of the regulars for the pursuance of religious exercises.[24] Under the present law, entry to the monastic church will always be available apart from all need of passing through the cloistral limits.[25] Consequently there will be no necessity for invoking the privilege. However, if there be posited a case wherein it will be necessary, for the pursuance of religious duties, to enter a chapel which is situated within the cloistral limits, then the privilege may be used. It appears, then, that the affirmations of Vermeersch and Schaefer must be understood in the light of the limitation placed by Pope Benedict XIV and within the framework of the present law which, wherever its provisions are followed, offers the facility of attendance at Mass in a monastic church without presupposing the need of passing through or of entering the cloister.

Much consideration has been given to the lawfulness on the part of women to enter the cloister of regulars at the time of processions and divine services. It has been shown that Pope Pius V in his Constitution *"Decet"* [26] permitted women to enter the monastery to

[20] Cf. canons 4; 598, § 1.

[21] *Epitome,* I, n. 758, 1.

[22] *De Religiosis,* n. 350.

[23] *Commentaria,* I, 774.

[24] Const. *"Regularis Disciplinae,"* § 8: " . . . et dummodo nec vagandi, nec otiandi, nec comedendi cenandique, nec per ambulacra, cubicula, cenacula, aliaque loca, et officinas discurrendi causa, sed ad Ecclesias accedendi, Sacrosanctum Missae Sacrificium audiendi, aliaque erga Deum pietatis officia, et opera exercendi studio ingrediantur. . . ."—*Bullarium Benedicti XIV,* I, 128.

[25] Cf. canon 597, § 2.

[26] 16 iul. 1570—*Fontes,* n. 136; cf. *supra,* pp. 56-57.

attend Mass, processions, etc., and, when the size of the congregation forbade easy entry and egress through the doors of the monastic church, it was perfectly licit for women to use an entrance which led into the cloister, provided always that in so doing they continued immediately to the door of the monastery which led to the outside. The subsequent revocation of that privilege by Pope Gregory XIII [27] has been sufficiently proved, it seems, by the many decrees of the Roman Congregations.[28] Moreover, the Constitution *"Regularis Disciplinae"* of Pope Benedict XIV [29] revoked all privileges previously accorded by any Popes. Only those of which mention has been made above were permitted to remain. But the question concerning the continuance of the privilege granted by Pope Pius V has been and is today a topic of large discussion and of sharp disagreement among authors. Before the promulgation of the Code both the utter revocation of that privilege and its valid continuance in use were upheld by authors. Among the proponents of these divergent opinions it seems that those who denied the continuance of that privilege could and did invoke the stronger legal support for their doctrine. This view is held by the present writer because of the fact that these authors not only could and did cite the various revocatory decrees of the Sacred Congregations in support of their position, but also assumed the wording of the Constitution of Benedict XIV in its natural and apparent signification.[30] On the other hand, those who de-

[27] Const. *"Ubi gratiae,"* 13 iun. 1575—*Fontes,* n. 147.

[28] Cf. S. C. Ep. et Reg., 21 apr. 1577—*Fontes,* n. 1329; 24 ian. 1595—*Fontes,* n. 1531; 22 feb. 1595, ad 3—*Fontes,* n. 1594; S. R. C., 30 sept. 1628—*Fontes,* n. 5308; 11 iun. 1629—*Fontes,* n. 5315; 5 iul. 1631—*Fontes,* n. 5337; 24 nov. 1635—*Fontes,* n. 5360; 10 dec. 1667—*Fontes,* n. 5568.

[29] 3 ian. 1742—*Bullarium Benedicti XIV,* I, 128.

[30] Mocchegiani (*Iurisprudentia Ecclesiastica,* I, nn. 343-344) observed after a study of the decrees of the Sacred Congregations: "Non esse amplius locum concertationibus vel dubitationibus super re a quibusdam auctoribus, etiam Commentatoribus Const. *Apostolicae Sedis* excitatis." Cf. also J. Bucceroni, *Commentarii . . . de C. Pii IX Apostolicae Sedis . . .* (5. ed., Romae, 1899), p. 143 (hereafter cited *Commentarii*); St. Alphonsus, *Theologiae Moralis,* lib. VII, n. 221; Bachofen, *Compendium Juris Regularium,* p. 158; J. Téphany, *Constitution Apostolicae Sedis de Sa Saintete Le Pape Pie IX Limitant Les Censures Latae Sententiae* (Tours: 1883), n. 325.

nied the revocation of the privilege contented themselves with devious explanations and interpretations of the Constitutions of Popes Gregory XIII and Benedict XIV, and dismissed without mention the important and pertinent decrees of the Roman Congregations.[31]

Among the contemporary authors there is likewise a wide divergence of opinion. Schaefer,[32] Coronata,[33] Gerster a Zeil,[34] Beste,[35] and Prümmer [36] assert that the immemorial customs which exist in some places and grant to women entrance into the cloister on the occasion of processions may be tolerated by virtue of canon 5, if the bishop judges that such customs cannot prudently be suppressed. Can this view be accepted? It is evident, first of all, that the value of any opinion must be determined by the cogency of the reasons upon which it is founded. Particularly is this true when a position is taken with regard to a question which is widely discussed. But the view of these authors is simply stated without confirmatory proof. Moreover, in a footnote, Schaefer cites a decree of the Sacred Congregation of Rites which was issued in the year 1635.[37] In all appearance he cites that decree in confirmation of his opinion. But the decree itself obviously states quite the opposite.[38]

Secondly, the strength of the opinion expressed by these authors depends upon the actual presence of an immemorial custom which permits the bishop to invoke canon 5. Granting, but not admitting,

31 Ferraris, *Bibliotheca*, s. v. "Conventus," art. III, n. 26. Either Ferraris or his correctors added however: "Nunc autem quoad supradicta est omnino attendenda novissima dispositio Benedicti XIV." Cf. also Pennacchi, *Commentaria*, I, 797-802; A. Ciolli, *Commentario Practico Delle Censure Latae Sententiae Oggigi in Vigore Nella Chiesa* (4. ed., Siena, 1884), p. 131; P. Avanzini, *De Constitutione Apostolicae Sedis* (2. ed., Romae, 1874), n. 301.

32 *De Religiosis*, n. 350.

33 *Institutiones*, n. 612.

34 *Ius Religiosorum*, p. 188.

35 *Introductio in Codicem*, p. 407.

36 *Manuale Iuris Canonici*, q. 227, r. 3.

37 *De Religiosis*, n. 350, note 224.

38 ". . . an liceat mulieribus occasione Processionum ingredi septa Monasteriorum Regularium, etiam stante consuetudine ingrediendi? Et S. R. C. respondit: Nullo modo licere mulieribus ingredi septa Monasteriorum Regularium occasione quarumcumque Processionum, non obstante quacumque contraria consuetudine"—S. R. C., *Sulmonen.*, 24 nov. 1635—*Fontes*, n. 5360.

the presence of such a custom, can it be said that the custom is legitimate or canonical? Mocchegiani,[39] Bucceroni,[40] St. Alphonsus,[41] Téphany, [42] and Bachofen [43] have been previously cited as denying that it was legitimate for women to enter the cloister on such occasions. With the exception of St. Alphonsus, these authors wrote shortly before or after the turn of this century. Their opinions did not admit the presence at that time of a legitimate immemorial custom warranting the entrance of women into the cloister on the occasions of processions. And their view, it seems, was based upon stronger legal support than that of the opposing group.

Vermeersch [44] and Cocchi [45] approach this problem from another avenue. While not mentioning explicitly the custom on the part of women to enter the monasteries of regulars on the occasions of processions, Vermeersch does say that *all* century old customs in this regard were suppressed by Pope Pius IX in his Constitution *"Apostolicae Sedis"* [46] and consequently cannot today be admitted. Cocchi explicitly mentions the precise problem under consideration and maintains a position identical with that of Vermeersch. It must be admitted that this view appears rather weak. There is no mention in the Constitution *"Apostolicae Sedis"* pertinent to the suppression of all customs in this regard. The Constitution reaffirmed all the censures which had been decreed by the predecessors of Pope Pius IX. Moreover, it asserted that women may not enter the cloister of regulars. Apparently that reaffirmation and reassertion have been interpreted by Vermeersch and Cocchi as implying a suppression of all contrary customs. But it must be noted that the commentators upon that Constitution who have been consulted made no mention of such a suppression. And had that notion been prevalent when they wrote, it appears that they would have adverted to it.

[39] *Loc. cit.*

[40] *Loc. cit.*

[41] *Loc. cit.*

[42] *Loc. cit.*

[43] *Loc. cit.*

[44] *Epitome*, I, n. 758.

[45] *Commentarium*, IV, n. 99, note 3.

[46] Oct. 12, 1869—*Fontes*, n. 552.

In commenting upon the words "*sub quovis praetextu*" of canon 598, § 1, Blat asserts that not even the pretext of piety will avail to grant entry into the cloister of regulars.[47] Though he makes no mention of the question under discussion, it does seem that, when dwelling upon the pretext of piety, he would have made reference to the immemorial custom permitting entrance on the occasion of religious processions had he thought one to be in existence.

It does appear, then, that today canon 5 cannot be invoked by bishops to permit the continuance of the immemorial customs which allowed the entry of women into the cloister of regulars at the time of processions. This view is adopted for the following reasons: (a) the evident desire of the present day legislator is to be most rigid in excluding women from the cloister of regulars; the exception to this law is stated explicitly by the canon itself; (b) the decrees of the Sacred Congregations prove decisively that it was the mind of the Church to suppress all customs in this regard; (c) those authors who in the past centuries held for the continuance of the privilege granted by Pope Pius V ignored the decrees of the Sacred Congregations and the universal suppression of all privileges in this regard by Pope Benedict XIV; (d) present day authors who assert the validity of immemorial customs are content simply to state their position without offering any reasons; (e) the citation by Schaefer of the decree of the Sacred Congregation of Rites certainly does not strengthen his position in the opinion which he has chosen to defend.

The closing words of canon 598, § 1, vitiate all appeals on the part of women to justifying motives which could render legitimate their entry within the cloister. Under no pretext may they be permitted to enter into the cloistral limits.[48] If the examples used by authors can serve as a true criterion, it may be judged that the pretext most frequently apt to be invoked to gain entry into the cloister is that of visiting a very sick or dying son or relative.[49] This ex-

[47] *Commentarium,* II, n. 527.

[48] Canon 598, § 1: ". . . ne admittantur mulieres . . . sub quovis praetextu."

[49] Vermeersch-Creusen, *Epitome,* I, n. 758; Cocchi, *Commentarium,* IV, n. 99, a; Beste, *Introductio in Codicem,* p. 407; Claeys-Bouuaert, *Manuale,* I, n. 666.

ample can serve the purpose of manifesting not only the absolute rigidity of the law but likewise the inefficacy of the invocation of pretexts. When the law will not bend in favor of the natural craving of a mother to be at the bedside of her dying son, then it is useless to appeal to other pretexts. This one, it seems, is the ultimate, and it fails.[50]

As Blat wisely observes,[51] it would be wrong to interpret the inefficacy of invoking pretexts as applying only to the women who desire to enter into the cloister. Those who reside within the cloister are equally forbidden any and all recourse to pretexts for the apparent sake of warranting any woman's entry into the monastic cloister. There is no distinction made in the canon. Any other interpretation would obviously deprive the canon of its intended force.

Prescinding, then, from all valid indults and privileges, the all-embracing extent of this canon can be summed up in the words of Berutti who says: "No cause can, of itself, render legitimate the entry of women into the cloister; whether it be a question of infant girls or of decrepit old women, of matrons, of virgins or even of religious; whether it concern pious Catholics or non-Catholics and pagans; whether it regard those who have or those who have not the perfect use of reason; whether it relate to the poor or the rich, even to those who have been most beneficent to the regulars; whether it refer to those who in no manner are related by blood or by affinity or to those who are joined by the closest bonds with the religious." [52]

[50] A misconception of the true meaning of what the religious life implies may readily engender adverse criticism of the laws of the Church in this regard. An uninformed observer may accuse the Church of being harsh and merciless for enacting such an inflexible and austere law. But let it be remembered that absolute freedom accompanied the choice whereby the person decided to live within the cloister. Knowledge of what that life entailed was possessed, not only by the religious himself, but by his parents as well. The sacrifice was motivated by spiritual and not temporal values. It must, consequently, be judged by that norm alone. When it is, all aspect of harshness will disappear. Cf. Jombart, "Cloture et Rigorisme,"—*Revue des Communautés Religieuses*, XIV (1938), 83-86.

[51] *Commentarium*, II, n. 527.

[52] *Institutiones*, III, n. 114.

B. Exemptions From This Law

Canon 598, § 2, states that from the law of papal cloistral observance are exempted together with their retinue the wives of those who actually exercise supreme authority as the rulers of a people.[53]

The absolute exclusion of all women by the first paragraph of this canon is modified by this one exemption. Assuming the nature of a common law privilege, the favor which this canon grants to certain women is based upon the recognition by the Church of the dignity and prerogatives inherent in their state in life.[54]

The interpretation of this canon will follow a threefold division: (1) What is the meaning of the word *uxores?* (2) what is meant by the words *qui supremum actu tenent populorum principatum?* (3) what is the meaning of *cum comitatu?*

1. Who Are the Wives of Rulers?

The privilege expressed in this canon regards primarily not the faith of the rulers and of their wives, but rather the exalted position which they fill in a country or state. Since the legislator of the Code was well aware of the fact that not all the rulers and their wives were Catholics, and since, at the same time, he failed to place any distinction in his law, it can be concluded that this privilege applies even to non-Catholics and infidels.[55]

Much discussion among authors centers about the precise meaning of the word *"uxores."* Will it be necessary that the woman who invokes this privilege be the canonically lawful wife of the supreme government official? Interpreting the word in its strict sense, some authors demand, as a necessary condition for the legitimate use of

[53] The exemptions which were formerly granted to queens are now extended to women who enjoy a similar position in a country. " . . . Exceptio qua fruebantur reginae, ad personas aequiperatas extenditur. . . . "—Vermeersch-Creusen, *Epitome,* I, n. 758, 2. Cf. also, Cocchi, *Commentarium,* IV, n. 99, a; Schaefer, *De Religiosis,* n. 350.

[54] Cf. Oesterle, *Praelectiones Iuris Canonici,* I, 336. Similar beneficial concessions of the common law in favor of persons vested with ruling authority will be found in canons 1557, § 1, 1°, and 2227, § 1. Cf. Eichmann, *Lehrbuch,* p. 244, note 1.

[55] Cf. Coronata, *Institutiones,* n. 612; Berutti, *Institutiones,* III, n. 114.

this canon, that the woman be the canonically lawful wife of the ruler.[56] This opinion includes not only the valid marriage of Catholics, but all mixed or disparate marriages contracted with the proper dispensation, the valid marriages of baptized non-Catholics, the valid marriages of the non-baptized and, according to Blat,[57] all putative marriages. The statement of Blat that a merely civil marriage (*non ex mero civili*) is not to be included causes some confusion. If he means a merely civil union which is contracted by those who are bound to the Catholic form of marriage,[58] then his position is clear. But the merely civil marriage of all others can be a valid union. The issue is made more confusing by his admission of a legitimate marriage, that is, a marriage validly contracted by two non-baptized persons.[59] But certainly that marriage could be a merely civil one. He may, however, have reference to a marriage which is contracted as a merely civil union which excludes all of the duties and obligations which marriage implies. But that would be no marriage at all.

The strict opinion of these authors is weakened considerably, however, by the interpretation of those who adopt a more lenient view in this matter. Oesterle,[60] Vermeersch-Creusen,[61] Fanfani,[62] Coronata,[63] and Berutti [64] assert that the status of a woman as the wife of a ruler is not to be determined by an application of the canonical principles of marriage, but rather by the dictates of the common estimation of men. In other words, it is not a question of law, but one of fact. In line with this opinion the problem will be settled by

[56] ". . . uxores appellanter feminae, quae nuptias secundum ius canonicum validas inierunt . . ."—Pejska, *Ius Canonicum*, p. 155; ". . . si femina talis non esset legitima uxor, non eximitur a lege clausurae . . ."—Gerster a Zeil, *Ius Religiosorum*, p. 188; ". . . non ex mero civili, sed putativo saltem matrimonio, etsi tantum legitimo. . . ."—Blat, *Commentarium*, II, n. 527.

[57] *Loc. cit.*

[58] Cf. canon 1099.

[59] Cf. canon 1015, § 3.

[60] *Praelectiones Iuris Canonici*, I, 337.

[61] *Epitome*, I, n. 758, 2.

[62] *De Iure Religiosorum*, n. 306, B.

[63] *Institutiones*, n. 612.

[64] *Institutiones*, III, n. 114. This opinion is inferred from his statements.

the uniform answer which is given by lay persons to the question: "Is this woman the wife of the ruler?"

Because of the disregard prevalent today among Protestant sects and in civil laws for the indissolubility of the marriage bond, it can happen that a woman who is not the true wife of a man will nevertheless be considered as such. With this in mind, Vermeersch presents the case wherein a non-Catholic ruler has divorced his wife and then has married another woman. He then asks whether the latter of these women may enjoy the exemption which is mentioned in canon 598, § 2.[65] It is assumed, of course, that canonically the second marriage is invalid. But that fact does not merit primary consideration. If the second woman is commonly reputed to be his true wife, she may be included among those who enjoy the right to enter the papal cloister.[66]

It could happen that there has taken place a divorce which is generally unknown. This could be the case if a ruler married a woman who previously lived in another country and had been divorced there. But the case as presented by the authors assumes that the divorce is public and that it was obtained by the ruler from his lawful wife. If, despite this knowledge, the woman is generally conceded to be the true wife of the ruler, she will, then, be granted the exemption of canon 598, § 2. Gerster a Zeil asserts that if there is doubt about the validity of her marriage, the woman may enjoy the exemption. It appears, however, in view of the canonically valid marriage which he requires, that he has reference here to a strictly canonical doubt and not merely to a factual doubt among lay persons.[67] The opinion of Vermeersch and his followers seems to refer only to the divorce and subsequent marriage of non-Catho-

[65] " . . . Supponas principem protestantem qui, facto divortio, aliam ducere uxorem tentarit. Quid tunc iuris?"—*loc. cit.*

[66] "Arbitramur ad communem aestimationem respiciendum esse. Admitti poterit quae passim pro vera uxore habetur. . . ."—Vermeersch, *loc. cit.* Since it appears that the other mentioned authors have been content to follow Vermeersch in this question, what is expressed in the opinion of Vermeersch may be assumed to reflect their opinion also.

[67] "Si femina talis non esset legitima uxor, non eximitur a lege clausurae; quamdiu legitimitas dubia est, eximitur."—*Ius Religiosorum*, p. 188.

lics. In view of the fact that the Catholic laws about the indissolubility of marriage are well known, even to those of different faiths, it appears that the common estimation of lay persons would not regard the second "wife" of a divorced Catholic ruler as being his true and lawful wife.

This is the theory of the opinion as held by the authors who have been cited. Fanfani seems to express the mind of all when he says that the canon is granting a privilege and henceforth deserves a wide and lenient interpretation.[68]

Because some of these authors have qualified their opinions with the necessary condition of always excluding scandal and wonderment in lay persons, the practical application of this interpretation will assume quite a different aspect.[69] This shifts the entire problem so as to connect its solution with a practical judgment concerning the scandal or wonderment which would arise in lay persons were the Church to grant the same exemptions to a legitimately married woman and to one not validly married. Oesterle and Vermeersch make no distinction with regard to the persons who would suffer scandal. It can be presumed, then, that they include Catholics as well as non-Catholics. Furthermore, they simply assert that if there is scandal or wonderment present, the privilege may not be used. Schaefer [70] asserts that the invalidly married wife of a ruler may not enter the cloister because there would *always* be scandal and wonderment on the part of *Catholics* if the Church were to grant equal privileges to validly and invalidly married women. This opinion seems to be the safest and most prudent. The topic of divorce is prevalent today. And the teachings of Christ and of His Church on this subject are widely denied. It is quite proper to interpret widely the privileges which the Church grants. But when that benign interpretation offers favors to those who ill deserve them, and, at the same time, causes scandal among others who are striving to live a good life, then it appears that the Church desires first to pro-

[68] *De Iure Religiosorum,* n. 306, B.

[69] Cf. Vermeersch, *Epitome,* I, n. 758, 2; Oesterle, *Praelectiones Iuris Canonici,* I, 337.

[70] *De Religiosis,* n. 350.

tect her own, and only then allow favors to others. It appears, then, that the privilege granted in canon 598, § 2, may be invoked only by those women who are the legitimate wives of rulers. It would be licit for one to hold the opposite view *if* he could prove that the common estimation of men regards as a true wife the woman who is married to a divorced ruler, *and* that no scandal, wonderment or bewilderment would be present for Catholics if the Church were to permit that woman to enter the cloister.

Schaefer states that the wife of a divorced ruler could enter the cloister if she were to obtain a new privilege.[71] This statement must be understood in the correct sense, however. For special reasons she could be authorized, like any other woman, to enter the cloister. In such a case scandal would not, or at least need not, necessarily ensue.

2. *Qui Supremum Actu Tenent Populorum Principatum*

The sense of these words is not that a man must be vested with absolute, supreme power over a people before his wife may enjoy the exemption which canon 598, § 2, grants. This is neither the sense of the words nor is it the general interpretation of the authors.

As the first meaning of the word "*principatus*" Forcellini gives: "the first place, pre-eminence, preference." Its secondary sense he gives as: "the chief place in the state." [72] The use of this precise word by the legislator makes it evident, then, that a change from the old law was being introduced. The terminology formerly employed was similar to the following: *imperatores, imperatrices, reges reginasque, etc.* The concept expressed by the present terminology is more extensive.[73] During the past few centuries the forms of government have undergone radical changes. Provided only that it is just and legitimate, each and every form of government is recognized by the Church.[74] Catholics reside in every land and under every

[71] *Loc. cit.*

[72] *Totius Latinitatis Lexicon* (4 vols., Schneebergae-Lipsiae: 1831-1839), s. v. *Principatus.*

[73] Eichmann, *Lehrbuch*, p. 244, note 1.

[74] Cf. Pope Leo XIII, ep. encycl. "*Immortale Dei,*" 1 nov. 1885—*Fontes*, n. 592.

form of government. And where Catholics are, there usually are monasteries. Were the use of the exemption granted by canon 598, § 2, confined only to the wives of those rulers in whom is vested complete governing authority, very few would be permitted to enjoy it. There would, consequently, be many countries and states in which the use of this privilege would be unknown. In view of the facts, then, that all legitimate forms of government are recognized by the Church, that the privilege here in question is a common law privillege, and that it is granted by the Church as a favor to governmental heads, does it not appear that the purpose and intention of the legislator is defeated by the application of a rigid interpretation of his law? The interpretation of reputable authors certainly does not restrict the extent of the privilege. On the contrary, their interpretation is most extensive.[75]

In the face of such a practically unanimous interpretation, the opinion of Augustine that "the President's wife, and the governor's wife, we are sorry to say, are not included in this privilege, because their husbands are not actual rulers in the commonly accepted sense of the word," cannot possibly possess any probability.[76] Commenting upon this opinion, Vermeersch exclaimed that he could not understand the scruple of Fr. Augustine.[77]

While authors generally admit that the wife of the President of a Republic enjoys this privilege, few of them refer specifically to the President of the United States and the Governors of the individual states.[78] It is true that the President and the Governors in

[75] ". . . populorum principatum, sive reges sint, imperatores, principes, reipublicae praesidentes, aliove nomine designentur. . . . "—Blat, *Commentarium*, II, n. 527; ". . . ergo non tantum reginae, sed etiam uxores praesidum reipublicae, principis regnantis, etc. . . . "—Fanfani, *De Iure Religiosorum*, n. 306, B; cf. also Pejska, *Ius Canonicum*, p. 155; Vermeersch-Creusen, *Epitome*, I, n. 758, 2; Beste, *Introductio in Codicem*, p. 407; Schaefer, *De Religiosis*, n. 350; Cappello, *De Censuris*, n. 317; Oesterle, *Praelectiones Iuris Canonici*, I, 337.

[76] *Commentary*, III, 314. Note that this opinion is expressed in the 1938 edition of his work.

[77] ". . . nec intelligimus scrupulum R. P. Augustine de uxore praesidis reipublicae americanae, quasi talis praeses non satis principetur. . . . "—*Epitome*, I, n. 758, 2.

[78] Cf. Beste, *loc. cit.;* Oesterle, *loc. cit.;* Schaefer, *op. cit.*, n. 350, note 219.

this country represent only one branch of our government—the executive branch. They alone, however, are in personal and sole possession of that distinction. The powers of the legislative and judicial branches are divided among many. Consequently the President and the Governors of States occupy a position unique in eminence and jurisdiction. It is that position which canon 598, § 2, recognizes and honors. Their wives, therefore, may invoke the privilege of entering into the cloister of regulars. It also appears conclusive that this same privilege is enjoyed by the wives of the Governors of United States Territories.

In conclusion, the following norm appears to be a safe one in the determination of this problem: Who is considered to be the first lady in any given territory? The present practice of social life attributes that honor to the woman who is the wife of him who occupies the pre-eminence in governmental positions. In this country, the first lady of the land is the wife of the President; the first lady of any State is the wife of the Governor of that State.

Canon 598, § 2, demands that her husband be actually in office before the wife of any ruler enjoys its exemption. Consequently, before the ceremony of induction into office as demanded by the various forms of government is carried out by her husband, whether it be the voicing of the oath of office, or some other solemn rite of installation, the wife does not possess this privilege. When the term of office ceases, regardless of the manner, unless of course it be the manifest consequence of an unjust usurpation of power, the privilege likewise ceases. It is given to the person through the medium of the office and ceases with the latter.[79] There is, naturally, an even greater reason why this singular exemption should be accorded to a woman who personally occupies the position of ruler in any country. In modern governmental standards she fulfills a position similar to that of queens.

Another problem provoked by this canon concerns the precise monasteries with relation to which this privilege accords the option of entry to the wives of the heads of governments. Does this privi-

[79] Cf. Vermeersch-Creusen, *Epitome,* I, n. 758, 2; Beste, *Introductio in Codicem,* p. 407; Fanfani, *De Iure Religiosorum,* n. 306, B; Schaefer, *De Religiosis,* n. 350.

lege make the option available with regard to only such monasteries as are located within the confines of the territory over which the woman's husband rules? This aspect of the question was not discussed by the pre-Code authors. Hence it will be of little avail to turn to them for a solution.

The mind of Pope Benedict XIV, as expressed in his Constitution *"Regularis disciplinae"* issued on the third of January, 1742, seems to have been that the privilege could be used only within the confines of a definitely limited territory. When he permitted to remain the privileges which were enjoyed by women related by blood or affinity to temporal rulers, he limited the use of the privileges to the monasteries situated within the territorial boundaries of the domain over which their relatives ruled.[80]

There is no clause in the present law which restricts to one given territory the use of these privileges. Canon 6 gives the norm by which the canons of the Code are to be interpreted. The second number of canon 6 states that when the new law repeats in substance the old law, it is to be interpreted in accordance with the authority of the old law and its reputable interpreters. But does the present law repeat substantially, at least in this respect, the former legislation? It appears that it does not. The privileges which were enjoyed by persons of royal rank derived mostly from custom and from the interpretations of authors, and consequently were based more upon what the law did not explicitly prohibit than upon what the law specifically conceded.

It may be objected that Pope Benedict XIV explicitly granted privileges to favored persons. While that is true, still the limitation which permitted entry to only certain parts of the monastery and the necessity of a previous approval by papal Bull were invoked as conditions for the valid use of these privileges. Today the privilege is granted outright. In this respect it can be considered more lenient and more extensive than the former privileges. Consequently a true parallel cannot be obtained by comparing the present and the past law.

[80] § 8: ". . . sive feminae huiusmodi sint Consanguineae et affines eorum qui sunt Domini in Temporalibus locorum in quibus Monasteria sita reperiuntur. . . ."—*Bullarium Benedicti XIV*, I, 128.

Few modern authors among those whom the writer could consult have given any attention to this problem. And even among these few there is a divergence of opinion. Since canon 598, § 2, contains no restrictive clause, Augustine can find no reason for limiting territorially the application of the privilege which it grants.[81] In citing this opinion of Augustine Coronata suggests that, though it may not be opposed to the letter of the law, it does seem to be contrary to the mind of the Code.[82] Schaaf [83] on the other hand, adopts the teaching of Augustine, and it is the mind of Berutti [84] that any reasonable cause will suffice to permit the wives of rulers to enter the monasteries of regulars anywhere in the world.

Notwithstanding the restriction expressed by Pope Benedict XIV and the reluctance indicated by Coronata, it appears that the position of Augustine, Schaaf and Berutti is tenable in practice. The fact that the canon makes no distinction and contains no restrictive clause merits consideration. It is a practice employed in the diplomatic circles of all nations to welcome visiting rulers with manifestations of high honor and distinction. Does it not seem that the Church in the present consideration wishes to grant similar concessions in recognition of the position occupied by such men? It is, then, altogether reasonable to acknowledge that the use of this privilege will accompany the wives of rulers even when they journey into foreign countries.

3. What Is the Meaning of *cum comitatu?*

Above all, prudence and sound, practical judgment should dominate the determination of what constitutes the retinue of women entering the monastery of regulars. It is true that the Code is here granting a privilege. But there is something to be preferred even

[81] "If the wife of a European monarch should visit a monastery in our country, the law would admit her, because the text does not limit the privilege to their own country."—*Commentary,* III, 314. Augustine does admit, however, that the opposite opinion could not be considered too rigorous. Cf. *Commentary,* VIII, 372, note 11.

[82] ". . . quae extensio litterae Codicis non adversatur licet forte menti adversetur."—*Institutiones,* n. 612, note 8.

[83] *The Cloister,* p. 81.

[84] *Institutiones,* III, n. 114.

to privileges in this matter, and that is the proper safeguard of the religious house and its inhabitants.

The meaning of the word *"comitatus"* does not include all those persons who are officially retained as witnesses of the public doings of an eminent government official. Rather it signifies those persons who have been chosen by the ruler to be his special companions, his guard of honor, or his bearers (body servants).[85] Such persons are always easily distinguishable. This in the norm, then, which must be applied also to the retinue which accompanies the wife of that ruler. It is restrictive. And is not the retinue of any first lady confined to a select few? This restriction, moreover, is consonant with the mind of the Code which in canon 598, § 1, excludes all women from the cloister of men.[86] It may be objected that the Code has indicated no limit with respect to the number which may comprise the retinue. That is true. Authors recognize this fact and as a result assert that the number of the retinue may be many or few.[87]

But the concept of the retinue must always be preserved. It appears that there will be no difficulty in practice, since even the dictates of social etiquette demand that a retinue be select and not of a large number. Vermeersch offers the wise suggestion that the retinue be comprised of those who are worthy to associate with a queen or first lady.[88]

There was one exception to this restrictive norm of what constitutes a retinue. By virtue of canon 4 the privilege enjoyed by the King of Spain—which privilege permitted entry into the cloister of regulars to all those persons who were present with him when he entered—continued to remain in force also after the advent of the Code.[89]

[85] Cf. Forcellini, *Totius Latinitatis Lexicon*, s. v. *"Comitatus."*

[86] Cf. Goyeneche, "Consultationes,"—*CpR*, II (1921), 47-48; Schaefer, *De Religiosis*, n. 350.

[87] Fanfani, *De Iure Religiosorum*, n. 306, B; Gerster a Zeil, *Ius Religiosorum*, p. 188; Schaefer, *loc. cit.;* Coronata, *Institutiones*, n. 612; Beste, *Introductio in Codicem*, p. 408.

[88] *Epitome*, I, n. 758, 2; cf. Prümmer, *Manuale*, q. 227, r. 3.

[89] Goyeneche, "Consultationes,"—*CpR*, II (1921), 48; Schaefer, *loc. cit.;* Coronata, *Institutiones*, n. 612, note 10; M. Leitner, *Handbuch des katholischen Kirchenrechts* (2. ed., 2 vols., Regensburg: Kösel und Pustet, 1921-1927), I, 436. Hereafter this work will be cited as *Handbuch*.

Canon, 598, § 2, gives to the retinue of the wife of the ruler the privilege of entering the cloister of regulars. May this same privilege be enjoyed by the retinue composed of the women who accompany the ruler himself? The answer must be sought, it seems, through an application of the rule of canon 20 in relation to canon 600, 3°, which permits the wives of rulers to enter with their retinue (composed, apparently, even of men) the cloister of nuns. Since nothing is said in canon 598, § 2, about the ruler himself and a retinue, it does seem that the principle of canon 20, which provides the norm by which a suitable interpretation is to be obtained in such cases, can be coupled with canon 600, 3°, to permit that privilege even to the ruler and his retinue.[90]

The occasion may often arise when the ruler and his wife desire to enter a monastery together. In that event, may both be accompanied by their own individual retinue? Since the circumstance of simultaneous entry is only incidental to the rights which each one possesses individually, it appears certain that a retinue may accompany each. Here again, however, prudence should be the master of the situation. The discipline and normal mode of life within the monastery should not be permitted to suffer by the presence of a large throng of women within the cloister. The right to have their retinue accompany them is granted by the canon and vouched for by the authors for each of the two individually. But the monastery deserves due consideration also.

Article II. Unlawful Entry of Women

Canon 2342, 2°, declares that women who violate the cloister of regulars incur by that very fact the penalty of excommunication reserved in a simple manner to the Holy See. Before any consideration is given to the nature of this penalty, it will be necessary to clarify not only the meaning of the word *mulieres* as used in this canon, but likewise the concept of the term *violantes*.

[90] Oesterle, *Praelectiones Iuris Canonici*, I, 336; Schaefer, *De Religiosis*, n. 350; Berutti, *Institutiones*, III, n. 114; Beste, *Introductio in Codicem*, p. 408; Leitner, *loc. cit.*

A. Who Are the Mulieres *of Canon 2342, 2°?*

Canon 598, § 1, explicitly states that women may not be admitted into the cloister of regulars. It logically and obviously follows from the nature and purpose of this prohibition that, if women may not be admitted into the cloister by others, neither may they enter of their own volition. With a proper prescinding from the admitted exemptions, the law indicates that all women who, of their own volition, enter the cloister of regulars automatically incur the censure of excommunication. But it may be asked whether, in its reference to the volitional entry of women, canon 2342, 2°, includes in its scope all the women of whom mention is expressly made in canon 598, § 1.

Because a *latae sententiae* penalty is enacted by canon 2342, 2°, its application will be of a relatively restricted character. Certain definite requirements of age are always presupposed in the subject who incurs such a penalty. Whereas canon 598, § 1, demands only that the person be of the female sex, canon 2342, 2°, requires much more.

It is stated in canon 88, § 2, that puberty is presumed [91] to be reached by boys at the age of 14, and by girls at the age of 12. By a provision of ecclesiastical law, those persons who have not yet attained the age at which puberty is presumed to be present do not incur *latae sententiae* penalties.[92]

A comparison of the norms of canon 88, § 2, and 2230 appears to render the fact quite obvious that when they have reached the age at which puberty is juridically presumed or, in other words, when they have completed their twelfth year, girls incur the *latae sententiae* penalties contained in the Code for the commission of crimes. Among the pre-Code authors, however, as well as among those who have written since its publication, there are some who assert that *in re criminali* the age of puberty for girls is to be computed from their completed fourteenth year.

The opinion of the authors who hold for equality between boys and girls in this matter seems to proceed from the Decretals of Greg-

[91] Cf. Coronata, *Institutiones,* n. 120, A, note 3.

[92] Canon 2230.

ory IX.[93] In commenting upon this decretal Reiffenstuel explicitly stated that in criminal matters the age of puberty for both sexes was to be computed at fourteen years.[94] Other pre-Code authors also taught this same concept.[95]

Writing after the promulgation of the Code of Canon Law many authors clung to the pre-Code opinions, and, despite the explicit wording of canons 88, § 2, and 2230, excused girls from *latae sententiae* penalties until they had reached the age of fourteen.[96]

[93] "*Pueris* grandiusculis peccatum nolunt attribuere quidem, nisi ab annis 14, cum pubescere coeperint . . ."—c. 1, X, *de delictis puerorum*, V, 23; Vermeersch-Creusen, *Epitome Iuris Canonici cum Commentariis ad Scholas et ad usum Privatum* (3 vols., Vol. III, 5. ed., Mechlinae et Romae: Dessain, 1936), III, n. 424; B. Ojetti, *Commentarium in Codicem Iuris Canonici* (4 vols., Romae: Universitas Gregoriana, 1927-1931), II, p. 20. Hereafter cited *Commentarium*.

[94] *Jus Canonicum*, lib. V, tit. XXIII, n. 5.

[95] M. Lega, *Praelectiones in textum iuris canonici de iudiciis ecclesiasticis* (4 vols., Romae: 1896-1901), III, n. 28; Wernz, *Ius Decretalium*, VI, n. 20. The words of Wernz which state this opinion are found within parentheses. Immediately following the expression of this opinion, Wernz asserts that there is no ecclesiastical law which grants to *impuberes* immunity from penalties. Ojetti defends this apparent contradiction of the subject by Wernz with the explanation that, when his work was edited, Wernz was occupied with other duties which prevented personal correction of his manuscript. Ojetti asserts that the teaching expressed within the parentheses cannot be found in the original copy. Apparently, then, it is someone else's opinion which is found within the parentheses. Cf. Ojetti, *Commentarium*, II, p. 19, note 5.

[96] J. Sole (*De Delictis et Poenis* [Romae: Pustet, 1920], p. 24, note 2) based his opinion upon the statements of Reiffenstuel, Lega and Wernz; Fanfani (*De Iure Religiosorum*, n. 308, A) somehow finds this meaning in the words of canon 2230; Cappello (*De Censuris*, n. 17, 4) appeals to the statements of the pre-Code authors and to canons 6, 2°, and 23; G. Cocchi (*Commentarium in Codicem Iuris Canonici ad Usum Scholarum* [8 vols., Vol. VIII; *De Delictis et Poenis*, 3. ed., Taurinorum Augustae: Marietti, 1936], VIII, n. 44) distinguishes *aetas pubertatis* and *aetas impubertatis*. In criminal matters, he asserts that the age of puberty for both boys and girls is to be computed from the fourteenth year. Vermeersch-Creusen (*Epitome*, III, n. 424) hold this to be probable upon the authority of the old law and pre-Code authors; Beste (*Introductio in Codicem*, p. 950) asserts this teaching upon the authority of canon 2230; E. Genicot (*Institutiones Theologiae Moralis* [2 vols., 10. ed., quam recognovit J. Salsmans, Bruxellis: Dewit, 1922], II, n. 566) holds this teaching as probable; Prümmer (*Manuale*, p. 650, note 21) attributes probability to this opinion since maturity

Despite the large number of reputable authors who grant this favor to girls, there appears to be no foundation either in the pre-Code law or in the Code for such an opinion. In the first place, the decretal of Pope Gregory IX does not support the concept of equality which has been and is attributed to it relative to puberty in boys and girls. The reference made in that decretal pertained to boys and not to girls.[97] May the affirmations of present day authors be justified by an appeal to canons 2230 and 6, 2°-3°? Following that procedure, one could interpret the current law of the Code which excuses *impuberes* from *latae sententiae* penalties, as canon 6, 2°-3°, permits and commands, in accordance with the old law and its approved interpreters. But in the present case recourse to canon 6 is useless, for there was no former law. Canon 6 permits appeal to the old law and the interpretations of the authors upon that law. But it has been shown that the interpretations of the authors is based upon a law which did not exist.[98]

A similar argumentative retort can be lodged against Cappello in his appeal to canon 23, through which he seeks to support his opinion that in criminal matters the age of puberty for girls is to be computed from the fourteenth year.[99] Determining the procedure which is to be followed in cases of doubt, canon 23 states that the *revocation* of a pre-existing law is not presumed, but that later laws must be considered in conjunction with earlier laws, and, in as much as possible, the two must be reconciled. But, once again, this pre-

of judgment develops equally in boys and girls; F. Roberti (*De Delictis et Poenis* [Vol. I, Romae: Apud Aedes Facultatis Juridicae ad S. Apollinaris, 1938], I, n. 80) asserts that *in re criminali* the reason for any distinction between puberty in boys and girls ceases.

[97] "Nulla igitur exinde desumi potest probatio pro delicti imputabilitate ad annum 14um transferenda in casu *puellae* delinquentis. Praeterea, si qua ex illo capite desumi potest probatio, eius objectum illud unice esset, impuberes immunes esse a poenis quando agitur de delictis carnis, non vero quando agitur de aliis, ut de furtis, de mendaciis . . ."—Ojetti, *Commentarium*, II, p. 20.

[98] Cf. Ojetti, *op. cit.*, pp. 21-22.

[99] *De Censuris*, n. 17, 4. Beste (*Introductio in Codicem*, p. 895) likewise asserts that canons 6, 2°, and 23 can be invoked against the ruling of canon 88, § 2.

supposes the existence of a former law. There is none. Moreover, the present law of the Code is most definite. It must, then, be permitted to stand on its own merits.[100]

It is certainly valid and reasonable to presume that the legislator of the Code was acquainted with the opinions of former authors upon this subject. However, in drafting canon 2230 he chose simply to indicate that boys and girls were not subject to the incurring of *latae sententiae* penalties so long as they were ***impuberes***, and then by equally positive statement confirmed the corollary that they do incur the penalty if they are ***puberes***. Had any modification of canon 88, § 2, been desired, it appears that the specific age would have been expressed as accurately in canon 2230 as it is expressed in other canons of a similar nature.[101]

In conclusion, it appears certain that canons 88, § 2, and 2230 must be taken in conjunction with each other. Even in criminal matters the juridically assumed age of puberty for girls is twelve years. In confirmation of the arguments which have been adduced against the proponents of the opposite opinion, one may point to the conformable interpretation of many equally reputable authors.[102]

[100] Cf. Ojetti, *op. cit.*, pp. 22-23.

[101] Cf. canons 766, 1°, 1648, § 3; Berutti, *Institutiones Iuris Canonici* (6 vols., Vol. VI, *De Delictis et Poenis*, Taurini-Romae: Marietti, 1938), VI, n. 31, II. Vermeersch-Creusen (*Epitome*, III, n. 424) invoke canon 1648, § 3, in confirmation of the opposite opinion by asserting that this canon is proof that the Code considers the development of a girl's intellect and will to take place no earlier in life than the development of a boy's mental faculties. Prescinding from the disputed truth of that fact, one must note that in canon 1648, § 3, the age of fourteen is explicitly stated for both sexes. In canon 2230, however, the reference is made in a less determinative manner through the employment of the words *puberes* and *impuberes*.

[102] Schaefer, *De Religiosis*, n. 351; Gerster a Zeil, *Ius Religiosorum*, p. 189; Cerato, *Censurae Vigentes*, p. 121; M. Coronata, *Institutiones Iuris Canonici ad Usum Utriusque Cleri et Scholarum* (5 vols., Vol. IV, *De Delictis et Poenis*, Taurini [Italia]: Marietti, 1935), n. 1721, note 6; J. Raus, *Institutiones Canonicae iuxta Novum Codicem Iuris pro Scholis vel ad Usum Privatum Synthetice Redactae* (2. ed., Lugduni, Parisiis: Vitte, 1931), n. 448, hereafter cited *Institutiones Canonicae*; Eichmann, *Lehrbuch*, p. 686; R. Salucci, *Il Diritto Penale secondo il Codice di Diritto Canonico* (2 vols. in 1 Subiaco: Tipografia dei Monasteri, 1926-1930), II, n. 253 (hereafter cited *Il Diritto Penale*); M. Pis-

Cerato introduced a new doubt into the discussion when he asked whether nuns are included under the term *mulieres*.[103] Appealing to canon 6, 3°, he stated that if nuns were excluded by the old law, they must also be excluded today. That point is clear enough. Then he asserted that if they were exempted in the old law, they should enjoy equal exemption under the new law. It seems that he could have had similar recourse to canon 6, 3°, to substantiate this assertion also. But in the latter case, Cerato cited canons 2219, § 3, and 2246, § 2, as the foundation for his statement. Now granting, but not admitting, that Cerato had some foundation for his assertion that nuns were exempt from the prohibition against entering the cloister of regulars as it was expressed in the old law, it is difficult to determine just how he could protect that exemption today by virtue of the two canons which he has cited. Canon 2219, § 3, forbids the use of analogy and of *a fortiori* reasoning in convicting one of a crime punishable with a canonical penalty. It appears that Cerato anticipated the use of the following deduction and wished to show its lack of value: If women are punished for entering the cloister of regulars, so also should nuns equally be punished, for they too are women.

But this confuses the issue. If nuns are exempted from the law of cloister relative to the houses of regulars, there can never be any question of its being violated by them. Why, then, the appeal to canon 2219, § 3? His recourse to canon 2246, § 2, seems likewise to prove of no value. That canon asserts that reservations should receive a strict interpretation. But surely no vindication for the existence of an exemption on the part of nuns which permits them to enter the cloister of male regulars can be concluded from that canonical principle. Furthermore, the present writer has not been able to discover in the old law any reference to the exemption of nuns in this regard. On the contrary, the old law, as the law

tocchi, *I Canoni Penali del Codice Ecclesiastico Esposti e Commentati* (Torino-Roma: Marietti, 1925), p. 133, hereafter cited *I Canoni Penali*; Wernz-Vidal, *Ius Canonicum*, VII, n. 60, II, note 16; A. Blat, *Commentarium Textus Codicis Iuris Canonici* (6 vols., Liber V, *De Delictis et Poenis*, Romae: Collegio "Angelico," 1924), VI, nn. 50, 183 (hereafter cited *De Delictis et Poenis*); J. Biederlack, M. Führich, *De Religiosis* (Oeniponte: 1919), p. 235.

[103] ". . . Moniales afficiuntur?"—*Censurae Vigentes*, p. 121.

today, rendered it almost impossible for a nun ever to be given the opportunity to enter the cloister of regulars. The laws of her own enclosure forbade her to leave it.

The notion of a censure [104] makes it impossible for a non-baptized woman who enters the cloister of regulars to be included in the scope of canon 2342, 2°. One must note well, however, that this is true only with respect to the woman herself, and may not be applied to those who admit or introduce such a woman into the cloister.

B. What Is Violation of the Cloister?

Any woman who enters beyond the cloistral limits of a monastery without having first obtained proper permission is considered to have violated that cloister. This is the simple meaning of violation: entrance without permission.[105] The proper permission to enter the cloister of regulars can ordinarily be given only by the Holy See. Having been established by common law, this legislation is withdrawn from the jurisdiction of intermediate or lesser superiors. Usually the application for this permission will be directed to the Sacred Congregation of Religious.

The precise manner in which entry within the enclosure is gained is of no practical consequence in reference to the penalty involved. The law simply states without distinction that a violation of the cloister is punished with excommunication. Entry may be effected by the use of force, threats or stealth. On the other hand, however, a woman may violate the cloister by entering unnoticed and without having recourse to any of these means.[106]

Any one of several purposes might motivate a woman to violate

[104] Cf. canon 2241, § 1.

[105] Cf. Mocchegiani, *Iurisprudentia Ecclesiastica*, I, n. 365; Bucceroni, *Commentarii*, p. 143; Cappello, *De Censuris*, n. 316, 4; Sole, *De Delictis et Poenis*, p. 292; Pejska, *Ius Canonicum*, p. 150; P. Ciprotti, *De Consummatione Delictorum Attento eorum Elemento Objectivo in Iure Canonico*, pars I (Romae: apud Custodiam Librariam Pont. Instituti Utriusque Iuris, 1936), n. 78 (hereafter cited *De Consummatione Delictorum*); S. Sipos, *Enchiridion Iuris Canonici* (Pecs: Ex Typographia "Haladas R. T.," 1926), p. 369, note 12 (hereafter cited *Enchiridion*).

[106] Cf. Pejska, *Ius Canonicum*, p. 156.

the cloister of regulars. Regardless of its nature any motive on her part may lead, under normal and ordinary circumstances, to her incurring of the penalty. By no means is it demanded that the woman who violates the cloister be possessed of evil desires or purposes.[107] This aggravating circumstance would constitute a new sin, but it would exercise no substantial influence upon the question of the incurred censure as such. It can be said, in fact, that a woman who possesses the privilege to enter the cloister does not incur excommunication even if in the use of that privilege she is motivated by evil purposes. Such an act would simply connote the abuse of a legitimate privilege.[108] Inefficacious endeavors to enter the cloister do not result in the penalty decreed by canon 2342, 2°. This is true regardless of the reason which renders the attempts fruitless. The canon supposes violation. And violation can be effected only by a true entry, not by mere attempts.[109]

The dictates of justice have always insisted that penalties may not be inflicted in an arbitrary or haphazard manner. A penalty is a just punishment for a crime which has been committed. The essential and all important consideration is that a crime has been committed. In the Fifth Book of the Code of Canon Law this fundamental truth is accurately portrayed.

Violation of the cloister results in the most severe of all ecclesiastical penalties, excommunication. In a study of this nature, then, it is necessary to determine, as far as possible, when the exact and specific crime of cloistral violation has been committed. This will necessitate the treatment of a twofold consideration. The first of these will relate to the subjective elements, or the requisites of the law regarding the person who violates the cloister. The second will consider the objective factors, or what constitutes physical violation of the cloister.

[107] Cf. Sipos, *loc. cit.*; Cappello, *loc. cit.*; Cocchi, *Commentarium*, VIII, n. 185; Coronata, *Institutiones*, n. 1982.

[108] Pennacchi, *Commentaria*, I, 723; Coronata, *loc. cit.* It appears, however, that such a woman deserves to have her privilege revoked. Cf. canon 78.

[109] Cf. canons 2212; 2213; Salucci, *Il Diritto Penale*, II, n. 250; Cappello, *De Censuris*, n. 318, 1.

1. Subjective Requisites

Pertinent to the delict and penalty involved, the responsibility of a woman who has violated the cloister of regulars will depend in general upon the knowledge and freedom which she possessed at the time she entered the cloister.

(a) Knowledge

There is no possibility of imputing to a woman the crime of violation of the cloister unless she was aware (i) of the law of papal cloister, (ii) of the precise penalty for the violation of that law; (iii) of the cloistral boundaries which she has transgressed.

With the exception of affected ignorance,[110] the Code shows a very lenient attitude toward crimes committed in ignorance. This is especially true of crimes punished with *latae sententiae* medicinal penalties. It is this type of penalty which is incurred for the violation of the cloister.[111]

(i) Ignorance Regarding the Law of Papal Cloister

If the existence, extent or meaning of a law is not known, there is ignorance of the law. If a law does not contain the words ***praesumpserit, ausus fuerit***, etc., then ignorance of that law, provided it is not crass, will excuse from *latae sententiae* medicinal penalties.[112] The penal law which relates to the violation of the cloister does not contain the words ***praesumpserit, ausus fuerit***, etc. It appears, then, that a woman who is not crassly ignorant of that law will not incur any penalty for its violation. Before any fuller determination concerning the probability of the existence of ignorance relative to this law, the concept regarding ignorance which is not crass deserves a few words of clarification. The most effective method of reaching

110 ". . . a directly voluntary lack of obligatory knowledge, which is procured by positive effort and from a wrongful motive"—I. Swoboda, *Ignorance in Relation to the Imputability of Delicts*, The Catholic University of America Canon Law Studies, n. 143 (Washington, D. C.: The Catholic University of America Press, 1941), p. 140. Cf. also pp. 139-144.

111 Cf. canons 2229, § 3, 1°; 2241, § 1; 2342.

112 Canon 2229, § 3, 1°.

an understanding of what is meant by ignorance which is not crass will, it appears, look to a prior explanation of the notion of crass ignorance itself.

Swoboda distinguishes two characteristics which of necessity attend the correct concept of crass ignorance.[113] First of all, crass ignorance is a total lack of diligence. "Crass ignorance is, on the subjective side, a complete and total failure to use any effort to fulfill the obligation of knowing the law or the pertinent facts falling under the law." [114] Secondly, the truth must be easily ascertainable. "Hence, only the ignorance of those things which might easily be learned can be considered crass or supine. When it is evident that a serious effort would be futile, it is difficult to see how a person could be obliged, so to speak, under the pain of becoming guilty of crass ignorance for not making the sterile effort." [115] These are the two characteristics which enter into the concept of what constitutes crass ignorance. It can be said, then, that "ignorance which lacks either of these two elements is grave ignorance, provided there is sufficient culpability for the commission of a mortal sin." [116]

Will it be probable, then, that crass ignorance concerning the law of the cloister can be attributed to any women? Two classes of women may here be considered. The first class is composed of those women who have some familiar knowledge about the monasteries of regulars. Into this class may be placed the mothers, sisters, close friends of regulars; female religious; women who have worked at the monasteries of regulars; women who have been repeated visitors at such monasteries. It seems reasonable to assume that to these the law of cloister is well known. If they have not been told outright by some regular, their natural curiosity, aroused by the precautions

[113] *Ignorance in Relation to the Imputability of Delicts*, pp. 146-151. The conclusions of Swoboda are being adopted here for two reasons. First of all, he has made a complete study of this question, not only in accordance with the old law, but likewise in relation to the Code. Secondly, it is beyond the scope of this work to delve deeply into the concept of ignorance and its relation to delicts.

[114] Swoboda, *op. cit.*, p. 148.

[115] Swoboda, *op. cit.*, p. 149.

[116] Swoboda, *op. cit.*, p. 151.

which they must have observed in this matter, would have led them to make inquiries. The second classification is constituted of those women who have had neither association with regulars or with their families and friends, nor any opportunity to visit monasteries. Certainly there is a greater probability that this group of women will be ignorant of the law of cloister. But in either case, may it be said that their ignorance will be less than a crass ignorance, or, in other words, that it will exist as a factor which is not of sufficient import to entail their incurring of the penalty when they physically enter the cloister without due permission?

In answer to this question it appears that ordinarily only the opinion which dictates a negative answer can be considered tenable. This view is based upon the assumption that the injunction of canon 597, § 3, which demands that the parts of the monastery subject to cloister be plainly indicated, has been faithfully carried out. If each entrance which leads into the cloister bears a sign in indication of the cloistral limits and of the consequent prohibition to enter therein, it is difficult to conceive how any woman who is capable of reading the sign can pass through that entrance and yet at the same time profess ignorance which it not at least crass. It is sufficient that she be able to read. Couple this with her realization of the nature of the house in which she is, and it appears that any normal woman will appreciate and recognize that she must keep out. It is assumed in this discussion that the doors leading into the cloistered parts of the house and bearing the signs which indicate the cloistral law are kept closed, for an open door, even though it bear the required sign, is more or less, an invitation to enter, at least to curious persons. The posted sign would obviously be deprived under such circumstances of much of its intended force and purpose. It may be objected that a woman may consider such a notice as just a regulation of the house which leads to the keeping of proper order. That objection may be perfectly justified. It may also be true that as a result she will deem the sign not to be of great consequence. But, on the other hand, it is evident that the very purpose of the sign as demanded by the Code consists in furnishing to the woman the necessary information about the cloistral law. Extreme efforts, however, need not be taken to acquaint women with this law. It appears, moreover, that generally there will be nearby in the house some one of whom she may easily inquire about the meaning of the sign. For these reasons it seems difficult to maintain that ordinarily her ignorance will not at least be a crass ignorance.

(ii) Ignorance Regarding the Precise Penalty for the Violation of the Cloister

Canon 2202, § 2, states that ignorance of the penalty of a law does not take away imputability for the committed delict, but diminishes it somewhat. Canon 2229, § 3, 1°, explains that, when not crass, *ignorantia solius poenae* excuses from medicinal *latae sententiae* penalties.[117]

From the wording of the canon it is not exactly clear whether the Code has reference to ignorance of the fact that this crime is punished by the Church or to ignorance of the precise penalty which is inflicted on one who commits this crime. Because of the cogency of his arguments, appeal will be made once again to Swoboda for an answer to this problem. Since the penalty incurred for the violation of the cloister is excommunication, consideration will be given this penalty only. Because of the unique detrimental nature of excommunication, Swoboda, basing his position also upon pre-Code authors, concludes that a person who is ignorant of the fact that a definite crime is punished by the *precise* penalty of excommunication can be considered in substantial error, even though he may be aware that it was punished in some way. If such ignorance did not excuse from the penalty, then the person would altogether unknowingly be placed absolutely outside the pale of the Church. But this would defeat the very purpose of the medicinal censure which seeks to effect the abandonment of contumacy by the guilty person.[118]

In an effort to determine whether crass ignorance regarding the

[117] It will be noted that the Church is not declaring in canon 2229, § 3, 1°, that there is any lessening in moral guilt. Because the essential nature of a censure demands contumacy, the Code excuses one from the incurring of the canonical punishment when contumacy is not present in one's act. It is not the will of the Church to impose her strict penalties upon those who would never know that they incurred the penalty.

[118] *Ignorance in Relation to the Imputability of Delicts*, pp. 222-225.

precise penalty, and not merely regarding the existence of the cloistral law, can be attributed to women who violate the cloister of regulars, it seems useless to appeal to canon 597, § 3. While the signs which are posted to designate the law of cloister disclose the existence of that law, it will be a very unusual or rare occurrence if the sign will give even the slightest clue to the nature of the punishment which ensues for those who disregard its warning. It is difficult to conceive that many women would even think, despite the prohibition which they know to exist, that by simply stepping across a threshold into the cloister they would incur the same penalty that results upon a voluntarily procured abortion or upon a marriage which is contracted before a non-Catholic minister. The knowledge that is had by lay persons concerning the precise penalties imposed by the Code for the violation of its laws can be regarded, it seems, as not being either extensive or exact. Because monastic life and discipline do not enter into the common experiences of lay persons, it appears that their knowledge relating to the cloistral penalties will be deficient in some way or other.

It will be profitable once again to give consideration to the twofold classification of women who may enter the monasteries of regulars. The mothers, sisters and intimate friends of regulars, religious women, and those who are familiar with the regulations of monasteries as the result of repeated visits can be presumed, it seems, to have some knowledge concerning the cloistral penalty. It appears that the natural curiosity of such women would eventually lead them to inquire about the penalty for the violation of the cloister. In that event they would undoubtedly be told. There is, however, another group. It is composed of those women who know nothing or very little about the strict cloistral regulations. When a woman of such a group visits a monastery, she will learn, at least through her observation of the signs, that a cloistral prohibition does exist. But it is assumed here that ordinarily she will be in almost total ignorance of the severe penalty attached to the violation of that prohibition. It is true to say that she should make inquiries. But can one not assume that very many women, if they do not even realize the existence of such a penalty, would fail, in absolutely good faith, to make any effort to ascertain the nature of the penalty? If inquiries were made, it seems that very often they would be directed to other women who, perhaps, would be equally unaware of the penalties involved.

There has been no endeavor herein to disregard the laws of the Code. Rather, the writer has made a sincere effort, founded upon the practical observations of everyday life, to determine what would be the normal reactions of women under such circumstances. It may seem that prejudice is directed in favor of liberty. But is not this leniency consonant with the doctrine of the Code concerning the juridical consequences which follow from ignorance?

(iii) Ignorance Regarding the Cloistral Boundaries

To incur the punishment which is enacted for the violation of the cloister, knowledge regarding the existing law of the cloister together with an awareness of the specific penal sanction of the law do not suffice. One must be aware, furthermore, of the cloistral limits. Certainly there can be no doubt that the penalty is not incurred by a woman who did not know that the room she entered was within the cloister. An argument similar to that which has been employed to disprove the ordinary existence of ignorance regarding the law can be used, it seems, in the discussion of the question of ignorance relative to the limits of the cloister. The purpose of the posters which canon 597, § 3, requires is twofold. One of these is the determination of cloistral limits. It seems then that a woman who can learn from a sign the existence of the law of cloister can also learn the determination of its boundaries. It is conceivable, however, that a woman could be unaware of the fact that the limits of the cloister are absolute and that even the slightest violation of the cloistral limits is strictly forbidden. Without intending boldly to walk into the forbidden cloister, many women, motivated by natural curiosity, may perhaps venture a step or two beyond the cloistral limits. To say that they could be ignorant of the fact that the law forbids even this seems perfectly logical. If, however, all doors leading into the cloister are faithfully kept closed, the concept of strict prohibition will, it seems, become more evident to women. An open door is all too often a very inviting gesture for unrestricted entry.

It appears reasonable to suppose, moreover, that ignorance relative to the cloistral limits of the grounds contiguous to a religious house could easily be present. Particularly would this be true if the barriers around the grounds are not of a nature sufficient to exclude entry, or if they are not well posted with informative signs. It can well be imagined that many women would not think that the law of cloister extended even to the grounds about the house. For this reason the thought may never occur to them to make inquiries before they venture to enter the grounds.

What has been said of ignorance in this discussion will apply also in the case of error or of a false judgment, which is but the usual consequence of ignorance, and in the case of inadvertence or of actual inattention, distraction and forgetfulness.[119]

(b) Freedom of Action

Besides the possession of knowledge, freedom of action is a necessary prerequisite for the valid infliction of medicinal penalties. In its penal legislation the Code makes ample provision for this dictate of justice. Certainly a woman who enters the cloister under the influence of physical force incurs no penalty for its violation.[120] The same may be said of a woman who acts under the stress of necessity, of grave inconvenience, or of grave fear, even though it be such not absolutely but only relatively.[121] When the occasion of necessity arises, the case must not be interpreted with hasty indulgence. It is to be understood, in view of the rigidity of the cloistral prohibition, that the necessity must be one which is truly grave. Centuries ago Pope St. Gregory I condemned as an abuse the practice of admitting into a monastery women who were seeking safety from barbarian invasions. Because other places of refuge were equally available, the Pope forbade women to enter within the walls of the monastery.[122]

119 Cf. canon 2202, § 3; Swoboda, *Ignorance in Relation to the Imputability of Delicts*, pp. 166-169; Sole, *De Delictis et Poenis*, p. 22; Coronata, *Institutiones*, n. 1658.

120 Cf. canon 2205, § 1.

121 Cf. canon 2205, § 2.

122 *Regestrum Epistolarum*, lib. I, ep. XLVIII—*MGH, Epistolae Gregorii*, I, tom. I, pars 1, p. 74; Jaffé, 1118.

During periods of extraordinary trials and dangers, such as are now being experienced, an occasion might arise when, though it be not absolutely necessary, it will nevertheless be permissible to allow the entry of women into the cloister of regulars. One may suppose, for example, the situation wherein a town or city is bombed and havens of refuge are sought in the monasteries. While there may be other available places, yet it appears that were the laws of the cloister to be strenuously insisted upon at such times, great opprobrium would result to the Church which preaches always the need of charity. At the least, under such circumstances the limits of the cloister could justifiably be altered to permit the housing of women.

It may be rare that a woman will be forced to seek the refuge of the cloister in order to avoid being killed or becoming seriously injured. Yet, if such danger is imminent, it would admit of an exception to the law of the cloister.[123]

The same would be true of the admittance of a nurse within the cloister, if she was absolutely necessary for the well-being of a sick religious. That this case will ever be a reality today is doubtful. It was admitted, however, by the old authors,[124] and could validly be invoked as a sufficient cause today *if* all other reasonable means had been exhausted.

2. Objective Requisites

(a) Concept of Entry

It has been shown that the violation of the cloister consists in entry without permission.[125] Canon 2342, 2°, requires as a necessary condition for the violation of the cloister that the entry truly take place. It may be asked, then, what constitutes such a physical entry? The idea seems obvious in itself. It can be said with Cappello[126] that the common estimation of people will dictate what is

[123] St. Alphonsus, *Theologiae Moralis,* lib. VII, n. 231; P. De Siena, *Commentarius Censurarum iuxta Novum Codicem Iuris Canonici* (Neapoli: 1918), p. 44 (hereafter cited *Commentarius Censurarum*); Genicot-Salsmans, *Institutiones Theologiae Moralis,* II, n. 599.

[124] St. Alphonsus, *loc. cit.*; Genicot-Salsmans, *loc. cit.*

[125] Cf. *supra,* pp. 143-144.

[126] *De Censuris,* n. 316, 4.

meant by this term. And certainly the understanding which they have of this word requires complete bodily passage from one space to another. The natural request, for example, which would be spoken to a welcome visitor standing outside of a door or even on the threshold would be: Come in! The conclusion to be drawn from that request is that a person is not considered to have entered a room until he has completely passed into it. This will be the norm by which one will judge whether the cloister has been violated. True entry is required. And true entry will be realized *only* when the *entire* body has overstepped the cloistral boundaries. Consequently, a woman will not violate the cloister when, in keeping her feet on the outside, she leans within the cloistral limits. Again, to keep one foot outside the cloister and to place the other foot within the cloister is not violation. Such a position does not imply an entry into the cloister. The most that can be said of such a position is that the person is partially within. But it can equally be said that the person is also partially without. Neither of these implies an entry in the true sense. This concept of entry is not only the universally accepted one of all persons, but it is the commonly expressed opinion of the authors.[127] Cappello strongly insists upon the requirement of a true bodily entry and resolutely repudiates the contrary opinion of some authors.[128] It may be remarked here with Ciprotti,[129] however, that no expression of the opposite opinion on the part of authors can anywhere be found. One wonders whether Cappello is not confused about what the opinion of the supposedly many other

[127] Bonacina, *De Clausura,* q. I, p. VIII, n. 6. The opinion of Bonacina is expressed regarding the *egress* of *nuns.* The same principle will apply with regard to the factor of entry, however. Cf. also Pennacchi, *Commentaria,* I, 723; Bucceroni, *Commentarii,* p. 140; Ciolli, *Commentario Practico,* p. 130; St. Alphonsus, *Theologia Moralis,* lib. VII, n. 229; Salucci, *Il Diritto Penale,* II, n. 248; Schaefer, *De Religiosis,* n. 355, a; Coronata, *Institutiones,* n. 1978; Pejska, *Ius Canonicum,* p. 156; Fanfani, *De Iure Religiosorum,* n. 308, A; De Siena, *Commentarius Censurarum,* p. 42; I. Teodori, "Consultationes,"—*Apollinaris,* V (1932), 110; J. Cavigioli, *De Censuris latae sententiae quae in Codice Iuris Canonici continentur Commentariolum* (Torino: 1919), n. 129 (hereafter cited *De Censuris*).

[128] *De Censuris,* n. 316, 4.

[129] *De Consummatione Delictorum,* n. 78, note 4.

authors really is. Many of the above mentioned authors state that one step into the cloister is sufficient. But they state that this implies a completed step which is sufficient to introduce the entire body into the cloister. Apparently Cappello interprets them as implying that to enter the cloistral boundaries even partially is to violate the cloister.[130]

Cerato offers the opinion that a woman would not be guilty of violating the cloister if she were to climb upon the wall surrounding the cloistral grounds.[131] This opinion seems to be not only a tenable one, but also the only acceptable one. The wall surrounds the grounds which are cloistered. The case appears to be analogous to that of the threshold of a room. Until a woman would cross the threshold or leap down from the wall, there would be no violation of the cloister. This opinion is consonant with the principles stated in canons 19 and 2219, § 1.[132]

It may happen that a woman learns of the cloistral prohibition only after she has entered within the cloister. Or again, one who knows of the strict prohibition may realize too late that she has crossed the cloistral boundaries. In either case there can be no question of a formal violation. But can it be said that, if she does not leave the cloister upon her realization of these facts, she will incur the censure? It cannot. The law is directed toward the prohibition of entry into the cloister. It is on account of the entry, and on that account alone, that the penalty is incurred. There is no law which demands under severe penalty that such a woman leave the cloister. In such a case there can, of course, be question of sin, but not of any canonical penalties. This applies also in the case wherein women tarry within the cloister long after the reason which permitted them to enter has ceased. In fact, it may be extended even to the case wherein a woman arbitrarily exploits throughout the entire cloister a privilege which permitted her to enter but a certain part of it. Once a woman is within the cloister, the possibility of

[130] ". . . at, contra non paucos doctores, putamus omnino requiri, ut quis *vere* ingrediatur, h. e. *toto corpore,* non autem *uno passu* seu *pede . . .*"—*loc. cit.*

[131] *Censurae Vigentes,* p. 119.

[132] Cf. Ciprotti, *De Consummatione Delictorum,* n. 78, note 4; Pistocchi, *I Canoni Penali,* p. 132.

violating it has ceased. Though she continue farther into the cloister, there is no *penal* law which invokes any further sanction against such an act.[133]

(b) *Slightness of Matter*

The law of the Code relative to entry into the cloister is clear and explicit. The question now arises: Will this law admit slightness of matter? Relative to the violation of the cloister, slightness of matter may be considered as a step of two within the cloister, or an entry for a very brief space of time. This problem is discussed by authors mostly with regard to the egress of nuns from the enclosure. However, if slightness of matter may be admitted in connection with egress from the enclosure, then it is also admissible in connection with entry into the cloister. The law makes no distinction and is equally strict in its penalty regarding egress and entry.[134]

The admissibility of slightness of matter is a disputed question among authors. Adhering rigidly to the concept of violation, those who deny that slightness of matter is admissible state that once the cloistral limits have been completely crossed, the act of entry and the consequent act of violation have taken place.[135]

[133] Cf. Bonacina, *De Clausura,* q. V, p. IV, nn. 15-16. St. Alphonsus (*Theologia Moralis,* lib. VII, n. 229) excuses from censure a nun who remains outside the enclosure beyond the time allotted by her permission. The analogy is valid, it seems. Bucceroni (*Commentarii,* p. 140) states a like position; Salucci (*Il Diritto Penale,* II, n. 257) likewise excuses from censure the nun who remains outside of the cloister beyond her allotted time; and Cappello (*De Censuris,* n. 323, 7) cites the same case that St. Alphonsus cited. Cf. also Cavigioli, *De Censuris,* n. 129; Cerato, *Censurae Vigentes,* p. 119; Coronata, *Institutiones,* n. 1978.

[134] Cf. Coronata, *Institutiones,* n. 1978, p. 419, note 6.

[135] Cf. Bonacina, *De Clausura,* q. I, p. VIII, n. 6. St. Alphonsus (*Theologia Moralis,* lib. VII, n. 229) accepts this doctrine as representing the more probable opinion. Cf. also Ciolli, *Commentario Practico,* p. 130; Bucceroni, *Commentarii,* p. 140; Sipos, *Enchiridion,* p. 371; J. Chelodi, *Ius Poenale et Ordo Procedendi in Iudiciis Criminalibus iuxta Codicem Iuris Canonici* (4. ed., recognita et aucta a V. Dalpiaz, Tridenti: Ardesi, 1935), p. 105 (hereafter cited *Ius Poenale*). A. Ballerini-D. Palmieri (*Opus Theologicum Morale in Busembaum Medullam* [2. ed., 7 vols., Prati: 1892-1894], tract. IX, cap. I, n. 161) affirm that *pro foro externo* the violation does not admit slightness of matter, but that the nature of the intention which motivated the act may and often will have some effect upon the decision.

Many authors hold the opposite view. But in practice, it appears their opinion frequently becomes the equivalent of the opinion which does not admit any slightness of matter. Great care is taken to explain precisely what in their opinion constitutes slightness of matter. It consists in the taking of one or two steps into the cloistral limits followed by an immediate withdrawal from the cloister. Moreover, it is specifically supposed that the entry takes place at an entrance where none of the regulars of the monastery will be encountered.[186]

This opinion appears to be founded upon the fact that the claustral observance is of merely ecclesiastical precept. It will consequently admit of exceptions or slight relaxations in favor of human frailty. Moreover, as the admitted slightness of matter is defined by the proponents of this view, it will result in no immediate danger to the inhabitants of the cloister. The end of the law will suffer no harm.

It is admitted here that this opinion enjoys some degree of probability. Yet it does seem that the stricter view is the more acceptable one. The law of the cloister certainly binds whether or not anyone is residing within the house. The end of the law is one thing; the means by which that end will be safeguarded is quite another thing. The fact that in a given case no immediate or even remote danger to the end of the law will result certainly offers no reason for making light of the binding force of the law. It exists in all its rigidity and force until it is revoked.

Again, to admit slightness of matter in this regard is to open up an avenue for possible abuses which can in the long run become a source of grave danger. A strict interpretation of this law will bet-

[186] F. Pellizzarius, *Tractatio de Monialibus* (3. ed., Venetiis: 1651), cap. V, sec. I, n. 19; Ferraris, *Bibliotheca*, s. v. "Moniales," art. III, n. 10; H. Noldin, A. Schönegger, *De Censuris* (32. ed., Oeniponte-Lipsiae: Rauch, 1938), n. 80; Cappello, *De Censuris*, n. 323, 5; Coronata (*Institutiones*, n. 1978) regards the opinion as probable. Moreover, he cites Chelodi as admitting this teaching. But while inclining to the opposite view, Chelodi only cites the existence of an opinion contrary to his own. Cf. also Salucci, *Il Diritto Penale*, II, n. 259; Cocchi, *Commentarium*, VIII, n. 185; Pistocchi, *I Canoni Penali*, p. 131; Gerster a Zeil, *Ius Religiosorum*, p. 189; Sole, *De Delictis et Poenis*, p. 290; Biederlack-Führich, *De Religiosis*, p. 239.

ter achieve the desired end of the law. The long history of cloistral legislation has shown most convincingly that the only certain method of preserving intact the cloister consists in the use of unflinching sternness in the application and enforcement of the enacted laws. It may be objected that all of this constitutes but an *argumentum ex convenientia.* One may grant that to be true. But through that fact the argument surely loses none of its force, for simultaneously it supports the interpretation which more intimately and efficaciously insures the achievement of the law's acknowledged purpose.

It appears, then, that the more acceptable opinion in this question is that which does not admit of any slightness of matter. Moreover, inasmuch as the realm within which the opposing view admits a slightness of matter is a rigidly restricted one, it is evident that the seemingly liberal opinion will have very little application in practical use. In the concrete the two opinions very nearly coincide. In theory the one opinion admits the possibility of slightness of matter and the other does not. But in practice there will almost always be lacking the full complement of conditions which are prerequired by the authors who subscribe to the admissibility of slightness of matter in the question of the cloistral violation. This acknowledged situation leads one to conclude that in actual life the two opinions fundamentally lead to an identical interpretation in practice.

ARTICLE III. *Introducentes et Admittentes*

Recognizing the lamentable fact that the violation of the cloister is not always effected without assistance, the legislator enacted a punishment also for those persons who introduce or admit women into the cloistral limits. So comprehensive is the language which he employed in this regard, that all the avenues of escape from the enacted punishment appear to be effectively foreclosed with reference to whosoever introduces or admits women into the cloister of regulars.[137] Included under the term *superiores* in this canon are all those who enjoy any power of jurisdiction, whether they be supreme, major or local superiors. The name under which they exercise their

[137] Canon 2342, 2°: ". . . Superiores aliique, quicumque ii sint, . . . introducentes vel admittentes. . . ."

power deserves no consideration.[138] The wording of the canon, *"aliique, quicumque ii sint,"* is more strict than was the enactment of the Constitution *"Apostolicae Sedis"* which employed the terminology, *"Superiores aliosve."* The interpretation which formerly limited the punishment to regulars or other religious [139] obviously can no longer be held. The present day law is all-inclusive, extending not only to all religious, novices and postulants, but also to all lay persons, whether they be men or women. No formal or official association with the monastery is required. The language of the Code clearly indicates that a departure from the old law is intended. Interpretations must be guided by that fact.[140] The concluding phrase of canon 2342, 2°, which enacts a *further* penalty against religious who are guilty of this crime, serves to disperse all doubts regarding the legislator's intention to make his penal enactment universally applicable.

A. Concept of the Terms

With some few exceptions, authors portray unanimity in their explanations of the meaning of the words *"introducentes et admittentes."* In general their concept of the word "introducing" embraces every actual assistance afforded for the entry of women, whether it be manifested by invitation, approval, removal of obstacles, opening of doors, indication of ways and means, accompaniment, etc. In a word, the term denotes the exercise of any influence which brings about, or at least renders more easy, the entry of women

[138] Cf. Coronata, *Institutiones*, n. 1982; Cappello, *De Censuris*, n. 321; Salucci, *Il Diritto Penale*, II, n. 254; Augustine, *Commentary*, VIII, 372.

[139] Cf. Hollweck, *Die kirchlichen Strafgesetze*, § 152, note 5; Mocchegiani, *Iurisprudentia Ecclesiastica*, I, n. 338; Pennacchi, *Commentaria*, I, 790-791.

[140] Cf. canon 6, 3°; Coronata, *op. cit.*, n. 1982, p. 423, note 5; Schaefer, *De Religiosis*, n. 351; Cappello, *De Censuris*, n. 321; Sole, *De Delictis et Poenis*, p. 292; Salucci, *Il Diritto Penale*, II, n. 254; Sipos, *Enchiridion*, p. 369; Beste, *Introductio in Codicem*, p. 950; H. A. Ayrinhac and P. J. Lydon, *Penal Legislation in the New Code of Canon Law* (revised edition, New York: Benziger, 1936), n. 285; Augustine (*Commentary*, VIII, 373) excludes "those who have nothing to do with the monastery. . . ." This canon will not affect persons who have not reached the age of puberty, since they are excluded by canon 2230. Canon 2227, § 2, exempts cardinals from this penalty.

into the cloister. Anybody may exert this influence or help.[141] While agreeing in substance with this concept, some authors assert that the help must proceed from a person who is within the cloister itself. Thus they maintain that a person who himself is outside of the cloister cannot introduce a woman into the cloister.[142] Though admitting that outsiders can be guilty of introducing a woman within the cloister, other authors exclude from this concept those who exercise the rôle of assistants or counselors in gaining entry for others.[143] The distinction which is made by these authors is finely drawn. But Cappello asserts that while such persons may not be included under the classification of "*introducentes*," they may incur the punishment in virtue of the general principles of co-operation as contained in the Code.[144] And Coronata rightly asserts that the differences among the authors assume no practical importance in view of the fact that the principles of co-operation as enacted in canons 2209 and 2231 will embrace all who are deserving of the penalty.[145]

The common opinion of authors classifies under the term "*admittentes*" those who permit unwarranted entry into the cloister or do not impede those who are in the act of entering. This concept, however, is confined by the authors solely to superiors, porters and

[141] Cf. Ferraris, *Bibliotheca*, s. v. "Conventus," art. III, n. 30; Mocchegiani, *Iurisprudentia Ecclesiastica*, I, n. 337; A. Lehmkuhl, *Theologia Moralis* (12. ed., 2 vols., Friburgi Brisgoviae: 1914), II, n. 1231; Noldin-Schönegger, *De Censuris*, n. 80; Salucci, *op. cit.*, n. 251; Sipos, *op. cit.*, p. 371, note 20; Cerato, *Censurae Vigentes*, p. 119; Genicot-Salsmans, *Institutiones Theologiae Moralis*, II, n. 599; De Siena, *Commentarius Censurarum*, p. 43; Coronata, *Institutiones*, n. 1978; Teodori, "Consultationes,"—*Apollinaris*, V (1932), 110; Biederlack-Führich, *De Religiosis*, pp. 239-240; Cl. Marc-F. X. Gestermann et J. B. Raus, *Institutiones Morales Alphonsianae* (19. ed., 2 vols., Lugduni: Vitte, 1933-1934), I, n. 1334.

[142] Pennacchi, *Commentaria*, I, 740-742; Hollweck, *Die kirchlichen Strafgesetze*, § 149, note 11; Augustine, *Commentary*, VIII, 373; Sole, *De Delictis et Poenis*, p. 289; Pistocchi, *I Canoni Penali*, p. 132.

[143] Cappello, *De Censuris*, n. 319; A. Cipollini, *De Censuris latae sententiae iuxta Codicem Iuris Canonici* (Taurini: Marietti, 1925), lib. II, *De singulis censuris*, n. 46. Hereafter cited *De Censuris*.

[144] *Loc. cit.*

[145] *Institutiones*, n. 1978, p. 418, note 1.

others upon whom is incumbent the duty of guarding the cloistral observance.[146]

It appears that only confusion will result from a detailed treatment of the various distinctions which are made regarding those who introduce and those who admit women into the enclosure. Practically it will avail nothing to say that one is guilty of the crime of introducing and others are guilty of admitting. Can it not be said with Prümmer [147] that the time for recourse to subtle distinctions in explaining these notions is past? The concepts of the canon can well be coupled with the doctrine of co-operation as expressed in canons 2209 and 2231 in an effort to determine when guilt is present and punishment is deserved.

The penalty which is stated in the Code is the same for the "*introducentes*" and the "*admittentes*." Furthermore, the authority of the Sacred Congregation of Religious can be invoked in defense of the opinion that there seems to be no foundation in the law for a distinction between superiors and others in the monastery in the determination of the term "*admittentes*." It is true that the Instruction which that Congregation issued pertains only to the convents of nuns. The subject matter, however, is identical with the corresponding legislation which relates to the monasteries of regulars. According to that Instruction, the superioress *or any other person* who would introduce *or only admit* any person into the cloister without permission, would not only sin gravely, but would incur at once an excommunication reserved in a simple manner to the Holy See.[148]

[146] Ojetti, *Synopsis*, s. v. "Clausura," n. 1182; Bucceroni, *Commentaria*, p. 143; Cappello, *De Censuris*, n. 319, 3; Fanfani, *De Iure Religiosorum*, n. 308, A. Vermeersch-Creusen, *Epitome*, I, n. 766; Schaefer, *De Religiosis*, n. 355, b; Noldin-Schönegger, *De Censuris*, n. 80; Ciprotti, *De Consummatione Delictorum . . .*, n. 79; Salucci, *Il Diritto Penale*, II, n. 251; Cerato, *Censurae Vigentes*, p. 120; Pistocchi, *I Canoni Penali*, pp. 132-133; Ayrinhac-Lydon, *Penal Legislation in the New Code of Canon Law*, p. 220; Coronata, *Institutiones*, n. 1978.

[147] *Manuale Iuris Canonici*, q. 227, 5. Cf. Coronata, *Institutiones*, n. 1978, p. 418, note 1.

[148] "Quod si antistita vel quaelibet alia, personam quamcumque sine legitima licentia in monasterium introduceret, vel solum admitteret, non tantum graviter peccaret, sed etiam ipso facto excommunicationem Sedi Apostolicae simpliciter reservatam incurreret (canon 2342, 1°)."—*Instructio*, IV.

The doctrine on co-operation is expressed in canon 2209. Canon 2231 determines the penal guilt of the various types of co-operators. Pertinent to the violation of the cloister, certain conclusions can be drawn from these canons.

All those who are in collusion with the person entering the enclosure and physically concur in that act incur excommunication.[149] There would be no difficulty in determining the guilt of persons who had taken such an obvious part as this in the violation of the cloister. If the crime of the violation would not have been committed had not certain assistance been given, then the person who afforded that aid is equally guilty and deserving of the penalty.[150] If, on the other hand, the help which was given rendered the commission of the delict only more easy, and, if even apart from the aid the violation would nevertheless have been effected, then the penalty is not incurred by the co-operator.[151] It may be objected here, however, that this principle would exempt from the penalty a person who opened the door of the cloister and allowed an intruder to enter. This action possibly rendered the violation only more easy in the sense that it relieved the woman of the task of employing more than ordinary means. The assumption in this case is that she would have gained entry even without his help. But such a case, it seems, can be judged in accordance with canon 2209, § 1. The two persons concur physically in the very commission of the crime. There seems to be some complicity present, for both intend that the crime be committed.

A superior who commands a subject to admit or introduce an unauthorized person can be considered the principal cause of the crime and consequently incurs the penalty. The same can be said of the superior who without cause authorizes a person to enter the cloister. If, however, a superior had given a command relative to the violation of the cloister, but fully withdrew that command in due time, he cannot be accused of guilty co-operation in the event that

[149] Canons 2209, § 1; 2231.

[150] Canons 2209, § 3; 2231.

[151] Canons 2209, § 4; 2231.

the persons to whom the command was given persist in effecting the violation apart from the command of the superior.[152]

Canon 2209, § 6, states that a person who concurs in the commission of a delict merely by neglecting his office is guilty to the extent to which his office binds him to impede that delict. Canon 2231 asserts that only those who co-operate according to one or the other type of co-operation mentioned in canon 2209, §§ 1-3, merit the same penalty as that which is incurred by the principal party. A negative co-operator then is guilty of neglecting his office. But it cannot be said that he is guilty of the delict, the commission of which he did not hinder. If one judge by this principle alone, it would seem that a superior who observes a woman entering or about to enter the cloister, and does nothing to prevent her, would not incur the excommunication. The only assistance which he offers, if assistance it can be called, is purely negative. To excuse such a superior, however, appears to repudiate the concept of the term "*admittentes*," which according to authors implies that a superior must prevent, whenever he can, all unwarranted entry of women into the cloister.[153] But this definition of the authors must be understood in accordance with canon 2209, § 6. Provided that the co-operation in this case remains purely negative, and is joined with no consent or permission that the cloister be violated, the crime is solely one of negligence of office. Foreseeing the violation, the superior failed to employ the diligence required by his office. His guilt, according to canon 2203, § 1, approximates *dolus*. But it is not of such a character as to entail the incurring of the penalty.[154]

If this principle is valid for the superior of the monastery who is bound by his office to exercise vigilance over the cloistral observance, then *a fortiori* it will hold for all others who may be guilty of similar neglect in allowing a woman to enter the cloister. The superior is bound in justice to fulfill his office of exercising care over the cloistral observance. The others in the religious house are bound only in charity to fulfill this same vigilance.

152 Canons 2209, § 5; 2231.

153 Cf. *supra*, pp. 159-160.

154 Schaaf, *The Cloister*, pp. 94-95.

B. May impuberes *or* infantes *Be Introduced or Admitted?*

Attention has been given [155] to the explanation, founded upon canon 2230, that those girls who have not yet attained the age of puberty do not incur the precise penalty of excommunication for the violation of the cloister. The question now arises concerning the guilt of those who introduce or admit within the cloister girls below the age of puberty, or even infants. The controversy which existed before the Code will prove of no value in rendering assistance for the proper interpretation of the current law.[156] This is true because the law has been altered to such a degree that recourse can no longer be had by virtue of canon 6, 2°, to the interpretations of former authors. Rather canon 6, 3°, must be invoked and the contemporary law must be interpreted on its own merits.

Whereas Pope Pius IX in his Constitution *"Apostolicae Sedis"* [157] excommunicated "women violating the cloister of regulars, and superiors or others admitting *them,*" canon 2342, 2°, excommunicates "women violating the enclosure of regulars, and superiors and others . . . who admit or introduce *"women of any age whatsoever."* Obviously there has been a distinct and intended departure from the former law. Moreover, canon 2342, 2°, when taken in conjunction with canon 598, § 1, which declares that "no women of any age . . . may be admitted within the enclosure . . . ," presents an irrefutable barrier to the argumentative devices of anyone who endeavors to defend the interpretation which excludes a universal meaning from these words. The authority of the supreme legislator has now put an end to all controversy.[158] Since the promulgation of the Code, this interpretation has been the common one of authors. They can

[155] Cf. *supra,* pp. 138-141.

[156] It was the opinion of some that excommunication was incurred only by those who admitted or introduced girls who had attained the age of reason. Cf. Pennacchi, *Commentaria,* I, 797; D. Annibale, *Summula Theologiae Moralis,* III, n. 227, note 3; Mocchegiani, *Iurisprudentia Ecclesiastica,* I, n. 336, b; Ojetti, *Synopsis,* s. v. "Clausura," n. 1187; Bucceroni, *Commentarii,* p. 143. Others favored the view that the admission even of an infant resulted in the punishment. Cf. Ferraris, *Bibliotheca,* s. v. "Conventus," art. III, nn. 18-19.

[157] § II, n. 7—*Fontes,* n. 552.

[158] Cappello, *De Censuris,* n. 322.

find nothing but a direct and express statement of exclusion in the canon.[159]

Consideration must be given, moreover, to the enactment of canon 2230. Though that canon exempts *impuberes* from *latae sententiae* penalties, it likewise states that *puberes* who, according to the norms of canon 2209, §§ 1-3, induce them or concur with them in the commission of a delict will incur the penalty which is stated in the law. And according to the norms of canon 88, §§ 2-3, there must be classed among *impuberes all* female persons up to the age of twelve.

Certainly the penalty of excommunication will be incurred by those who admit or introduce women of unsound mind. Prescinding from the fact that the law provides no basis for an exception in favor of the admission of such women into the cloister, and prescinding also from the comprehensive terminology of canon 598, § 1, one must still recognize the full possibility that the dangers which the law seeks to prevent can even be magnified by the presence of such women within the enclosure.[160]

What is to be said of the religious, or any other person, who detains within the cloister a woman who has entered it without the necessary permission? This problem was the object of considerable discussion among the pre-Code authors. It has also become the object of continued discussion among those who have written since the promulgation of the Code. Contradictory conclusions have been reached. The question proposed for solution is: Will a censure be incurred by that person who, by conversation or some other means, detains a woman from making her exit from the cloister? The supposition in this case is that the detaining party has had nothing to do with the entry of the woman into the cloister.

The common opinion of authors excused from the incurring of

[159] Cappello, *loc. cit.*; Fanfani, *De Iure Religiosorum*, n. 308, A; Schaefer, *De Religiosis*, n. 351, note 226; Beste, *Introductio in Codicem*, p. 950; Vermeersch-Creusen, *Epitome*, I, n. 766, 2; Augustine, *Commentary*, VIII, 373; Coronata, *Institutiones*, n. 1982; Ciprotti, *De Consummatione Delictorum . . .*, n. 80; Noldin-Schönegger, *De Censuris*, n. 80; Salucci, *Il Diritto Penale*, II, n. 255; Pistocchi, *I Canoni Penali*, p. 134; Chelodi, *Ius Poenale*, p. 104.

[160] Cf. Cappello, *De Censuris*, n. 322; Cerato, *Censurae Vigentes*, p. 121; Salucci, *Il Diritto Penale*, II, n. 255.

the penalty the ordinary religious whose actions were not the *cause* of the woman's remaining within the cloister.[161] On the contrary, authors did not and do not now excuse from the incurring of the penalty superiors and such others who are charged with the care of the cloister, if they do not expel from it every woman who is present therein without permission. The failure to fulfill this duty is considered by them as the equal of the prohibited admission of a woman into the cloister. This seems to be founded upon the concept which they had and have regarding the meaning of admission. They applied and apply their doctrine only to superiors.[162]

The modern authors who treat professedly of this problem and state the opinion that the penalty is not incurred by any religious, superior or subject, who detains a woman within the cloister, give no reasons for the position which they venture. Coronata does say that such friendly actions could in the wide sense be comprehended under the concept of admitting the person, but that the same actions would not constitute an admission in the sense in which the penal law assumes the term *"admittentes."* [163]

[161] Ferraris, *Bibliotheca,* s. v. "Conventus," art. III, n. 31; Reiffenstuel, *Jus Canonicum,* lib. III, tit. XXXV, n. 79; Mocchegiani, *Iurisprudentia Ecclesiastica,* I, n. 339; Hollweck, *Die kirchlichen Strafgesetze,* § 149, note 12; Lehmkuhl, *Theologia Moralis,* II, n. 1231; Biederlack-Führich, *De Religiosis,* p. 240; Cappello, *De Censuris,* n. 319. Bonacina (*De Clausura,* q. V, p. IV, n. 16) considered *all* detaining actions the equivalent of the acts of admitting and hence worthy of the penalty.

[162] Reiffenstuel, *loc. cit.*; Mocchegiani, *loc. cit.*; Lehmkuhl, *loc. cit.*; Biederlack-Führich, *loc. cit.*; Beste, *Introductio in Codicem,* p. 950; Noldin-Schönegger, *De Censuris,* n. 80; Salucci, *Il Diritto Penale,* II, n. 251; Cipollini, *De Censuris,* n. 47; Chelodi, *Ius Poenale,* p. 104. Cappello (*De Censuris,* n. 319) excuses from the censure only those who detain a woman who has entered legitimately; Genicot-Salsman (*Institutiones Theologiae Moralis,* II, n. 599) likewise imply this when, in excusing such actions on the part of ordinary religious, they make no mention of superiors, but rather prescind from them.

[163] *Institutiones,* n. 612, a; Vermeersch-Creusen (*Epitome,* I, n. 766), Schaefer (*De Religiosis,* nn. 351, 355, b) and Coronata (*Institutiones,* n. 1978) regard this as a probable opinion; Genicot-Salsmans (*Institutiones Theologiae Moralis,* II, n. 59) hold this opinion to be applicable at least for subjects. Cf. also Ciprotti, *De Consummatione Delictorum,* n. 79; Marc-Gestermann-Raus, *Institutiones Morales Alphonsianae,* I, n. 1334; Teodori, "Consultationes,"—

Pennacchi stood out among the authors who defended the position that one who detained a woman within the cloister did not thereby become a victim of the penalty.[164] The method which he employed will herein be coupled with a few canons of the Code to defend the opinion that excommunication is not incurred for detaining a woman within the cloister. This defense will include even superiors among those who do not incur the excommunication. Canon 2342, 2°, excommunicates a woman who violates the cloister of regulars. But it has been shown [165] that the violation consists in the act of entry without proper permission. For this reason a woman who has legitimately entered the cloister will not incur a penalty for remaining there beyond the time of her permission. If this be the correct concept of the cloistral violation, then it will be necessary that the delict of introducing or of admitting a woman into the cloister be very intimately connected with that concept. In other words, the prohibition of the canon is directed against those who assist a woman *to gain entry,* either by introducing or by admitting her. Had the legislator wished to extend the comprehensiveness of the concept of cloistral violation, he could readily have added to the canon the words *"detinentes"* or *"retinentes."* The precise sense of the word *"admittentes,"* as used in canon 2342, does not seem in its meaning to extend to the association of regulars with women who have already entered the cloister. Moreover, the present interpretation appears to be confirmed in the light of the penal principle which states that "a penalty established by law is not incurred unless the nature of the crime corresponded perfectly to the proper sense of the words of the law." [166]

The friendly actions of such a religious are akin to those which are contemplated by the legislator in canon 2209, § 7. There is in a certain sense a reception or harboring of the woman who has committed the crime. But such an act does not constitute a delict in

Apollinaris, V (1932), 111; Augustine, *Commentary,* VIII, 371. Coronata (*Institutiones,* n. 1978, p. 419, note 3) falsely attributes the opposite opinion to Augustine.

[164] *Commentaria,* I, 791-795; cf. also Schaaf, *The Cloister,* p. 96.

[165] Cf. *supra,* pp. 143-144.

[166] Canon 2228; cf. also canon 18.

itself unless the law has attached that effect to it. In the case of canon 2342 the law has not invoked any such specification.

Perhaps the objection may be raised that the danger which would probably result from laxity in expelling a woman from the cloister will not reasonably tolerate adherence to any mild opinions in this matter. It is readily admitted that dangers may well be consequent upon such actions by a religious. But such an argument seems to abstract from the strict canonical principles which obtain throughout the Church's penal legislation. Even though there be just and weighty reasons for extending penalties from one case to another, canon 2219 declares that such an extension may not be invoked. Penal law does not consist in the treatment of what crimes should be punished, but rather in a consideration of those precise crimes which the legislator has punished. In this matter there can be no recourse to arguments which derive solely from even a discreet person's persuasion regarding the proper fitness of things in any given issue. Consequently the present writer considers it as very probable that no religious incurs the penalty of canon 2342 by reason of detaining within the cloister a woman who has entered it without the requisite permission. And the writer furthermore recognizes this opinion as extending its favorable interpretation even to those who have placed some definite cause preventing the woman from leaving the cloister.

Article IV. The Penalty—Its Nature

The penalty which is incurred for the violation of the cloister in monasteries of men and for the delict of introducing or of admitting women into it, is the most severe among the penalties which the Church imposes, namely, excommunication.[167] Being a *latae sententiae* penalty, it is incurred immediately upon the commission of the delict.[168] This penalty is reserved *simpliciter* to the Holy See. Ordinarily, then, absolution from the censure can be obtained only from the Pope or from one to whom he has delegated the faculty. Numbered among the powers contained in the Quinquennial Faculties accorded to ordinaries in this country, however, is the

[167] Cf. canons 2342, 2°; 2257, § 1.

[168] Canon 2217, § 1, 2°.

faculty to absolve from this penalty provided that the delict was not committed for a purpose in any way gravely criminal, even though that purpose was not carried out, and provided that the case was never brought to the external forum. A suitable and salutary penance proportionate to the offense should be imposed.[169]

As is true of all *latae sententiae* penalties, so also in this case any person who is burdened with an excommunication which cannot be observed without infamy is excused from betraying himself through the observance of the penalty. Consequently, before a declaratory sentence [170] has been passed, one can at times conduct himself as if he were not under the penalty.[171] Care must be taken, however, to verify the condition of the canon which presupposes the presence of a danger of infamy before the person is freed of the public observance of the penalty.[172] Applicable likewise to this punishment will be the faculties granted by canon 2254, which permit the granting of absolution by an ordinary confessor when the required conditions are fulfilled.[173]

Contained in canon 2342, 2°, is the mention of a further penalty in punishment of religious who are guilty of introducing or of admitting women into the cloister. Such religious shall be deprived of any office which they may hold and also of any active and passive voice in the community elections. Unlike the penalty of excommunication, this punishment is a *ferendae sententiae* penalty.[174]

[169] This faculty is granted by the Sacred Penitentiary in Section 6, n. 6, of Formula IV of the quinquennial faculties which the bishops of the United States possess through the year 1944. A translation of this faculty will be found in T. Bouscaren, *Canon Law Digest* (2 vols. and one supplement, Milwaukee: Bruce Publishing Co., 1934-1941), *Supplement* (1941), p. 36.

[170] Cf. canon 2232, § 2.

[171] Canon 2232, § 1.

[172] Sole, *De Delictis et Poenis*, pp. 86-87; Coronata, *Institutiones*, n. 1723.

[173] Cf. F. Moriarty, *The Extraordinary Absolution from Censures*, The Catholic University of America Canon Law Studies, n. 113 (Washington, D. C.: The Catholic University of America, 1938), pp. 142 ff.

[174] Cf. canon 2217, § 1, 2°. In the old law this penalty was a *latae sententiae* penalty. Cf. Pope Pius V, Const. "*Regularium*," 24 oct. 1566—*Fontes*, n. 115. The Constitution "*Apostolicae Sedis*" of Pope Pius IX did not revoke this penalty. Cf. Pennacchi, *Commentaria*, I, 802; Ojetti, *Synopsis*, s. v. "Clausura," n. 1188.

It must, then, be imposed according to the norms of canon 2223.[175]

Embraced in this penal legislation are the religious of any Order or Congregation. It is by no means demanded that they be members of the monastery whose cloister has been violated. Novices and postulants, however, are not included in this punishment.[176] The active vote of which religious are deprived by this penalty is the right to cast a ballot in community elections; the passive voice is the right of having votes cast in one's favor. If, despite this prohibition, a religious should exercise the right of active vote, the ballot cast by him will be invalid, but the election in which he participated will remain unaffected, unless it is evident that solely by virtue of his invalid ballot the required number of ballots for the election was obtained.[177]

Section B. Active Violation

Article I. Egress of Regulars

In one respect the present law offers no appreciable departure from the old legislation which never entailed a universal *latae sententiae* penalty for the forbidden egress from the enclosure of regulars. In the penal legislation of the Code no mention is made of the active violation of the enclosure by regulars.[178] Canon 606, § 1, alone contains reference to this phase of the law. And even that canon deals specifically not only with regulars, but rather with all religious.[179]

The enactment of canon 606, § 1, does not descend to details, but urges only that superiors exercise care that the prescriptions of the

[175] Salucci, *Il Diritto Penale*, II, n. 256; Coronata, *Institutiones*, n. 1984; Pistocchi, *I Canoni Penali*, p. 134; Sipos, *Enchiridion*, p. 369; Ayrinhac-Lydon, *Penal Legislation in the New Code of Canon Law*, p. 221; Schaefer, *De Religiosis*, n. 351, b; Sole, *op. cit.*, p. 293.

[176] Cf. canon 488, 7°; Sipos, *loc. cit.*

[177] Cf. canon 167, § 2; Coronata, *Institutiones*, n. 231.

[178] There is certainly no prohibition which hinders particular laws from establishing penal legislation for egress from the cloister. Cf. canon 606, § 1; Schaefer, *De Religiosis*, n. 350.

[179] Cf. Berutti, *Institutiones*, III, n. 120, I; Vermeersch-Creusen, *Epitome*, I, n. 763.

individual constitutions pertinent to this matter be accurately observed. This general form of legislation presents a distinct departure from the universal law which was prevalent prior to the Code. The Council of Trent forbade regulars to leave their monastery even under the pretext of going to their higher superiors.[180] Pope Clement VIII (1592-1605) had prescribed that a regular could rightfully leave his monastery only after he had obtained specific permission from his superior. The granting of general permissions was explicitly excluded. Even special permissions were to be given only when they were justified by a worthy cause, and on the condition that the monk was to be accompanied by a companion of the superior's choice. A trustworthy guardian appointed by the superior was to guard the exits of the monastic cloister so diligently that only regulars in possession of the proper permission were permitted to leave the cloister. Severe penalties, even incarceration, were to be imposed by the superior upon all delinquents.[181] Berutti asserts that the Code has abrogated the enactment of Pope Clement VIII which demanded that a porter be assigned to the exit of the cloister to prevent all unlawful egress of religious.[182] Coronata [183] and Chelodi [184] regard as abrogated by the Code the more severe common law prohibitions relative to the egress of regulars.

The norm, consequently, which will determine the time, the frequency and the cause of egress from the cloister by regulars will be found in the constitutions governing the discipline of the individual Orders. And any severity which they may portray will in no way be contrary either to the letter or to the spirit of the Code. On the contrary, the legislator has expressed his desire that these precise regulations be rigidly observed. It is one of the duties of each religious superior to prevent, in so far as he is able, any laxity in the observance of the constitutions which govern the life of his religious community. In canon 606, § 1, the supreme legislator insists upon *special* care being exercised by religious superiors in the matter of

[180] Sess. XXV, *de regularibus*, c. 4; canon 616, § 1; cf. *supra*, pp. 53-54.

[181] Const. "*Nullus omnino*," 25 iul. 1599, § 12—*Bull. Rom.*, X, 664.

[182] *Institutiones*, III, n. 120, I. Cf. Schaefer, *De Religiosis*, n. 364, 1.

[183] *Institutiones*, n. 612, b.

[184] *Ius de Personis*, n. 277, p. 463, note 2.

the cloistral observance.[185] It is difficult to find in this canon, however, any further common law obligation as added to the prescriptions of the various constitutions.[186] The obligation is one which calls for the diligent exercise of care and watchfulness by superiors. Because very often certain points within the constitutions do not of themselves bind under pain of sin, a greater diligence is demanded of superiors in order that the proper observance of the cloister may be realized.[187]

Most of the deviations from the law of the cloistral observance will readily become known to any superior who exercises even the modicum of proper watchfulness. For this reason it will be relatively an easy matter for superiors to check abuses and to insist upon the constant fulfillment of the constitutional requirements. The legislator, moreover, desires to impress upon superiors the fact that they themselves should not adopt an attitude of imprudent laxity in granting permissions or in not insisting upon the request for permission to leave the monastery. The dangers which may be consequent upon a non-observance of this essential feature of religious life merit grave consideration. The lack of any severe penal legislation in the Code never must be construed as an indication that the supreme legislator regards this matter lightly.

Schaefer [188] and Chelodi [189] assert that the prohibition of arbitrary egress by regulars connotes of its very nature an obligation which is not light. To say, however, when there will be question of grave fault for the violation of this regulation is difficult. Certainly it seems that stealthy nocturnal excursions from the cloister would constitute grave sins.[190] It is obvious that there will arise certain contingencies which demand that a religious leave the cloister, even at night, without having first obtained permission. But in such cases, a presumed permission can readily be acknowledged as present.

185 Coronata, *loc. cit.;* Berutti, *Institutiones,* III, n. 120, I; Wernz-Vidal, *Ius Canonicum,* III, n. 376, III; Vermeersch-Creusen, *Epitome,* I, n. 763.

186 Berutti, *loc. cit.*

187 Coronata, *Institutiones,* n. 612, b.

188 *De Religiosis,* n. 350, note 215.

189 *Ius de Personis,* n. 277, p. 463, note 2.

190 Coronata, *Institutiones,* n. 612, b; Pejska, *Ius Canonicum,* p. 155.

It is entirely possible, moreover, for superiors to grant general permissions for such occasions. Oftentimes the nature of the work performed by religious, especially by priests, will necessitate egress from the cloister at times when the superior is not available. General permissions to leave the cloister at night for social motives seem certainly to be contrary to the letter and spirit of the canons.

One question which may possibly present difficulties in this matter concerns the privilege which is granted to religious of confessing to any confessor approved by the local ordinary.[191] It would be false to conclude from the grant of this liberty that a religious could leave the monastery without having first obtained permission for egress. Moreover, certainly the canon grants to no religious the right in such a way to leave the monastery that his egress will connote a concomitant obligation on the part of the superior to grant the permission. The laws of the cloister remain always intact. It is but part, however, of the wisdom and prudence demanded by their office that every superior grant such permissions when they are reasonably sought. Not to do so would be to adopt an attitude and a method of procedure which is contrary to the mind and intention of the Church.[192]

Article II. Residence Outside of the Enclosure

Community life is one of the essential features of the religious state.[193] It is the form of life within which it is desired that the religious will progress to the perfection which is demanded of his state. For these reasons religious should live in the houses of their own religious community. Realizing the enervating influence which residence outside of his community can exercise on a religious, and desiring its prevention, the legislator has forbidden religious superiors to permit their subjects to live outside of their own religious houses. Only with a grave and just cause may this be allowed, and then only for a brief time in accordance with the prescriptions of the

[191] Cf. canon 519.

[192] Goyeneche, "Consultationes,"—*CpR,* III (1922), 81-82; Coronata, *Institutiones,* n. 544, p. 676, note 2; Schaefer, *De Religiosis,* n. 167; Berutti, *Institutiones,* III, n. 39, I.

[193] Canon 487.

constitutions of the particular Institute. For an absence extending beyond six months' duration, unless it be for the cause of pursuing studies, permission of the Holy See is always required.[194] Specific provision has been made by the Code for those mendicant Orders which find it necessary to permit the absence of religious for the purpose of collecting alms.[195]

The interpretation of this law would fail, it appears, to correspond to the mind of the legislator were it to place undue emphasis upon the strict wording to the canon. The resulting conclusion would demand specific approval from the Holy See for every absence extending beyond six months. But this is not the interpretation of reputable authors. The ends and purposes of religious Orders must be given their due consideration. These ends and purposes have received the approval of the Holy See. Implicit then in that approval there seems to be contained the permission to fulfill the works for which the community was founded, even when the tasks connected with them necessitate a prolonged absence.[196] Most of the authors simply cite the views of Vermeersch on this question. Seeking to determine the meaning of the words *"extra propriae religionis domum,"* Vermeersch attributes to them the sense: *"extra domum ubi ratione vocationis suae religiosus degere vel commorari debet aut potest."* Thus he affirms that a religious can accept the position of spiritual director or of superior of a seminary when this is in accordance with the end of his Institute. The seminary thus becomes for him, in so far as the law is concerned, a religious house.[197] Thus

[194] Canon 606, § 2.

[195] Cf. canons 606, § 2; 621-624.

[196] Vermeersch, "De commoratione extra propriam religionis domum,"—*Periodica,* X (1922), (36)-(37); Vermeersch, "De religiosorum absentia secundum canon 606, § 2,"—*Periodica,* XX (1931), 144*-145*; Coronata *Institutiones,* n. 612, b; Schaefer, *De Religiosis,* n. 364, 1; Wernz-Vidal, *Ius Canonicum,* III, n. 382; Beste, *Introductio in Codicem,* p. 411; Berutti, *Institutiones,* III, n. 120, II; Cocchi, *Commentarium,* IV, n. 106, Biederlack-Führich, *De Religiosis,* p. 242.

[197] "Ac sane, qui secundum rationem sui Instituti, tamquam spiritualis director vel superior praeficitur cuipiam, nonne ibi degit sicut in domo propriae religionis?"—"De commoratione extra propriam religionis domum"—*Periodica,* X (1922), (37).

also may the law be applied with relation to his work in a parish, his preaching of missions, his serving as a chaplain in a hospital and other such works. It is very necessary, however, that care and prudence be exercised in adopting this interpretation. Any arbitrary extension of the works which serve the proper ends of a religious Institute will not justify the use of the interpretation which has been stated here. There are, in fact, authors who cling to the opposite view in this matter and stress the need of permission from the Holy See for every absence which is of more than six months' duration.[198] The correct and safe interpretation, then, will couple the constitutions of each individual community with the prescriptions of the canon and the interpretations of the authors. Foremost consideration must always be directed by superiors to the maintenance and preservation of the religious spirit for such regulars whose duties will call them from their monasteries. It will avail nothing if undue emphasis is placed upon the external works of the Order to the detriment of the religious spirit, the well-ordered life and the disciplined obedience of the priests who are called upon to perform them.

When the Code mentions a six months' period of time, it has reference to an uninterrupted duration.[199] Vermeersch sought to determine the length of time which would be sufficient to destroy moral coalescense between the various periods of absence when a religious returns to his house between assignments. His conclusions were as follows: (a) a religious who has been away from his community for a period of almost six months will require only one day in the community to break the continuity of time if the subsequent assignment which calls him away from the monastery is of a cause or of a nature different from the preceding; (b) if, however, an absence of

[198] Cf. Oesterle, *Praelectiones Iuris Canonici*, p. 340. Fanfani (*De Iure Religiosorum*, n. 318, C) places special emphasis on the word *semper* as used in canon 606, § 2.

[199] Fanfani, *loc. cit.;* Blat (*Commentarium*, II, n. 546) computes this time according to the rule contained in canon 34, § 2. This computation, however, appears to be wrong. The time should rather be computed according to the norm stated in canon 34, § 3. Cf. A. Dubé, *The General Principles for the Reckoning of Time in Canon Law*, The Catholic University of America Canon Law Studies, n. 144 (Washington, D. C.: The Catholic University of America Press, 1942), pp. 202-205.

over six months will be demanded by the assignment which is given to any religious, and this fact is foreseen, then an indult may be obtained at once from the Holy See, or the religious should, before the completion of the six months' duration of absence, return to his monastery for one month and then resume his assignment. Vermeersch derives this second conclusion in view of the present cases' analogy to the case in which there is a similar question relative to the length of time presupposed to effect an interruption, namely, the case of the religious novitiate.[200]

The interpretation of Vermeersch in the first postulated case, in which he requires only one day to be spent in the community after an assignment, appears to do violence to the letter and spirit of the law. Moreover, it appears to have no foundation in the canon itself. One day spent in the community will be almost negligible in restoring the vigor of the religious spirit which may have become impaired by the long-continued absence. It is true that the Code does not demand the permission of the Holy See for an absence of less than six months. But it is difficult to comprehend how a diversity of causes calling a religious away from his community will justify as sufficient the single day's interruption between assignments, which his return to the monastery connotes, when the sum-total of time spent outside of the community will far exceed the six months' period. Blat states that an interruption of one week would not be sufficient in a case of this kind.[201]

It does seem that a religious who has been away from his community for almost six months should be required to spend at least one month within the religious house, regardless of the nature of the subsequent assignment which will again call him away. Must it not be said that canonical interpretations are useless and even harmful when they entail the destruction of the prudent purpose for which the law was enacted?

Unlike the duty which canon 606, § 1, imposes upon religious

200 "De religiosorum absentia secundum canon 606, § 2,"—*Periodica,* XX (1931), 144*-145*. It will be noted that Vermeersch is not considering herein the religious who leaves the monastery to perform work compatible with the proper end of his Institute.

201 *Commentarium,* II, n. 546.

superiors, the obligation of which canon 606, § 2, makes mention must beyond all question be regarded as a grave one. Vromant, in fact, acknowledges that canon 606, § 2, imposes upon religious superiors a very grave obligation.[202] The requisite of a grave and just cause to warrant the grant of a permission by superiors manifests the obvious severity of the law. The existence of such causes in individual instances will necessarily be determined by the mature judgment of the superiors themselves. The necessity of hospitalization,[203] the pursuance of studies, the performance of works of piety and of charity will all fulfill the requirements of the law concerning the presence of a grave and just cause for a temporary absence.[204] The factors of age, the length of time one has spent in vows, the character and temperament of the religious—all these can exercise an important rôle in the matter of the superior's judgment about the advisability of granting the necessary permission.

Canon 606, § 2, demands that a religious live in a house of his own Institute. Consequently, even though a regular may be residing in a house of another religious Order, he must be considered as absent from his religious community life in the sense of this canon. Obviously, however, the canon does not demand that a religious reside in the house to which he has been permanently assigned. Provided that the house in which he is residing be one of his own Order, the regular will not be considered as absent in the sense of this canon.[205]

Among many religious communities it is an established custom that the members spend some time of their vacation at the home of their parents or relatives. Though he admits that such a practice is not entirely in consonance with religious life, Vermeersch allows

[202] ". . . sub peccato ex genere suo gravi . . ."—*De Personis*, n. 388.

[203] If it be foreseen that the period of hospitalization will require an absence of more than six months, then certainly an apostolic indult for this long-continued absence must be obtained. Cf. Schaefer, *De Religiosis*, n. 364; Vermeersch, "De commoratione extra propriam religionis domum,"—*Periodica*, X (1922), (36); Fanfani, *De Iure Religiosorum*, n. 318, C.

[204] Schaefer, *loc. cit.;* Berutti, *Institutiones*, III, n. 120, II.

[205] Schaefer, *De Religiosis*, n. 364, 1; Coronata, *Institutiones*, n. 612, b; Fanfani, *De Iure Religiosorum*, n. 318, C; Berutti, *Institutiones*, III, n. 120, II; Vermeersch-Creusen, *Epitome*, I, n. 763.

it on the ground that the difficulty of abrogating the long-received custom supplies the necessary just and grave reason demanded by the law for such an absence from the religious house. Such a vacation, however, should not be extended beyond a brief time.[206]

While it is true that canon 606, § 2, makes exception for regulars who will be sent away from the monastery for the purpose of study, yet even in these instances great care should be exercised by superiors. Canon 587, § 4, enumerates the precautions which must be taken. If a house of his own Institute is not readily accessible to the religious from his place of study, then the absentee religious should reside in some religious Institute of men, in a seminary, or in some other pious house which, with the approval of the proper ecclesiastical authority, is placed under the charge of priests.[207]

[206] *Epitome,* I, n. 763; cf. Coronata, *loc. cit.*

[207] Cf. Schaefer, *De Religiosis,* n. 291, 2.

CHAPTER VI

PASSIVE VIOLATION OF THE CLOISTER OF NUNS

ARTICLE I. EXTENT OF EXCLUSION

WITH one difference, the law of the Code which pertains to the question of entry into the cloister of nuns is identical with the corresponding legislation relative to the cloister of regulars. That difference consists in this: The law on the cloister of nuns excludes the entry not only of men but also of women; the law on the cloister of regulars excludes the entry of women only and not of men.[1] Since this one point of difference is so obvious that it requires no interpretation, the commentary which has been given in the discussion of canon 598, § 1, will suffice for canon 600.[2]

There arises, however, a distinct problem which is peculiar to the convents of nuns. It deserves special consideration here. Sometimes by virtue of a special permission from the Holy See nuns will travel from one convent to another. Will it be lawful to admit them overnight into the papal cloister of another convent which may be located in the city where they are stopping? Or are they to be excluded by virtue of the very rigid and comprehensive wording of canon 600? This problem received considerable attention from the pre-Code authors. Their opinions have been summarized by Vermeersch in a treatment of this question.[3]

The discussion followed a twofold procedure dependently upon whether the nun sought entry into a monastery of the same Order or of one of a different Order. Most of the authors admitted that a nun could be taken into a convent of the same Order. The gist of their argument was that such a nun could not be considered as an

[1] Cf. canons 600; 598, § 1.

[2] Cf. *supra*, pp. 116-126.

[3] "De Clausura Monialium,"—*Periodica*, XIX (1930), 12*-15*.

extern.[4] Others, however, denied the validity of this opinion. Castro-Palao (1581-1633) [5] based his contrary opinion upon the fact that the nun did not belong to the monastery. To make an exception in her case was tantamount to throwing open the door to all nuns of the same Order. He did admit, however, that permission could be granted by the superior to whom the convent was subject. Vermeersch rightly objects to the conclusion of Castro-Palao, namely that abuses would be consequent upon the admission of this opinion. It was only upon very rare occasions that nuns were outside of their own enclosure.[6]

Passerini (1595-1677) likewise objected to the opinions of those authors who permitted a traveling nun to enter the cloister of a convent of the same Order.[7] He objected that, unlike the monasteries of regulars, each convent of nuns was a distinct and separate unity and, consequently, a nun even of the same Order was an extern. He did admit the contrary interpretation only if the place where the traveling nun tarried was so full of dangers that she could not safely stay outside the convent. But even in that case permission was to be sought from the proper superior.

If the nun was a member of a different Order, there was again a discrepancy of opinion. Some based their opposing view upon the fact that in such a case she was an extern.[8] But when no other place of lodging was available, she could be admitted after permission had been obtained from the bishop and the regular superior, if the con-

[4] Bonacina, *De Clausure*, q. IV, p. I, n. 3; Llamas, *in methodo curationis, in append.* § 11 *in fine*, cited by Bonacina, *loc. cit.*; T. Sanchez, *Opus Morale in Praecepta Decalogi* (2 vols., Parmae: 1723), lib. 6, cap. 16, n. 10; Pellizzarius, *De Monialibus*, cap. V, sec. III, n. 107; Peyrinus, *De Officio Praelati Regularis*, in Const. 6 Pii V, quoted at length by Vermeersch, *loc. cit.*

[5] *De religione*, tr. XVI *De statu religioso*, Disp. IV. Punctum X, 1, cited by Vermeersch, "De Clausura Monialium,"—*Periodica*, XIX (1930), 14*.

[6] "De Clausura Monialium,"—*Periodica*, XIX (1930), 14*.

[7] *Commentaria in Tertium Librum Sexti Decretalium* (Venetiis: 1698), *de statu regularium*, cap. *Periculoso*, un., n. 123.

[8] Sanchez, *loc. cit.*; Castro-Palao, *loc. cit.*; Passerini, *loc. cit.*; Bonacina, *loc. cit.*

vent was subject to regulars. Others held that charity and the dignity of the nun's status in life required that she be admitted into the cloister, rather than that she be constrained to lodge outside.[9]

Vermeersch asks whether nuns may today be permitted to enter monasteries in like circumstances.[10] Canon 600 now reserves to the Holy See all permission to enter the cloister, with the exception of the stated exemptions. Formerly this was reserved to the bishop and, in certain monasteries, to the regular superior. Vermeersch asserts that canon 600 can be interpreted in accordance with the opinion of the old authors. When no recourse to the Holy See is possible, the principle of *epikeia* may be invoked to allow nuns of the same Order to enter the monastery when they are legitimately outside of their own monastery. The same principle may be applied to nuns of a different Order, but only when no suitable place of habitation outside of the enclosure is available. If time permits, however, the approbation of the local ordinary should be sought in accordance with canon 600, 4°.

In the year 1929 an indult was granted to a Carmelite nun whereby she was permitted while on a journey to enter another Carmel convent.[11] In commenting upon the grant of this indult, Vermeersch remarked that it was given only with some reluctance. However, an indult of this kind is not a direct interpretation of law.[12]

A rescript of the Congregation of Religious, which in 1936 granted for three years a special faculty to the Ordinary of Genoa, authorized him to permit all monasteries of nuns in that city to receive into the cloister for the duration of their stay all nuns of the same Order who were passing through the city.[13] This rescript also contains no authentic interpretation of law. For an unexpected case

[9] Pellizzarius, *De Monialibus*, cap. V, sec. III, n. 107; Peyrinus, *loc. cit.*

[10] "De Clausura Monialium,"—*Periodica*, XIX (1930), 14*. Schaefer (*De Religiosis*, n. 353, p. 722) adopts the conclusion of Vermeersch.

[11] "De Clausura Monialium,"—*Periodica*, XIX (1930), 15*.

[12] *Periodica, loc. cit.*

[13] Cf. "Acta et Documenta,"—*CpR*, XVII (1936), 209. The Latin translation of this rescript can be found in "Monumenta"—*Periodica*, XXVI (1937), 81-82.

which allows of no recourse to the Holy See, Ellis concludes that it will be licit for a nun to enter a monastery of the same Order according to the norms of the old authors. The approbation of the local ordinary should be obtained if time permits. If the nun is of a different Order, the principle of *epikeia* coupled with the permission of the local ordinary will permit her to enter the cloister if no other suitable place is available.[14]

Larraona does not extend his interpretation to such limits, but rather asserts that the Congregation of Religious is most generous and lenient in granting indults for all cases of this nature. He regards as a sufficient reason for the grant of an indult the opportunity it affords to the nuns, namely, of lodging within a papal enclosure in the course of their journey. It is his opinion, moreover, that there now exists in some Orders either a privilege or a prescribed custom whereby nuns of the same Order are taken into the cloister on such occasions. He anticipates no great difficulty in obtaining a favorable answer to a petition sent to the Sacred Congregation for the faculty to allow nuns of a different Order to enter the cloister of monasteries situated in large cities.[15]

Article II. Exceptions to the Law of Exclusion

A. Canonical Visitation of the Cloister

Canon 600, 1°, permits the local ordinary or his delegate to enter the cloister for the purpose of inspection. This same privilege is accorded to regular superiors and their delegates. It is required always that at least one cleric or male religious of mature age accompany the visitor at the time the inspection is made.

1. Visitation of the Local Ordinary

Consideration will be given first to the visitation of the convents of those nuns who are subject to the jurisdiction of the local ordinary or immediately to the jurisdiction of the Holy See. To convents of

[14] "Annotationes,"—*Periodica,* XXVI (1937), 84.

[15] "Annotationes,"—*CpR,* XVII (1936), 210.

this type a quinquennial visitation must be made by the local ordinary.[16]

Amplification of this legislation will be found in the *Instruction* of the Sacred Congregation of Religious. Permission to enter the enclosure is valid only for *local* inspection, and not for the personal visitation of the nuns which must be made at the grill.[17]

At least one cleric or male religious, who may be a lay brother of mature age,[18] must accompany the visitor, and must never become separated from him during the entire time of the visitation.[19] The use of the term *saltem* in canon 600, 1°, and in the *Instruction* seems to favor more than one companion. Certainly, greater assurance of the fulfillment of the purpose of the law will flow from the use of a pair of companions. Two or three companions may be allowed, then, to accompany the visitor.[20] On all other occasions the rigid prohibition of the cloister applies equally to local ordinaries. Let it not be thought that their office entitles them to enter the cloister

[16] Canon 512, § 1, 1°. The local ordinary is not necessarily bound to a five-year period in making his visitation. Whenever he deems it necessary he may enter the enclosure for a tour of inspection. This may be done every year or, in extraordinary circumstances, even more often. Cf. canon 603, § 1; Berutti, *Institutiones*, III, n. 115, I; Coronata, *Institutiones*, n. 613, 3; Schaefer, *De Religiosis*, n. 353.

[17] *Instructio*, III, 2°, b. Considering the situation in which infirm nuns would be unable to present themselves at the grill for personal visitation of the bishop, Jombart ("Visite Canonique et Cloture,"—*Revue des Communautés Religieuses*, VIII [1932], 25) permits the bishop to conduct such a personal visitation when he is within the cloister for his local visitation.

[18] Blat (*Commentarium*, II, n. 533) places this age at about 40 years. The nonfulfillment of this precaution, however, will certainly not imply a violation of the cloister. Maturity oftentimes will not be so much a question of years as a question of ripe and considerate judgment and discretion. It is not required, moreover, that the lay brother be a member of any special religious order. The *Instruction* does not distinguish.

[19] *Instructio*, III, 2°, e.

[20] Coronata, *Institutiones*, n. 613, a; Vermeersch-Creusen, *Epitome*, I, n. 759; Berutti, *Institutiones*, III, n. 115, I; Schaefer, *De Religiosis*, n. 353, note 250; Blat, *Commentarium*, II, n. 533. The former legislation confined the number of companions to a few (*paucis*)—cf. Mocchegiani, *Iurisprudentia Ecclesiastica*, I, n. 410-413.

except for the execution of the duties of visitation.[21] Thus the examination which is to be conducted before investiture or profession [22] does not admit of any exception. Neither may the local ordinary enter the cloister when he presides at the ceremonies of investiture or of profession, or at the election of a superioress.[23]

Larraona raises a question in reference to the entry of the local ordinary at the time of the elections. May such entry be permitted to prevent subornation? Though Larraona admits that the case is highly hypothetical, he favors the use of canon 5 in order to determine the validity of customs in this regard. Noting also the explicit terminology of the Council of Trent,[24] he states that any contrary practice antedating that Council and contrary to the Code should be judged in accordance with the prescriptions of canon 4.[25] Coronata cites without comment the statement of Larraona.[26] Schaefer notes the treatment of Larraona but asserts that the present law will be found in the *Instruction.*[27] Strict adherence to the letter of the law appears to be the better interpretation of this question.

The election of a superioress in a monastery of nuns presents for solution another knotty problem. Canon 506, § 2, enacts that two priests shall be appointed tellers for the election. The question now presents itself: May those priests enter the cloister to receive the ballot of an infirm nun who is unable to cast her ballot at the grill? In the present law canon 168 requires that, unless particular laws or legitimate customs have provided for some other method of pro-

21 *Instructio,* III, 2°, b.

22 Canon 522, § 2.

23 *Instructio,* III, 2°, c; cf. canon 506, § 2.

24 ". . . Is vero qui electione praeest, episcopus sive alius superior, claustra monasterii non ingrediatur; sed ante cancellorum fenestellam vota singularum audiat, vel accipiat. . . ."—Sess. XXV, *de regularibus,* c. 7.

25 "Commentarium Codicis,"—*CpR,* VIII (1927), 23. He cites Petra (*In Constitutiones Apostolicas,* IV, p. 478) in favor of the lawfulness of such an action by the bishop. Pennacchi (*Commentaria,* I, 735) and A. Lucidi (*De Visitatione Sacrorum Liminum* [3. ed., 3 vols., Romae: 1883], II, 153) likewise granted this exemption in favor of the bishop.

26 *Institutiones,* n. 538, p. 659, note 5.

27 *De Religiosis,* n. 131, note 266; cf. Blat, *Commentarium,* II, n. 127.

cedure, the tellers shall obtain the ballots of all infirm persons. May it be concluded from this canon that the Code is implicitly granting to tellers the privilege of entering into the cloister for such a purpose? It seems that in canon 168 there is not implied any obligation which demands that the ballots be *personally* obtained by the tellers. The use of the verb *"exquiratur"* in the canon seems not to imply in any necessary manner that the tellers must personally go to the infirm voters. Moreover, this conclusion seems to be strengthened by the *nisi* clause which appears in the canon. When the obligation of preserving intact the cloister of nuns is weighed in the balance with the obligation of procuring the ballots of an infirm nun, it appears that the scale of canonical principles will indicate the preponderance of the former.

An occasion such as this will warrant the appointment of two nuns to serve in the capacity of tellers. This appointment will proceed from the presiding officer in the event that the Constitutions or particular customs do not specifically provide some other method. Proper precautions can well be taken to prevent danger of revelation in the act of voting by providing the two nuns with a box into which the ballot of the infirm nun can be placed.[28]

Canon 512, § 2, 1°, obliges the local ordinary to visit quinquennially the monasteries of nuns who are subject to regulars, but only for the purpose of inspecting the cloistral observance. It is evident, then, that the visitation of the local ordinary may extend to the choir, the dormitory, the cells, the recreation room, etc., but only in so far as they relate to the law of the cloister. During the time of this visitation the local ordinary may conduct a personal visitation of the nuns. This latter visitation will be made at the grill. Its subject matter will relate only to the cloistral observance. It shall be made in accordance with canon 513, § 1.[29] Should it happen that the regular superior has not visited such a monastery of nuns within the five year period, then the local ordinary is empowered to supply

[28] Cf. Larraona, "Commentarium Codicis," *CpR,* VIII (1927), 25, notes 337-338; Schaefer, *De Religiosis,* n. 129, note 241; n. 130; Fanfani, *De Iure Religiosorum,* n. 100, D.

[29] Cf. *PCI,* 24 nov. 1920—*AAS,* XII (1920), 575.

his negligence and to conduct an investigation of the accounts, the dowry funds, the administration, the discipline, etc.[30]

2. Visitation of the Regular Superior

Canon 511 states simply that major superiors shall visit the monasteries of nuns who are subject to them. Relative to the time of this visitation and to the precise superiors who will conduct it, nothing is said either in the canon or in the *Instruction*. The determination of these factors is left to the religious Constitutions. What has been said relative to the visitation conducted by the local ordinary will be equally applicable to the visitation undertaken by the regular superiors.[31]

B. Minister of the Sacraments and the Confessor

1. The Administration of the Sacraments to the Sick and the Dying

Canon 600, 2°, states that the confessor or his substitute may with the observance of due precautions enter the cloister to administer the sacraments to the sick or to assist the dying. This bare statement of the law is greatly expanded by the *Instruction* of the Congregation of Religious. The faculty of administering the sacraments and of assisting the dying pertains to the ordinary confessor [32] of the monastery or to that priest who, in accordance with canon 514, § 2, takes his place. If either of these priests is absent, any other priest may enter the cloister for this purpose.[33] Who is the priest who will substitute for the ordinary confessor? This can be the chaplain of the convent [34] or any other priest who is deputed or

[30] Cf. canon 512, § 2, 1°.

[31] Cf. T. F. Reilly, *The Visitation of Religious*, The Catholic University of America Canon Law Studies, n. 112 (Washington, D. C.: The Catholic University of America, 1938), pp. 80-83.

[32] Cf. canon 520, § 1.

[33] *Instructio*, III, 2°, f.

[34] Cf. canon 529.

designated by the ordinary confessor to fulfill this duty.[35] If it should happen that the ordinary confessor and his substitute are both absent, then any priest may licitly enter the cloister for the administration of the sacraments. It was formerly required that, before such a priest could lawfully enter the cloister, he had to have in his possession at least the habitual permission of the bishop.[36] It seems, however, that the wording of the *Instruction* no longer requires any such permission.[37]

Whenever the extraordinary confessor [38] is exercising his duties, then it will be his right to enter the cloister to administer the sacraments to the nuns. At such a time the ordinary confessor will remain away from the monastery.[39] If, however, it is the occasional, the supplementary or some substitute confessor who is hearing the confession of a nun, the right of the ordinary confessor to administer the sacraments still remains.[40] It seems advisable, however, that on such occasions the ordinary confessor cede his rights.

Since the *Instruction* makes no distinction, necessity need not be present to permit, in the absence of the ordinary confessor of the monastery or of him who takes his place, any priest to enter the cloister for the administration of the sacraments. The desire of an infirm nun to receive Holy Communion purely for reasons of devotion will constitute a sufficient reason. The superioress can permit any priest who says Mass in the convent to fulfill this function.[41]

There is no limitation of number placed upon the visits to the cloister which may be made by the ordinary confessor or his sub-

[35] Coronata, *Institutiones,* n. 613; Schaefer, *De Religiosis,* n. 353; Beste, *Introductio in Codicem,* p. 409; Oesterle, *Praelectiones Iuris Canonici,* p. 337; Fanfani, *De Iure Religiosorum,* n. 416; A. Jardí, *El Derecho de las Religiosas* (2. ed., Vich: Serafica, 1927), n. 285.

[36] S. C. de Rel., 1 sept. 1912—*AAS,* IV (1912), 625-626.

[37] Coronata, *op. cit.,* n. 613, p. 800, note 7; Schaefer, *op. cit.,* n. 353, note 245.

[38] Cf. canon 521, § 1.

[39] Coronata, *op. cit.,* n. 613, p. 800; Jardí, *El Derecho de las Religiosas,* nn. 365-366; Cocchi, *Commentarium,* IV, n. 40.

[40] Coronata, *Institutiones,* n. 613, p. 800, note 8.

[41] Vermeersch-Creusen, *Epitome,* I, n. 759; Beste, *Introductio in Codicem,* p. 409; Fanfani, *De Iure Religiosorum,* n. 310, A.

stitute. The desire of an infirm nun to receive Holy Communion will permit daily entry into the cloister.[42] Whenever they deem it necessary, be it day or night, or many times a day, the ordinary confessor and his substitute may enter the cloister to assist the dying.[43]

Once the priest has completed the duty which brought him into the cloister, he must depart immediately.[44] The obvious purpose of this regulation is to prevent any loitering or unnecessary visiting of other nuns, whether they be sick or not.[45] An unswerving interpretation which adheres rigidly to the strict wording of the law fails, however, to take into consideration the fact that it is not merely the bare administration of the sacraments that is permitted by the Church. Such an inflexible compliance with the letter of the law would repeatedly result in the deprivation of the company and assistance of the priest in the dying moments of some nun. Ripoli permits a confessor to spend an entire night within the cloister if a nun is in imminent danger of death.[46] Berutti allows a priest to remain at the bedside of a dying nun for a long time (*diutius*).[47] Ferreres does not go so far as expressly to permit the ministering priest to attend at the bedside of the dying nun throughout the night, but he does permit a priest to remain in the cloister for a great part of the night.[48] Once the fact is granted, however, that a nun is in imminent danger of death, one would have difficulty in proving that a priest could not spend an entire night with her within the cloister.

[42] Schaefer, *De Religiosis*, n. 353, note 253; Berutti, *Institutiones*, III, n. 115, p. 262; Chelodi, *De Personis*, n. 277, c; J. Ferreres, *Compendium Theologiae Moralis* (13. ed., 2 vols., Barcinone: Subirana, 1925), II, n. 233. Blat (*Commentarium*, II, n. 533) asserts that in order to avoid abuses this practice should receive prior episcopal approbation.

[43] Schaefer, *op. cit.*, n. 353, p. 720; Coronata, *Institutiones*, n. 613, p. 801; Berutti, *loc. cit.*

[44] *Instructio*, III, 2°, k.

[45] Creusen, Garesché, Ellis, *Religious Men and Women in the Code*, n. 287.

[46] *Novisimas instituciones de derecho canonico* (2 vols., Madrid: 1920), I, n. 1052, 6.

[47] *Institutiones*, III, n. 115, p. 262.

[48] *Compendium Theologiae Moralis*, II, n. 233.

Certainly canon 600, 2°, and the *Instruction* state no limitation of time. When the *Instruction* demands that a priest leave the cloister immediately upon the completion of his tasks, this must be widely interpreted. The Church desires that every benefit be accorded to those who are at the threshold of death. Surely it cannot be maintained that an exception is to be made when it is a question of nuns. In a case of this nature the consideration of prior importance favors the presence of the priest and not the rigid interpretation of the cloistral laws.

May the chaplain enter the cloister for the burial services of a nun when the cemetery is situated therein? The former law progressed from rigidity to relative leniency on this question.[49] On the 24th of April, 1903, the Sacred Congregation of Bishops and Regulars "in virtue of special faculties" tolerated in the diocese of Zamora in Spain the continuance of a custom which permitted several priests together to enter the cloister for the conducting of a funeral.[50] Jombart defends the position that such customs may now be tolerated in accordance with canon 5. He asserts that the "special faculties" which the Congregation sought from the Holy Father in the Zamora case were sought not for the sake of enabling the diocese to retain and use its custom, but for the sake of allowing an unusual number of priests to enter the cloister on the occasion of the funeral. One or two servers may now be permitted to accompany the chaplain who will conduct such services in accordance with canons 1204 and 1230, §5. Nuns should be regarded as meriting all of the funeral rites which are accorded to other Catholics, even when it involves entry into the cloister.[51] Other authors also admit the validity of

[49] Cf. S. C. Ep. et Reg., 10 mart. 1577, which forbade a priest to enter the cloister, but granted permission to the bishop to allow two workmen to fulfill the task of burial—Lucidi, *De Visitatione Sacrorum Liminum*, II, 158. Cf. also S. C. Ep. et Reg., 30 iun. 1582; 11 aug. 1610—Lucidi, *loc. cit.* Ferraris (*Bibliotheca*, s. v. "Moniales," art. V, nn. 51-53) did not for any reason admit the validity of a custom which permitted priests to enter the cloister for the purpose of burial.

[50] *Acta Sanctae Sedis*, XXXVI (1903), 203-204.

[51] "Consultationes,"—*Revue des Communautés Religieuses*, III (1927), 121-122.

any contrary custom which permits the chaplain to enter the cloister for burial services.[52]

Both canon 600, 2°, and the *Instruction* demand that certain precautions be observed in the administration of the sacraments within the cloister. The *Instruction* states what these will be when Holy Communion is distributed.[53] Four nuns, of mature age, if possible, shall accompany the priest from the moment he enters the cloister until he leaves it. The priest shall carry the consecrated Particles in a pyx and observe all of the rubrics contained in the Roman Ritual relative to the administration of Holy Communion to the infirm.

2. The Confessor

The ordinary, extraordinary and supplementary confessors may enter the cloister to hear the confessions of the nuns who are confined to their rooms by sickness. In accordance with canon 523, any priest approved for hearing the confessions of women may enter the cloister to hear the confession of a seriously ill nun who has called upon his services.[54]

To the confessors who are mentioned in canon 521, § 2, the *Instruction* gives the name *"adjuncti."* They are the priests whom the bishop has named as supplementary confessors for certain convents. They may be called to the convent in particular cases when the oc-

[52] Cf. Schaefer, *De Religiosis*, n. 252, p. 720; Coronata, *Institutiones*, n. 613, p. 801; Jardí, *El Derecho de las Religiosas*, nn. 936-939. Berutti (*Institutiones Iuris Canonici* [6 vols., Vol. IV, *De rebus*, Taurini-Romae: Marietti, 1940], IV, p. 163, note 2) cites the decision rendered in the Zamora case, but nevertheless requires that an apostolic indult be obtained to permit burial services by a priest in the cloister.

[53] *Instructio*, III, 2°, h. The legislation in the *Instruction* on these precautions is borrowed from a decree of the Congregation of Religious issued on Sept. 1, 1912—*AAS*, IV (1912), 626.

[54] *Instructio*, III, 2°, g. No mention is made either in canon 600, 2°, or in the *Instruction* concerning the confessor whom a sister in time of good health can approach in a church or even in a semi-public oratory for the sake of making her confession in accordance with the liberty granted to her by the rule of canon 522. Such a confessor may not enter the cloister unless a sick nun specifically calls for his services in the capacity of a confessor. Cf. Schaefer, *De Religiosis*, n. 177; Berutti, *Institutiones*, III, n. 46, Scholion.

casion warrants. With the exception of the confessor who is mentioned in canon 523, the other confessors will possess expressly granted faculties for hearing the confessions of nuns.[55]

The privilege of calling into the cloister the priest who has been approved for the hearing of women's confessions pertains only to the nun who is seriously ill. But the canon readily states that the enjoyment of this privilege does not demand that any danger of death be present.[56] What is serious illness in the sense of this canon? If the services of a doctor are prudently deemed necessary, then the illness may be considered serious, since nuns are not prone to call a physician for passing infirmities. An illness which confines a nun to bed for a week or two will be serious. A forthcoming operation, even though it be not of a serious nature, will fulfill the requirements. In a word, any illness which can give occasion to worry and concern. The common head colds, headaches and other everyday ailments are not of a nature sufficiently serious to merit the invocation of this privilege.[57] It cannot be said, for instance, that a nun with a broken leg, though she is naturally obliged to remain in her room, would come within the meaning of this canon. The canon requires serious illness. Only when it is present may the privilege be employed.[58] If such an injury may be construed as a serious illness, the privilege may be used.

A morally certain judgment concerning the existence of serious

[55] The faculty to hear the confessions of women as required by canon 523 may come from the local ordinary or derive from the common law itself. To qualify under this heading it seems to be sufficient if a priest possesses simply the faculties of hearing the confessions of women religious in some house of the diocese. Cf. A. Sobradillo, *Tractatus de Religiosarum Confessariis* (Torino: Berruti, 1932), p. 232; Berruti, *Institutiones*, III, n. 47, II.

[56] Cf. canon 523; *Instructio*, III, 2°, g. There can be no doubt that any priest may enter the cloister to hear the confession of a nun who is in danger of death. Cf. canon 882; Coronata, *Institutiones*, n. 613, p. 801, note 3; Schaefer, *De Religiosis*, n. 353, p. 720; Vermeersch-Creusen, *Epitome*, I, n. 759; Jardí, *El Derecho de las Religiosas*, n. 344; Beste, *Introductio in Codicem*, p. 347.

[57] Schaefer, *op. cit.*, n. 177; Coronata, *op. cit.*, p. 684, note 2; Wernz-Vidal, *Ius Canonicum*, III, n. 203; Jardí, *op. cit.*, n. 343; Blat, *Commentarium*, II, n. 217; Sobradillo, *Tractatus de Religiosarum Confessariis*, p. 232.

[58] Creusen-Garesché-Ellis, *Religious Men and Women in the Code*, n. 123.

illness is all that is required by this canon. The subsequent revelation that objectively no serious infirmity was ever present need give no cause for alarm or worry. To enter the cloister licitly a priest needs only moral certitude of the illness.[59]

Once again there is no limitation attached to the number of times a confessor may enter the cloister to visit a sick nun. The *Instruction* explicitly states that this may be done as often as it is judged necessary.[60]

The obvious reading of canon 523 leads to the conclusion that an infirm nun may call any priest who is approved for the hearing of women's confessions in order that she may confess to him. There are authors, however, who assert that, since confession has not been stated in the canon as a necessary condition for the approach of this priest, he may enter the cloister to afford consolation, comfort, ease of conscience or spiritual advice without hearing her confession.[61] Other authors either explicitly disagree with this interpretation,[62] or simply state that the purpose for which the priest will enter the cloister is to hear the nun's confession.[63]

It rather seems that it was the mind of the legislator to grant this privilege in favor of confession. Canon 523 explicitly states that the infirm nun can invite the priest for the purpose of confession. Moreover, this canon is contained within the chapter of the Code which treats of the confessors of religious. The obvious mean-

[59] Beste, *Introductio in Codicem*, p. 347; Schaefer, *De Religiosis*, n. 177; Blat, *Commentarium*, II, n. 217; Sobradillo, *loc. cit.*; Fanfani, *De Iure Religiosorum*, n. 137, B.

[60] *Instructio*, III, 2°, g.

[61] Goyeneche, "Consultationes,"—*CpR*, VII (1927), 102. This interpretation is expressed in a letter sent to Goyeneche by a person who calls himself P. G. R. He favors the opinion expressed in it. Cf. Coronata, *Institutiones*, n. 552, note 3; Berutti, *Institutiones*, III, n. 47, II.

[62] Schaefer, *De Religiosis*, n. 353, p. 721; Oesterle, *Praelectiones Iuris Canonici*, I, 338.

[63] Wernz-Vidal, *Ius Canonicum*, III, n. 202; Ferreres, *Compendium Theologiae Moralis*, II, n. 233; Beste, *Introductio in Codicem*, p. 347; Genicot-Salsmans, *Institutiones Theologiae Moralis*, II, n. 339; Gerster a Zeil, *Ius Religiosorum*, p. 292; Pejska, *Ius Canonicum*, p. 300; Augustine, *Commentary*, III, 164; Jardí, *El Derecho de las Religiosas*, n. 343; Creusen-Garesché-Ellis, *Religious Men and Women in the Code*, n. 123; Raus, *Institutiones Canonicae*, n. 181.

ing of confessor points to one who is approached for sacramental absolution. It seems, then, that the opinion which favors the use of this privilege solely for the making of a sacramental confession is the more probable opinion.

The precautions which must be observed in the hearing of confessions within the enclosure are outlined in the *Instruction* of the Sacred Congregation.[64] Two nuns shall meet the confessor at the door of the monastery and accompany him to the room of the infirm nun. They will wait outside of the room, the door of which will remain open, until the confessor has completed his ministrations. They shall then accompany him to the door of the monastery.

It is true that the ordinary confession may be heard without closing the door of the nun's room. The companions of the confessor will, of course, remain beyond earshot. In the event, however, that the nun who is confessing is partly deaf and the voice of the confessor must be raised, it will be licit to close the door of the room. The preservation of the seal of confession takes precedence over the regularly prescribed precautions.[65]

When grave reasons render it inconvenient to conduct sermons at the grill in convents of nuns, the Holy See is accustomed to grant permission for preachers to enter the enclosure to exercise their duties either in the choir or in the chapter room. On such occasions, however, the precautions stated for the ingress of confessors must diligently be observed.[66]

C. Exceptions Granted to Dignitaries

1. Rulers and Their Wives

Rulers and their wives may enter with a retinue the cloister of the monasteries of nuns.[67] Vermeersch observed that one might

[64] *Instructio,* III, 2°, i.

[65] Cf. Jombart, "Cloture et Visite des Malades,"—*Revue des Communautés Religieuses,* VIII (1932), 108-109; "Confession des Malades,"—*op. cit.,* XIV (1938), 122; Vermeersch, "Annotationes,"—*Periodica,* XIII (1925), 67.

[66] *Instructio,* III, 2°, 1.

[67] Canon 600, 3°: "Possunt clausuram ingredi qui supremum actu tenent populorum principatum eorumque uxores cum comitatu . . ."; cf. also *Instructio,* III, 2°, m.

conclude from the position of the words "*cum comitatu*" that the retinue is permitted only to the *wives* of rulers. But since a retinue was permitted to kings before the Code, and since also grave difficulties would stem from its prohibition now, it seems that rulers are also permitted a retinue when they enter the cloister.[68]

Oesterle also expresses with certainty that the privilege of taking his retinue with him is accorded to the ruler when he enters the cloister of nuns. The words "*cum comitatu*" are placed after the entire phrase and by no means need be regarded as necessarily modifying only the word "*uxoresque.*" To deny to the ruler what is granted to his wife, and precisely because she is his wife, would be to honor in a greater fashion the person who is the lesser in dignity.[69]

Further commentary on this canon would only involve a repetition of what has already been stated in the discussion of canon 598, § 2.[70]

2. Cardinals

By virtue of the dignity which they possess as princes of the Church, Cardinals are permitted to enter the cloister of nuns. This privilege becomes operative for them from the day on which they are promoted in Consistory.[71]

Discussion in the early years after the appearance of the Code centered on the question of the lawfulness for a Cardinal to have his retinue accompany him into the cloister. It is the rather concise wording of the law in canon 600, 3°, that apparently gave rise to the

68 *Epitome,* I, n. 759. When speaking about the privileges extended to Cardinals, however, Vermeersch asked whether they may not enjoy the retinue which is expressly given to *rulers* and their wives. On this occasion he found no textual difficulty. Cf. "De Clausura Monialium,"—*Periodica,* XIX (1930), 15*.

69 *Praelectiones Iuris Canonici,* I, 338. Cf. also Schaefer, *De Religiosis,* n. 353, p. 721; Jardí, *El Derecho de las Religiosas,* n. 802; Cocchi, *Commentarium,* IV, n. 100, c; Blat, *Commentarium,* II, n. 533, p. 463; Coronata, *Institutiones,* n. 613, p. 802.

70 Cf. *supra,* pp. 127-137.

71 Cf. canon 600, 3°; *Instructio,* III, 2°, m; canon 239, § 1. This universal privilege originates with the legislation in the Code. The former law was not so generous. Cf. Pope Gregory XIII, Const. "*Dubiis,*" 23 dec. 1581—*Fontes,* n. 148; Pope Benedict XIV, Const. "*Salutare,*" 3 ian. 1742—*Fontes,* n. 323.

difficulty which precipitated this discussion.[72] This canon does not explicitly include the words *"cum comitatu"* in the clause which mentions the Cardinals. The force of the word *"itemque,"* however, is sufficient to convey that meaning. The opinion of Blat, which denied to Cardinals the right to take their retinue with them into the cloister, engendered the erstwhile discussion. But this author now admits that he has relinquished the opinion which he expressed in the first edition of his *Commentarium,* and thus he agrees with the commonly proposed doctrine.[73]

D. Exceptions Conceded in Favor of the Monastery

Canon 600, 4°, grants to the superioress of the monastery the faculty of permitting into the cloister doctors, surgeons and others whose skill or whose work will be necessary. Before granting the permission the superioress must obtain at least the habitual approbation of the local ordinary.[74] If, however, an urgent necessity arises and there is no time to approach the local ordinary, then it is rightfully assumed that his approbation is granted. Certain precautions must be observed, however.

This legislation is both old and new. Concessions made in favor of the needs of the monastery are as old as the cloistral observance itself. The right, however, of the superioress to grant the required permission derives from the Code.[75]

To determine in a general manner those who are comprehended in a classification of this type is very difficult. Whereas the Code has confined itself to an enumeration of doctors, surgeons and other

[72] Canon 600, 3°: "Possunt clausuram ingredi qui supremum . . . cum comitatu; itemque S. R. E. Cardinales."

[73] *Commentarium,* II, n. 533. Cf. also Beste, *Introductio in Codicem,* p. 409; Schaefer, *De Religiosis,* n. 353; Vermeersch-Creusen, *Epitome,* I, n. 759; Jardí, *El Derecho de las Religiosas,* n. 802, b; Fanfani, *De Iure Religiosorum,* n. 310, A; Gerster a Zeil, *Ius Religiosorum,* p. 183; Vermeersch, "De Clausura Monialium,"—*Periodica,* XIX (1930), 15*.

[74] This approbation may be given by the vicar general, unless the local ordinary has reserved the right to himself. Cf. canon 368, § 1.

[75] Cf. *e.g.,* c. un., *de statu regularium,* III, 16, in VI°; Council of Trent, sess. XXV, *de regularibus,* c. 5; Pope Gregory XIII, Const. *"Ubi gratiae,"* 13 iun. 1575—*Fontes,* n. 147.

necessary persons, the *Instruction* has explained this notion in greater detail. It will be noted, first of all, that the required necessity will always have reference to the needs of the monastery itself or of its inhabitants.[76] The fact is thus made evident that in reality the privilege is granted primarily in favor of the monastery itself, and only indirectly to those who enter it. It is obvious that the services of doctors will be necessary in every monastery. Nurses likewise will be included in this category.[77] The *Instruction* enumerates gardeners, cellarers, artisans and other similarly needed workmen.[78] It is quite manifest that the needs of any given monastery may be occasioned by divers kinds of causes. The nature of the cause will correspondingly determine the character of the need. It is for this reason that anything like a complete classification of the causes and of the consequent needs can at most be approximated. Plumbers, carpenters, painters and electricians are persons whose services will usually be required. It seems, too, that a periodic visit by a fire inspector may be regarded as necessary for the safety of the monastery. Stretcher bearers can enter the cloister for the sake of transferring an infirm nun to an ambulance. Cases must be judged as they present themselves.[79]

It has been noted that the permission to enter comes from the superioress.[80] The approbation of the local ordinary must be habitual, at least. The use of the word *saltem* indicates that the local ordinary could demand that he be approached for approbation each

[76] *Instructio*, III, 2°, o.

[77] *Instructio, loc. cit.*

[78] ". . . operarios pro horto, pro cella vinaria, pro stabulis opifices, et alias huiusmodi personas. . . ."—*Instructio, loc. cit.*

[79] It has been stated that an artist may enter the cloister to paint a portrait of one of the nuns. Cf. Martinez de Antoniana, "Clausura Papal," *Ilustracion del Clero*, 1936, pp. 143-147 cited in "Ex Ephemeridibus excerpta,"—*Jus Pontificium*, XVI (1936), 321-322.

[80] This permission cannot be given by the regular superior to whom the nuns are subject. Cf. Fanfani, *De Iure Religiosorum*, n. 312, C. Coronata (*Institutiones*, n. 613, p. 802, note 4) asserts that by reason of custom the permission of the regular superior may also be required; Berutti (*Institutiones*, III, n. 115, I) thinks that the regular superior can demand that his own consent be obtained before the superioress seeks the approbation of the local ordinary.

time that the superioress intends to grant permission. He could not do so, however, in situations of necessity. Habitual approbation by the local ordinary must not be confused with a general approbation. The bishop must exercise vigilance and care regarding the cloister. Were he to grant a general approbation, the superioress would then be acting simply on her own authority and would be exercising a judgment which the Code has reserved to the local ordinary.[81] The *Instruction* has noted the manner in which this habitual approbation may be obtained. At the beginning of each year the superioress will enumerate in a book all the services which, as she foresees, will be required during the year. In this book the local ordinary will write his approbation.[82] The local ordinary will exercise prudence and sound judgment in granting his approvals. This is implied in the precautions which are demanded by the *Instruction* and in the fact that their certification must stand attested by the superioress. Care must be observed so that the permission of entering the cloister will be granted only to those persons who are known to be morally sound and of an upright character.[83] The bishop, it appears, is better able to determine these factors than is the cloistered superioress. He should give his approval, then, for only such doctors, nurses and workmen of whom he knows that they will satisfy the requirements of the law.[84] The other precaution enjoined by the *Instruction* requires that two of the older nuns accompany to the place of his work the person who enters the enclosure. Only those nuns whose office requires it may speak to the person who enters the cloister.[85]

There may arise certain contingencies which will demand that some persons enter the cloister at once. On such occasions, if there is not time to obtain the approbation of the local ordinary, the law itself presumes that the approbation is given.[86]

Pertinent to section four of canon 600 are a few cases which

[81] Vermeersch-Creusen, *Epitome*, I, n. 759; Schaefer, *De Religiosis*, n. 353.
[82] *Instructio*, III, 2°, o.
[83] *Instructio*, III, 2°, p.
[84] Vermeersch-Creusen, *Epitome*, I, n. 759.
[85] *Instructio*, III, 2°, p.
[86] *Instructio*, III, 2°, o.

present themselves for solution. The first involves the right of a priest to enter the cloister to pick up a Sacred Host which he has dropped. Authors formerly disagreed on this question. Pellizzarius did not permit the priest to enter, for an emergency of this type permitted a nun to pick up the Host by means of a paten. He asserted that many learned men to whom he wrote agreed with his opinion.[87] Ferraris cited authors who permitted the priest to enter if there was present no nun within the cloister who was able to pick up the Host. There were others who for such an emergency unconditionally allowed the priest to enter.[88] This case can be judged and settled in the light of the principles of canon 600, 4°. In the event of such a perplexing case, the due respect for the Holy Sacrament would demand that the Host be picked up at once. This urgent necessity would not permit recourse to the local ordinary. Consequently the superioress could permit the priest to enter. In stating this opinion, authors admit that the particular circumstances of the case will best determine what is to be done. A nun may, of course, pick up the Host. Prudence will dictate whether a nun is to do this or whether the priest will enter the cloister to pick up the Host.[89]

Ciprotti asks whether an ecclesiastical judge may enter the cloister to conduct a local inspection which he deems necessary in accordance with the expressed rule of canon 1806.[90] Canon 600, 4°, makes no mention of this case and, with a presupposed acknowledgement of the exception which attaches to exempt places, canons 1806-1811 do not restrict the objects of the inspection. It is true that ordinarily permission could and would be given for this inspection by the superioress with the approbation of the local ordinary. The judge should seek it. But if it could not be given, or would not be given, and the trial would suffer from the delay occasioned by the seeking of direction from the Holy See, then it seems that the judge

[87] *De Monialibus*, cap. X, sec. III, subsec. I, n. 239.

[88] *Bibliotheca*, s. v. "Moniales," art. V, n. 63; Lucidi, *De Visitatione Sacrorum Liminum*, II, n. 159; Pennacchi, *Commentaria*, I, 732.

[89] Goyeneche, "Studia Canonica,"—*CpR*, XIII (1932), 38-39; Schaefer, *De Religiosis*, n. 353, p. 722; Coronata, *Institutiones*, n. 613; Cavigioli, *De Censuris*, n. 129, p. 103, note 3.

[90] "Consultationes,"—*Apollinaris*, IX (1936), 139-140.

could enter the cloister without incurring the penalty. Not only will an ecclesiastical law—and the law of the cloister is such a law—cede its binding force to the demand which grave inconvenience interposes, but canon 200, § 1, could be invoked to give to the judge those faculties without which his jurisdiction could not be employed.[91]

May the same be said for the civil judge? If it be granted that all rights deriving from the *privilegium fori* have ceased and that the judge has obtained the proper permission to exercise his jurisdiction in immune ecclesiastical places, then it appears, according to Ciprotti, that the civil judge could enjoy, in similar circumstances, those rights which are allowed to the ecclesiastical judge.

Forced by the difficulties of obtaining the services of suitable lay persons, many convents of nuns formerly sought permission from the Holy See to possess outside sisters (*sorores externae*) who could perform certain necessary tasks outside of the cloister, which, by reason of the strict cloistral laws, could not be done by the nuns themselves. The number of these requests prompted the Sacred Congregation of Religious to formulate certain Statutes which were thenceforth to be observed by those outside sisters who were already in existence and also by all those who, with permission of the Holy See, were in the future to be attached to monasteries of nuns. The Statutes were approved and confirmed by Pope Pius XI.[92] The extern sisters profess simple vows. They live outside of the cloister. The comments upon the Statutes which pertain to the government of these sisters will here be confined solely to the regulations which deal with the cloister.

Article 7 of the Statutes explains in a general manner the relationship of the outside sisters to the cloister. They may not enter the cloister except to undergo their year of canonical novitiate, and

[91] It is true that canon 200, § 1, has reference to delegated jurisdiction. But it seems that it could be applied *a fortiori* to ordinary jurisdiction.

[92] S. C. de Rel., "Decretum," et "Statuta a Sororibus externis Monasteriorum Monialium cuiusque ordinis servanda," 16 iul. 1931—"Act et Documenta,"—*CpR*, XII (1931), 409-425; Schaefer, *De Religiosis*, nn. 655-670. For a complete commentary upon all of these Statutes cf. Vincentius La Puma, "Acta et Documenta,"—*CpR*, XII (1931), 426-430; XIII (1932), 245-249, 340-352; XIV (1933), 31-37, 157-168, 247-251, 339-344, 407-415; XV (1934), 13-17, 106-109.

for the causes expressed in articles 3 and 107. Postulants may never enter the cloister. Article 3 states that the special purpose of the sisters consists in the performance of those duties which pertain to the outside monastery and the Church. Only occasionally, and then for a brief time, may they enter the cloister to undertake duties therein. On such occasions their assistance must be necessary. Before the superioress may give permission, she must seek at least the habitual approbation of the local ordinary. The presumed or interpretative approbation of the local ordinary will not suffice. If special necessities demand more ample faculties, La Puma asserted that the Sacred Congregation will readily grant them. La Puma and Schaefer assert that this strict cloistral observance applies even to those monasteries which do not possess the papal cloister.[93]

Article 22 states that the period of postulancy will be passed in the proper house of the extern sisters. Canon 540, § 3, which states that postulants are bound by the enclosure, will consequently not apply to these sisters.[94] Article 31 requires that the canonical year of novitiate be spent within the enclosure in that place which is reserved to the lay novices. Though the second year of novitiate is spent outside of the enclosure, article 36 permits that two months before profession the novices will enter the enclosure to make preparations for their profession.

In accordance with article 107, if an extern sister is afflicted with an infirmity the gravity and nature of which will not permit that she be properly cared for in her own house, she may be given a bed in the infirmary which is within the enclosure. The permission, however, of the local ordinary will be necessary. The same may be said of those sisters who have become so old that they can no longer perform their duties. If other reasons render a sister equally useless in her work, she too may be brought within the enclosure.[95]

In 1932 La Puma was of the opinion that the Statutes for extern sisters did not annul or abrogate ancient, approved Constitutions

[93] La Puma, "Acta et Documenta,"—*CpR,* XIII (1932), 345-346; Schaefer, *op. cit.*, n. 654.

[94] La Puma, "Acta et Documenta,"—*CpR,* XIV (1933), 37; Schaefer, *De Religiosis*, n. 657.

[95] Schaefer, *De Religiosis,* n. 667.

which differed from them.[96] In many ways these Statutes were little honored by observance during the years following their promulgation.[97] In 1936 the Cardinal Archbishop of Genoa asked the Sacred Congregation whether immemorial customs or the prescriptions of old directories and books permitting extern sisters to live within the enclosure could be approved notwithstanding the Statutes of 1931. The reply stated that all such customs and prescriptions had been abrogated by the Statutes. Consequently, those monasteries which possessed suitable places for the extern sisters outside of the enclosure were bound by the Statutes. On behalf of the monasteries which did not possess such places the Sacred Congregation granted a quinquennial faculty which enabled ordinaries to permit such sisters to live within the enclosure. During the interim, however, suitable places for extern sisters had to be provided outside of the enclosure.[98] Larraona considered that the general terminology of the rescript would permit the faculty which it granted to be extended benignly to other territories.[99]

Only with the permission of the local ordinary may girls enter the papal enclosure for the purpose of beginning their postulancy.[100]

It is not allowed to admit young girls into the cloister for instruction or for any other reason, even though it be a good and pious one, without the permission of the Holy See.[101] Definite norms which were to be observed by the monasteries which had schools attached

[96] "Acta et Documenta,"—*CpR*, XIII (1932), 249.

[97] Larraona, "Annotationes,"—*CpR*, XVII (1936), 211.

[98] "Acta et Documenta,"—*CpR*, XVII (1936), 209; "Monumenta,"—*Periodica*, XXVI (1937), 81-82.

[99] "Annotationes,"—*CpR*, XVII (1936), 212.

[100] *Instructio*, IV. Fanfani (*De Iure Religiosorum*, n. 190, F) falsely asserts that as soon as girls are accepted as postulants, they may enter the enclosure without any special permission. This was written after the promulgation of the *Instruction*.

[101] *Instructio*, IV, Coronata (*Institutiones*, n. 613, p. 802, note 8) asserts that a general permission of the Holy See will suffice in this case. He thinks that such a permission may be presumed by the convents which are already engaged in this type of work.

to them were recently issued by the Sacred Congregation of Religious.[102]

Article III. Unlawful Entry Into the Cloister

Consideration has already been given, in the treatment of the cloister of regulars,[103] to the concept of cloistral violation, the requisite subjective and objective elements, and the question of slightness of matter. Any repetition of those principles here will serve no practical purpose. There are, however, a few considerations regarding the cloister of nuns which do deserve separate treatment.

Is it admissible to maintain that crass ignorance which would be sufficient to excuse one from incurring the penalty of excommunication can be present in one who violates the cloister of nuns? Ordinarily, at least, it seems not. This opinion is founded upon the fact that the enclosure is so constructed materially that any entry into its confines will usually necessitate the use of force. Sufficient informative evidence to convey the notion of strict prohibition will usually be posted. This opinion holds true, it appears, at least with regard to ignorance concerning the prohibition and the cloistral limits. Whether it holds true also with regard to ignorance concerning the penalty is more difficult to answer. It does seem that ordinary persons are more cognizant of the strict cloister of nuns than they are aware of the cloister of regulars. For this reason they would be more inclined to conclude that some penalty is incurred for violating the cloister of nuns. They would, then, be led to make the inquiries which every person should make. And certainly in a monastery of nuns there would ordinarily be some one present who would readily give an answer to all questions of this nature. Failure to make these inquiries could hardly excuse one from crass ignorance, and, in consequence thereof, also excuse one from incurring the penalty.[104]

A legitimate use of the faculty which canon 600 grants for entry

[102] S. C. de Rel., "Rescriptum de instituendo collegio pro educatione puellarum penes monasterium monialium Ordinis Sancti Dominici,"—*CpR*, XVI (1935), 419; "Monumenta"—*Periodica*, XXVI (1937), 78-80.

[103] Cf. *supra*, pp. 143-157.

[104] Cf. canon 2229, § 3, 1°.

into the cloister supposes that one is entering the cloister in view of the reasons for which the permission was granted. If those reasons are not present, permission is not given, and entry by any person constitutes a true violation. A bishop, for instance, who enters the cloister for reasons other than that of local inspection is excommunicated. The same may be said of the regular superior.[105] If this is true of bishops and regular superiors, it is equally true of all others who enjoy a conditioned right to enter the cloister but do not honor the conditions of this right when they enter. It must not be concluded from these statements, however, that the penalty would be incurred if no necessity which demanded their presence within the cloister was *objectively* verified. Judgment in this matter is subject to mistakes. And such mistakes made in good faith certainly do not entail the strict penalty of this canon. The opposite would be true, however, if a person were to invoke a fictitious necessity as a pretense for gaining entry. If, on the other hand, a legitimate permission in such an event is valid, the additional presence of other underlying reasons or motives does not of itself suffice to constitute the entry as an act of cloistral violation.[106]

Article IV. *Introducentes et Admittentes*

The concept of these two words has been sufficiently explained elsewhere.[107] There is, however, one problem which is peculiar to the cloister of nuns and therefore calls for consideration. Will the censure of excommunication be incurred for admitting or introducing into the cloister children who have not yet attained the age at which puberty is presumed juridically to be present? Relative to the cloister of regulars this question offers no difficulty, for canon 2342, 2°, explicitly imposes the penalty upon all those who admit or introduce girls of any age. Canon 2342, 1°, does not, however, employ the same terminology.

[105] Cf. canon 600, 1°; *Instructio*, III, 2°; Cappello, *De Censuris*, n. 317; Coronata, *Institutiones*, n. 1978; Schaefer, *De Religiosis*, n. 355, a; Vermeersch-Creusen, *Epitome*, I, n. 766.

[106] Pennacchi, *Commentaria*, I, 723; Coronata, *loc. cit.*; Ayrinhac, *Penal Legislation in the New Code of Canon Law*, n. 284, b.

[107] Cf. *supra*, pp. 158-162.

Canon 600 explicitly states that no one of any age may be admitted into the cloister of nuns. But canon 2342, 1°, contains no reference to age in its enactment of the penalty against violators of the cloister. When this same canon enacts the penalty against those who introduce of admit others into the cloister, it employs the term *eos,* which grammatically refers to *violantes.* Again, in failing to make any reference to age in the clause which modifies the word *violantes,* canon 2342, 1°, portrays a distinct departure from the Constitution *"Apostolicae Sedis."* [108]

The terminology employed in canon 2342, 1°, has engendered among authors a wide divergence of opinion. Basing their argument upon the absence of any reference to age in canon 2342, 1°, and upon the use of the word *eos,* which refers to *violantes,* some authors excuse from the penalty all those who introduce or admit into the cloister boys and girls below the age of puberty. Since *violantes* in the sense of canon 2342, 1°, seems to refer to those who in entering of their own volition incur the penalty, it cannot include children below the age of puberty.[109] Consequently, anyone who introduces or admits them does not incur the penalty.[110]

Other authors hold the opinion that the penalty is incurred for an act such as this. The force of this argument is found in its recourse to canon 2230, which states that all persons above the age of puberty who induce children to violate a law, or concur with them in the commission of a delict, are guilty of the penalty stated in the law. The co-operation of these persons must be one or the other of the types of co-operation classified in canon 2209, §§ 1-3. Ciprotti argues that the word *violantes* must be considered objectively. In

[108] "Clausuram monialium violantes, cuiuscumque generis aut conditionis vel sexus sint, in earum monasteria sine legitima licentia ingrediendo, pariterque eos introducentes vel admittentes . . ."—canon 2342, 1°; "Violantes clausuram monialium, cuiuscumque generis aut conditionis, sexus vel aetatis fuerint . . . pariterque eos introducentes vel admittentes. . . ."—Pope Pius IX, Const. *"Apostolicae Sedis,"* 12 oct. 1869, § II, n. 6—*Fontes,* n. 552.

[109] Cf. canons 2230; 12.

[110] Coronata, *Institutiones,* n. 1978; Cavigioli, *De Censuris,* n. 130; Sipos, *Enchiridion,* p. 371, note 22; Cerato, *Censurae Vigentes,* p. 120; Jardi, *El Derecho de las Religiosas,* n. 809; Sole, *De Delictis et Poenis,* p. 289; Schaefer, *De Religiosis,* n. 355, a; Teodori, "Consultationes,"—*Apollinaris,* V (1931), 112.

accordance, then, with canon 600, all of any age who enter the enclosure must objectively be considered as *violantes*. Consequently, all who admit or introduce them are excommunicated.[111]

A distinction is made by other authors. They state that the penalty is incurred only by those who admit or introduce *impuberes* who are above the age of seven. They appeal to canons 2204, 600 and 2230 to show that the *violantes* can be only those who are capable of possessing *dolus*. In as far, then, as the element of *dolus* does not actually attach to their act, such *impuberes* are subject to the cloistral law and consequently incur guilt in the act of cloistral violation, though they are exempt from incurring the *latae sententiae* penalty. On the other hand, anyone who concurs with them in any of the ways indicated in canon 2209, §§ 1-3, will incur the censure enacted in canon 2342, 1°.[112]

The *Instruction* on the cloister which was issued by the Sacred Congregation of Religious states that the superioress or anyone else who introduces or only admits, without permission, *any person* into the cloister will not only sin gravely, but will incur excommunication simply reserved to the Holy See.[113]

There can be no thought of attributing to this *Instruction* the force of an authentic interpretation of the canon. To render such an interpretation is the prerogative of the Pontifical Commission for

[111] Ciprotti, *De Consummatione Delictorum*, I, n. 79; Biederlack-Führich, *De Religiosis*, p. 239; Leitner, *Handbuch*, p. 440; Blat, *Commentarium*, V, n. 183; S. Woywod, *A Practical Commentary on the Code of Canon Law* (2 vols., New York: Wagner, 1925), II, 493; J. Mothon, *Institutions Canoniques* (2 vols., Paris: Desclée, 1922-1924), II, art. 3031; Prümmer (*Manuale*, q. 228, 6) holds this as probable.

[112] Cappello, *De Censuris*, n. 319; Beste, *Introductio in Codicem*, p. 950; Chelodi, *Ius Poenale*, p. 104; Vermeersch-Creusen, *Epitome*, III, n. 541. Ferreres (*Compendium Theologiae Moralis*, II, n. 236) hold this as a probable opinion. In the first volume of their work (*Epitome*, I, n. 766) Vermeersch-Creusen assert that, since there is no reference to the factor of age in canon 2342, 1°, all those who introduce or admit into the cloister anyone who is below the age of puberty are excused from incurring the *latae sententiae* penalty of excommunication which is mentioned in that canon.

[113] "Quod si antistita vel quaelibet alia, *personam quamcumque*, sine legitima licentia in monasterium introduceret, vel solum admitteret, non tantum. . . ." *Instructio*, IV.

the Authentic Interpretation of the Code which was established by Pope Benedict XV in his Motu proprio *"Cum iuris canonici."* [114] It seems that not even a strict legal force can be attached to the *Instruction*.[115] The most that can be said is that it reflects the force of an administrative power which commands the fulfillment of the law. Consequently it must be obeyed in the manner in which the command is given.[116] The *Instruction* possesses likewise the force of a doctrinal interpretation. As such, then, it will certainly possess great authority to be followed in the settlement of this question.

Upon the force and interpretation of this *Instruction*, then, it is here maintained that excommunication is incurred by those who admit or introduce into the cloister any child who is below the age of puberty. This is the law as it is commanded to be obeyed today in view, particularly, of the approval which Pope Pius XI gave to this *Instruction.*

Among the authors who have been consulted Schaefer alone has made reference to the *Instruction* concerning this question. He relegates this mention to a footnote and it does not change his opinion. Moreover, it is somewhat doubtful whether his citation of the *Instruction* is meant to bear specific reference to canon 2342, 1°.[117]

Article V. The Penalty

The crime of violating the cloister of nuns or of admitting or introducing persons within its limits is punished with a *latae sententiae*

[114] 15 sept. 1917—*AAS*, IX (1917), 483-484.

[115] Maroto ("Annotationes,"—*CpR*, V [1924], 141) asserts that this particular *Instruction* is more than a mere Instruction. He claims that it has the force of law which derives from the Congregation which issued it.

[116] Cf. J. R. Schmidt, "The Juridic Value of the *Instructio*,"—*The Jurist* (Washington, D. C., 1941—), I, (1941), 289-316.

[117] In the text of his work (*De Religiosis*, n. 355, a.) Schaefer asserts: "Locutio *cuiuscumque aetatis* deest in canone [2342, 1°], idcirco ii non excommunicati sunt, qui impuberes in clausuram inducunt aut admittunt." But in a footnote (*op. cit.*, n. 355, note 278) he says: "Habetur autem in Instructione de clausura (cf. *infra*, b.) haec locutio de hoc praecepto.". The apparent sense of the word *"locutio"* in the text implies a reference to the phrase *"cuiuscumque aetatis"* which is missing from canon 2342, 1°. In the footnote, however, Schaefer seems to relate to the precept of canon 600 what is contained in the *Instruction* of this point.

excommunication reserved in a simple manner to the Holy See.[118] What has been said in commenting upon the penalty for the violation of the cloister of regulars will apply equally well here.[119]

Beyond the penalty which is imposed upon all guilty persons, canon 2342, 1°, states that clerics [120] who enter the cloister, or who introduce or admit unauthorized persons into it, are to be suspended from office and benefice [121] by their ordinary for the time which he will determine as being proportionate to the gravity of the guilt. This penalty is of a vindictive character. It contemplates primarily the atonement of the crime.[122]

It will be noted that in canon 2342, 1°, reference is made to the *ordinary,* and not to the *local ordinary.*[123] The local ordinary can inflict this penalty not only upon his own subjects but also upon transients and exempt religious.[124] The major superiors of clerical exempt religious institutes may, for a violation of the papal cloister of nuns in monasteries which are subject to their jurisdiction, inflict suspension upon the clerics who are their subjects. Exempt religious who are not clerics are punishable for a similar crime either by the local ordinary [125] or by their own religious superior.[126]

It is quite true that canon 603, § 2, speaks only of the regular superior. And in the common law the superiors of religious congregations are not called *regular* superiors. Nevertheless, if in actual fact a religious congregation enjoys the privilege of exemption (Canon 613, § 1), then the superior of such a congregation has equal rights with a regular superior in this matter. The Code of course does not point to the actual possession of such a privilege by any specific religious congregation, but it leaves room for such a possibility, for example, in canon 512, § 2, 2°.

[118] Canon 2342.

[119] Cf. *supra,* pp. 167-169.

[120] This embraces all classes of ecclesiastics who have received at least tonsure. Cf. canon 108, § 1.

[121] Cf. canon 2278, § 2.

[122] Cf. canon 2286.

[123] Cf. canon 198 for a descriptive definition of the two distinct terms.

[124] Cf. canon 1566.

[125] Canon 603, § 1.

[126] Canon 603, § 2.

CHAPTER VII

ACTIVE VIOLATION OF THE ENCLOSURE OF NUNS

CANON 601 legislates that after her religious profession no nun may leave the monastery, even for a brief time or under any pretext, without a special indult of the Holy See. Exception is made for cases of imminent danger of death, or of some other very grave evil. If this danger is present, then, time permitting, it must be recognized in writing by the local ordinary. Canon 2342, 3°, states that any nun who leaves the enclosure against the prescriptions of canon 601 incurs excommunication reserved in a simple manner to the Holy See. These two canons will be considered together in an endeavor to determine which nuns incur the penalty for leaving the enclosure.

ARTICLE I. WHICH NUNS INCUR THE CENSURE FOR LEAVING THE ENCLOSURE?

It is beyond all doubt that postulants and novices do not incur the penalty for leaving the enclosure, even though they are bound by its law. In no sense of the law are they *moniales.*[1]

The crux of this problem centers about those religious who have, in accordance with canons 572, § 2, and 574, § 1, made their religious profession for a three years' period of simple vows in preparation for their solemn vows, and also about lay sisters who have professed simple perpetual vows. Does the censure of canon 2342, 3° apply to them?

[1] Cf. canon 540, § 3; *Instructio,* III, 1°, e: "Quamvis adspirantes . . . dum postulatum peragunt, lege clausurae teneantur, tamen libere et absque licentia Sanctae Sedis e monasterio egredi possunt quando ad saeculum sponte eas redire aut a superioribus dimitti contingat; et idem de novitiis dicendum. . . ." Sole (*De Delictis et Poenis,* p. 289) formerly held that, since canon 540, § 3, bound postulants to the enclosure, they, too, incurred the censure for leaving it. Cf. also Pistocchi, *I Canoni Penali,* p. 135.

The discussion of this problem has divided canonists into two groups. Generally considered their opinions are formed by the interpretation which they give to canon 488, 7°. In defining the word *monialium,* that canon states that they are "women religious of solemn vows or, unless the contrary appears from the nature of the case or from the context, women religious whose vows are normally solemn but which, by a dispensation of the Holy See, are simple in some regions." From this definition some authors derive the interpretation that nuns are women religious who actually are bound by solemn vows. Inasmuch, then, as canons 601 and 2342, 3°, refer to professed nuns, they encompass only the solemnly professed, and not those who have taken only simple vows. The penalty, then, does not affect the simply professed nuns.[2]

Affirming this same position, other authors assert that theoretically, at least, the word *moniales* does not include even those who are simply professed in monasteries wherein solemn vows are taken. Though these may be included within the scope of that word, *moniales* refers only to solemnly professed nuns, and because a strict interpretation in accordance with canons 19 and 2219 must be employed in this question, they excuse from the censure all those who have not actually professed solemn vows.[3]

[2] Cavigioli, *De Censuris,* n. 133; Coronata, *Institutiones,* n. 1979; Beste, *Introductio in Codicem,* p. 950; Cappello, *De Censuris,* nn. 323-324; Augustine, *Commentary,* VIII, 374; Sipos, *Enchiridion,* p. 371; Woywod, *A Practical Commentary on the Code of Canon Law,* II, 494; Cerato, *Censurae Vigentes,* p. 123; Marc-Gestermann-Raus, *Institutiones Morales Alphonsianae,* I, n. 1336; Ciprotti, *De Consummatione Delictorum,* n. 82, note 15; Chelodi, *Ius Poenale,* p. 104; Ayrinhac-Lydon, *Penal Legislation in the New Code of Canon Law,* n. 286; Raus, *Institutiones Canonicae,* p. 272, note 6; Vermeersch (*Epitome,* I, n. 766) speaks of "*moniales stricte tales*"; Creusen (*Epitome,* III, n. 541) admits the probability of this opinion of Vermeersch; Schaefer (*De Religiosis,* n. 355, c) holds this as probable. But in another place (*op. cit.,* n. 352, 2) he favors the opposite opinion.

[3] Chelodi, *De Personis,* n. 277; Salucci, *Il Diritto Penale,* II, n. 257; Jardi, *El Derecho de las Religiosas,* n. 808; Jombart, "Consultations,"—*Revue des Communautés Religieuses,* III (1927), 122-123; Jombart, "Les Moniales a Voeux Simples,"—*Nouvelle Revue Theologique* (Paris, 1869—), LI (1924), 351-352.

The opposing opinion is held by some equally reputable authors.[4] This opinion derives from an interpretation of the definition furnished in canon 488, 7°, and concludes that the word *moniales* embraces even those who profess simple vows in monasteries wherein solemn vows are taken. Since, therefore, the Code has made no distinction, either in canon 601 or in canon 2342, 3°, all professed nuns incur the penalty for leaving the enclosure without permission.[5]

Larraona [6] and Schweiger [7] are the chief exponents of this opinion. Commenting upon canon 488, 7°, Larraona asserts that the word *moniales* is the counterpart of the word *regulares*. *Moniales* are, then, women religious who profess vows in an Order, whether those vows be simple or solemn. His proof for this is threefold: (a) The word *regularium* as found in canon 488, 7°, is applied to all members of an Order who profess vows, regardless of the nature of the vows. It is the generic term for all members of an Order of regulars. Should not, then, the word *monialium*, which is the feminine generic term, be applied to all women who profess vows in an Order? (b) When the Code refers to women religious who are professed with simple vows in a religious Order, it calls them *moniales*.[8] (c) If the name *moniales* is given to perpetually professed women religious whose perpetual profession *according to the Rule of their Order* normally connotes the taking of solemn vows, even though in

[4] Cocchi, *Commentarium*, IV, n. 101; Fanfani, *De Iure Religiosorum*, n. 313, B; Berutti, *Institutiones*, III, n. 115, II, c; Sole, *De Delictis et Poenis*, p. 289; Larraona, "Commentarium Codicis," *CpR*, IV (1923), 11-14, Schweiger, "Questio Canonica," *CpR*, IV (1923), 140-145; A. De Meester, *Iuris Canonici et Iuris Canonico-Civilis Compendium* (ed. nova, 3 vols., Brugis: 1921-1928), II, p. 463, notes 2-3 (hereafter cited *Compendium Iuris Canonici*). Creusen, Garesché, Ellis (*Religious Men and Women in the Code*, n. 289) favor this opinion in theory.

[5] There can be no doubt that the simple vows which are professed by nuns in some regions do not bind them to the papal enclosure. An Apostolic indult which is still in force excuses them from the observance of the papal enclosure. Cf. canon 597, § 1; *PCI*, 1 mart. 1921—*AAS*, XIII (1921), 178; Maroto, "Annotationes"—*CpR*, II (1921), 164-168. Schaefer (*De Religiosis*, n. 47) gives a list of the places in which these simple vows are taken.

[6] "Commentarium Codicis,"—*CpR*, IV (1923), 11-14.

[7] "Questio Canonica,"—*CpR*, IV (1923), 140-145.

[8] Cf. canons 580, § 3; 647, § 1.

some specific instance, or in some particular regions, by virtue of an apostolic indult, their perpetual profession is attended with the taking of only simple vows, then, unless the contrary is clearly evident, the word *moniales* ought likewise to be employed in designation of those women religious who have as yet professed only temporary simple vows in a monastery wherein the perpetual profession is actually attended with the taking of solemn vows.

Explaining what is meant by the phrase *ex natura rei* of canon 488, 7°, Larraona states that, when a canon treats of solemn vows,[9] or of those things which juridically suppose solemn vows or are the consequence of them,[10] it does not comprise under the name *monialium* those who have made profession in monasteries wherein according to the Rule of the Order solemn vows are not taken. From the context, one must conclude to the type of vows which is intended by the legislator. If some paragraph or number of a canon treats of nuns of solemn vows, or of monasteries in which solemn vows are taken, the presumption is that the entire canon relates to the same type of vows.[11] If a canon treats of nuns of simple vows, then that canon presumptively applies to the simply professed in all the monasteries of nuns.[12]

Larraona concludes his discussion by offering a list of the canons which, in his opinion, embrace all women religious who come under the name *moniales,* and by drawing up a list of the canons which refer to only such nuns who have actually professed solemn vows, or who have made their profession (regardless of its nature) in a monastery wherein solemn vows are actually taken. Within the latter classification he includes canons 600-603 and 2342, 1°, 3°.[13]

Schweiger [14] traces his argument both from history and from an interpretation of the Code. From the time of Pope Pius V (1566-

[9] Cf. canon 2388, § 1.

[10] Cf. canons 600-603.

[11] Cf. canon 603.

[12] Cf. canon 580, § 3.

[13] Schaefer (*De Religiosis,* n. 49) has adopted this entire interpretation of Larraona.

[14] "Questio Canonica,"—*CpR,* IV (1923), 140-145.

1572),[15] solemn vows and papal cloister were always necessarily interrelated and mutually complementary factors. It was permitted to profess only one type of vows, and they had to be solemn.[16] The year 1902, however, witnessed a change in the matter of vows in the religious Orders of women.[17] Thenceforth at the completion of the novitiate year simple vows of three years' duration were to be professed. Nothing, however, was said relative to the law of the cloister for the sisters (*sorores*) who were thus only temporarily professed. Schweiger notes that authors failed to comment upon the obligation of these sisters to observe the enclosure. There was, moreover, doubt whether those who professed only simple vows in the Orders of regulars truly belonged to the religious state.[18] Since, then, the Constitutions "*Decori*" [19] and "*Apostolicae Sedis*" [20] restricted to *moniales* the penalty enacted for the active enclosure violation, those who professed only simple vows were not subject to it.

Must the word *moniales* receive today the strict interpretation which it formerly had? There can be no doubt today that even those who are professed in simple vows are true religious.[21] Considering the appeal of some authors to a very restrictive interpretation of canon 2342, 3°, Schweiger denies the validity of such an interpretation inasmuch as there is no longer present any *dubium iuris*. The principle of employing a restrictive interpretation exists merely as a reflex principle and cannot be used when the sense of the law is evident. Canon 2342, 3°, must receive its interpretation from canon 601. It does, therefore, embrace all nuns who are professed, even such as are professed with simple vows.

[15] Cf. Const. "*Circa Pastoralis,*" 29 maii 1566—*Fontes,* n. 112.

[16] This prescription was never fully observed. Cf. B. Farrell, *The Rights and Duties of the Local Ordinary Regarding Congregations of Women Religious of Pontifical Approval,* The Catholic University of America Canon Law Studies, n. 123 (Washington, D. C.: The Catholic University of America Press, 1941), pp. 20-25.

[17] Cf. S. C. Ep. et Reg., Decretum "*Perpensis,*" 3 maii 1902—*Fontes,* n. 2039.

[18] Cf. S. C. super Statu Reg., 15 iun. 1856—Bizzarri, *Collectanea,* p. 745, note; Mocchegiani, *Iurisprudentia Ecclesiastica,* I, nn. 33-34.

[19] Pope Pius V, 1 febr. 1570—*Fontes,* n. 133.

[20] Pope Pius IX, 12 oct. 1869, § II, nn. 6-7—*Fontes,* n. 552.

[21] Cf. canon 488, 7°.

If canon 601 refers only to nuns who have taken solemn vows, then, relative to the question of the enclosure, the Code contains no legislation regarding those who are professed with simple vows in the monasteries of nuns wherein it is the rule to take solemn vows at the final profession. Arguing exegetically from the title [22] of the Code under which canon 601 is placed, Schweiger states that this title affects all religious, unless expressly or equivalently a canon rules otherwise. Canon 601 has done so by imposing the obligation of the active enclosure merely upon professed nuns. The canon does not invoke any distinction regarding the nature of the profession made by the nuns. In the chapter on religious profession [23] the Code considers religious profession in all its forms. When it desires to attribute some peculiar efficacy to any one form of profession, the Code clearly so determines.

Schweiger draws three conclusions from his study of this question: (a) the wording of canon 601 encompasses those nuns who take simple vows in preparation for solemn profession; (b) canon 2342, 3°, receives its interpretation from canon 601, and hence its enacted penalty is incurred by simply professed nuns who leave the enclosure; (c) the legal definition of the word *moniales* as contained in canon 488, 7° (though it is imperfect) coupled with the authority of the old law give probability to the opposite opinion.

One might further ask whether there is justification for the opinion which requires that the word *moniales* in canon 2342, 3°, receive its interpretation from the phrase *"nemini monialium . . . post professionem"* in canon 601. May it not be said that, in referring to canon 601, canon 2342, 3°, is manifesting *only* the circumstances under which egress from the enclosure is forbidden to nuns? This appears to be the sense of the phrase *"exeuntes contra praescriptum can.* 601." Canon 2342, 3°, has itself used the word *moniales*. But it does not state under what conditions egress from the enclosure is permitted and prohibited. For this precise legislation it makes reference to canon 601. Were canon 2342, 3°, to read, *"Moniales, secundum praescriptum can. 601, exeuntes e clausura, etc.,"* then

[22] De obligationibus et privilegiis religiosorum.

[23] Canons 572-586.

it seems that it would be valid to interpret the word *moniales* according to the norm and reading of canon 601.

In view of the foregoing, it seems that the sense of canon 2342, 3°, may be rendered thusly: "Nuns who leave the enclosure, even for a brief time or under any pretext, without a special indult of the Holy See, except in the case of imminent danger of death or on account of some other very grave evil, *ipso facto* incur an excommunication which is reserved in a simple manner to the Holy See."

In the adoption of this rendering, an interpretation of the phrase "*post professionem*" will prove to be unnecessary, since it does not appear in canon 2342, 3°. A strict interpretation must be given to the word *moniales* as it appears in canon 2342, 3°. This interpretation follows the clear sense of canon 488, 7°, and restricts the incurring of the penalty to only those nuns who have actually been professed with solemn vows. It is consonant with the past legislation which has always restricted to nuns professed with solemn vows the penalty of excommunication for unlawful egress from the enclosure. Moreover, had the legislator intended to introduce a distinct change in his law, it certainly appears that he would have been very definite in so doing. The presence of so much discussion and doubt among authors on this point leads rather to the conclusion that clarity is absent from this law.

Let it be granted that the phrase "*post professionem*" in canon 601 includes even the nuns who are professed with simple vows. All nuns, then, are forbidden to leave the enclosure. But not all the nuns who contrary to this prohibittion do leave the enclosure also incur the penalty. It is affirmed here that it is most probable that canon 2342, 3°, restricts the penalty to only such nuns who have professed solemn vows.

The *Instruction* of the Sacred Congregation of Religious makes no reference to the penalty which is incurred for leaving the enclosure. It does make mention, however, of those who are professed with simple temporary vows. It states that they are bound by the law of enclosure and may not leave it except when their vows have expired or when they have been legitimately dismissed from the community.[24]

[24] *Instructio*, III, 1°, e.

Article II. Unlawful Egress From the Enclosure

Consideration has already been given to the question of the confines of the cloister in the monasteries of nuns.[25] Passage beyond these limits without the necessary permission constitutes an active violation of the enclosure. In expressing this idea canons 601, § 1, and 2342, 3°, use different terminology. Canon 601, § 1, employs the phrase "*exire e monasterio*"; canon 2342, 3°, makes use of the clause "*exeuntes e clausura.*" This divergence in language has led Cerato to defend the opinion that a nun indeed incurs the excommunication for leaving the monastery, but contracts simply the guilt of sin without any accompanying censure if she trespasses beyond the limits of the enclosure.[26] The penalty for unlawful trespass beyond the enclosure is expressed in canon 2342, 3°, and it is that canon which uses the word "*clausura.*" There is no indication that a change has been introduced in this law. The expression "*exeuntes e clausura*" should, then, be interpreted in accordance with the former legislation which accepted it as connoting a violation of the enclosure, even though the law also employed other terminology to express the same concept.[27]

The *Instruction* of the Sacred Congregation of Religious today permits nuns to enjoy an ambulatory which is situated on the roof of the monastery.[28] This is a noteworthy departure from the former legislation.[29] In accordance with canon 602 this ambulatory must be sheltered on all sides by a structure which will conceal the

[25] Cf. *supra*, pp. 108-113.

[26] *Censurae Vigentes*, p. 123. Cerato appeals to the use of the word "*monasterio*" by the Council of Trent (Sess. XXV, *de regularibus*, c. 5) and by Pope Pius V in his Constitution "*Decori*" (*Fontes*, n. 133). This word, however, was plainly used in the sense of the cloister and was acknowledged as expressing that concept. Very often the expression "*e septis monasterii*" was employed in connection with the notion of passing beyond the cloister. This expression is used even today. Cf. *Instructio*, III.

[27] Cf. canon 6, 3°.

[28] *Instructio*, III, 1°, c.

[29] Cf. S. C. Ep. et Reg., *in Lycien*, 16 sept. 1609; *in Comen*, 18 sept. 1609—Ferraris, *Bibliotheca*, s. v. "Moniales," art. III, 11; Mocchegiani, *Iurisprudentia Ecclesiastica*, I, n. 388.

nuns who are using it. Moreover, it should be accessible only to the nuns.[30]

The enclosure cannot be violated unless a nun places herself entirely beyond its limits. What has been said with reference to the question of entry into the cloister may be applied with equal validity to the question of egress. The one concept is but the correlation of the other.[31] In the past, authors presented for solution curious examples of possible enclosure violation.[32] It can be said with Ciprotti,[33] however, that the solution of any difficulties in this matter will be found in the answer to the question: Was the entire body of the nun placed beyond the enclosure limits? An affirmative reply will lead to the conclusion that the enclosure was violated. It is unlikely that one would observe a nun hanging on the outside of a window, sitting on a window sill in equestrian fashion, or employing a swing so vigorously that its impetus would carry her across the enclosure limits.[34] One of the mentioned cases may, however, be considered here. If a nun placed herself in the revolving structure which is situated at the enclosure limits and turned it around, may it be said that she violated the enclosure? The opinion has been expressed that such an act would not constitute an enclosure violation.[35] But such an opinion cannot be held. A nun who performs such an action is outside of the enclosure at some point in the full turn of the structure. And this is sufficient to constitute the violation.[36] Canon 601, § 1, states that egress from the enclosure must not take place even for a short time. With all due deference to the opinion of those authors who admit slightness of matter in the ques-

[30] Coronata, *Institutiones*, n. 613, p. 804, notes 2, 3; n. 1979.

[31] Cf. *supra*, pp. 116, ff.

[32] Most of these examples are foreign to the dignity which will be found inherent in the behavior of nuns today. Ciprotti (*De Consummatione Delictorum*, I, p. 70, note 16) gives a list of the proposed cases.

[33] *De Consummatione Delictorum*, I, p. 70, note 16.

[34] Cf. Ferraris, *Bibliotheca*, s. v. "Moniales," art. III, nn. 11-15; Pellizzarius, *De Monialibus*, cap. V, sec. II, nn. 76-78.

[35] Pellizzarius, *op. cit.*, cap. V, sec. II, n. 72.

[36] Cf. Ferraris, *Bibliotheca*, s. v. "Moniales," art. III, n. 72; Sole, *De Delectis et Poenis*, p. 290; Salucci, *Il Diritto Penale*, II, n. 257; Cappello, *De Censuris*, n. 323; Coronata, *Institutiones*, n. 1979.

tion of cloistral violation,[37] the sense of the canon seems to be that all types of egress are forbidden. The fact that only a brief time is spent outside of the enclosure does not excuse one from a violation of the enclosure law. The *Instruction* explicitly asserts that postulants may not leave the enclosure except when they are dismissed or when they wish to return to the world.[38] Taking cognizance of this provision of the *Instruction,* authors nevertheless admit the legitimate maintenance of a century old custom which permits postulants to leave the enclosure for about an hour in order that they may receive their habit in a more solemn fashion in the church.[39]

The history of the cloistral legislation justifies the use of the phrase "*quovis praetextu*" as found in the law today.[40] Any cause which cannot be comprehended within the scope of excusing necessities as they are admitted by the Code will not permit egress from the enclosure. The Church is reasonable in its legislation. The law regarding egress from the enclosure will follow the pattern set by the legislator, and not that which may in some way or other derive from the imagined necessities of the subject. If a cause is worthy of calling for an exception to the law of the enclosure, it will be recognized as such when, through the proper channels of competent authority, its merit is established. Pretexts are generally invoked when sufficient causes are lacking.

The church which is annexed to the monastery is outside of the cloistral limits.[41] It is forbidden, then, for the nuns to enter it. Very often, however, respect and honor for the House of God de-

[37] Cf. *supra,* pp. 155-157. Cf. *e. g.,* Cappello (*loc. cit.*), who denies that a nun could complete a turn within the rotating structure apart from incurring the penalty, and yet is ready to concede the admissibility of a slight matter in the question of enclosure violation.

[38] *Instructio,* III, 1°, e.

[39] Cf. canon 5; Vermeersch-Creusen (*Epitome,* I, n. 763) regard this practice as being *praeter Codicem* rather than *contra Codicem.* Cf. also Coronata, *Institutiones,* n. 613; Beste, *Introductio in Codicem,* p. 410.

[40] Canon 601, § 1. This same language was contained in the legislation of the Council of Trent (Sess. XXV, *de regularibus,* c. 5).

[41] Canon 597, § 2.

mand that nuns go into the church to clean it or to adorn it on the occasion of great feastdays. The Church has declared herself very willing to grant faculties which will permit the superioress to designate, as often as necessity demands, certain nuns to fulfill these duties.[42] The fulfillment of this declaration is reflected in the quinquennial faculties granted to the ordinaries of the United States.[43] Attached to this faculty, however, is the condition that all externs, including the confessor and those who serve the monastery but live outside of the enclosure, first leave the church, the door of which must then be locked. The inner door of the church must be closed with a double lock, and one key will be kept by the superioress and the other by a nun deputed by the ordinary. The door shall not be opened except in the cases specified and together with the prescribed precautions. This faculty may not be used to permit a nun to enter the church alone.

The penalty which is incurred for the active violation of the enclosure is an excommunication which is reserved in a simple manner to the Holy See. Relative to this type of violation there is no explicit penalty enacted by the Code for those who exercise assistance corresponding to that of introducing or of admitting persons into the cloister. Such actions, however, must be judged in accordance with the principles of co-operation as expressed in canon 2209, §§ 1-3. The local ordinary, moreover, can punish even with censures those who assist in this violation of the enclosure. Relative to the monasteries of nuns over which they exercise jurisdiction, regular superiors may punish their subjects, including the nuns themselves, if they be guilty of such enclosure violation.[44]

Article III. Causes Permitting Egress From the Enclosure

Canon 601, § 1, couches in language that is new the expression of admitted exceptions to the law of the strict active enclosure

[42] *Instructio*, III, 1°, d.

[43] Formula IV, 4—Faculties from the Sacred Congregation of Religious, n. 8—Bouscaren, *Canon Law Digest—Supplement* (1941), p. 33.

[44] Canon 603.

observance.[45] It states that the only admitted exceptions are those which consist in an imminent danger of death or in some other very serious evil. If time permits, then the existence of this danger must be acknowledged in writing by the local ordinary.

The *Instruction* of the Sacred Congregation of Religious furnishes examples of what these dangers may be. Thus it enumerates fire, flood, an unsafe building, invasion of soldiers, etc. Moreover, dangers can emanate from the nuns themselves. Thus a nun who is dangerously unsound of mind or afflicted with an infectious disease must leave the monastery lest harm come to the others of the community.[46]

Without the permission of the Holy See a nun may not be transferred, even for a brief time, from one monastery to another, though it be of the same Order. She may not leave her monastery for the purpose of founding a new one, or of acting as abbess, superioress or mistress of novices in another monastery. The motives of seeking good health or of supervising the erection of a new monastery are equally insufficient to warrant egress from the enclosure. In all these cases, however, the Sacred Congregation of Religious will, under certain prescribed conditions, readily grant the necessary permission if a just cause merits it.[47] Canon 601, § 1, has established the criterion according to which the specific causes which justify egress from the enclosure will be judged. The judgment, however, is reserved to the local ordinary. In this manner an impartial deci-

[45] This law has been expressed in various degrees of severity during the course of the centuries—". . . nisi forte tanto et tali morbo evidenter earum aliquam laborare constaret, quod non posset cum aliis absque gravi periculo seu scandalo commorari . . ."—c. un., *de statu regularium*, III, 16, in VI°; ". . . nisi ex aliqua causa, ab Episcopo approbanda . . ."—Conc. Trident., Sess. XXV, *de regularibus*, c. 5; ". . . nisi ex causa magni incendii vel infirmitatis leprae aut epidemiae. . . ."—Pope Pius V, Const. "*Decori*," 1 febr. 1570—*Fontes*, n. 133; ". . . itemque moniales ab illa [clausura] extra casus ac formam a S. Pio V in Const. *Decori* praescriptam. . . ."—Pope Pius IX, Const. "*Apostolicae Sedis*," 12 oct. 1869—*Fontes*, n. 552.

[46] *Instructio*, III, 1°, a.

[47] *Instructio*, III, 1°, b.

sion will the more readily be assured.[48] Permission to leave the enclosure is not granted by the local ordinary. It is his prerogative only to judge concerning the sufficiency of the cause which the law has honored as a reason for the departure. Can it be said, however, that in an ordinary case the failure to seek this recognition will result in the penalty of excommunication? Among the post-Code authors who have been consulted, Blat appears to be the only one who has treated this question. He affirms that since the permission for egress does not come from the local ordinary, a nun who neglects to procure his approbation will not incur the penalty.[49] This presupposes, of course, the existence of a just and sufficient cause.

Arguing from the fact that canon 601 and canon 2342, 3°, must be interpreted in conjunction one with the other, and from the opinion of pre-Code authors, Schaaf proposes the opposite opinion.[50] Following the opinion of Blat, one may state, with reference to this opinion, that the provision of canon 601, § 2, is directed primarily to the safeguarding certification of the justifying causes which permit egress. The approbation of the local ordinary does not beget the cause. And it is the existence of a sufficient cause which permits a nun to leave the enclosure. It may also be indicated here that the position which denies the opinion held by Blat would lead to the conclusion that, if an obvious justifying cause were present, but the local ordinary refused to recognize it, excommunication would be incurred by a nun who disregarded his non-approval and left the enclosure. More emphasis, it seems, would thus be placed upon the acknowledgment of the cause than upon the very existence of the cause itself.

All of this, however, seems to beg the question. Canon 2342, 3°, explicitly states that egress from the enclosure must be judged according to the norms of canon 601. Canon 601 requires the recog-

[48] Cf. Pennacchi, *Commentaria,* I, 760; Cappello, *De Censuris,* n. 325; Sole, *De Delictis et Poenis,* p. 291; Pistocchi, *I Canoni Penali,* p. 136; Cipollini, *De Censuris,* n. 50

[49] *Commentarium,* II, n. 535 and V, n. 183.

[50] *The Cloister,* p. 146. Cf. Mocchegiani, *Iurisprudentia Ecclesiastica,* I, n. 386; Ferraris, *Bibliotheca,* s. v. "Moniales," art. III, n. 32; Bonacina, *De Clausura,* q. I, p. VIII, n. 5.

nition of the local ordinary, if time permits that it be obtained. It seems, then, that a cause is not complete in itself until it is possessed of that recognition.

The Code anticipates, of course, that very often recourse to the local ordinary will not be possible. In such cases the nuns may themselves exercise judgment and leave the enclosure. In most of the cases this judgment will probably be exercised by the superioress. It certainly cannot be asserted, however, that a nun must rely upon the judgment of the superioress when grave danger is present. The canon does not demand it.

Canon 601, § 1, restricts to the local ordinary the right to grant recognition to causes which warrant egress from the enclosure. The regular superior, then, cannot by Code law demand that his approbation be obtained. The various Constitutions, however, may require this.

Though canon 601 demands that each recognition of a cause by the local ordinary be judged in accordance with the phrase "*excepto casu imminentis periculi mortis vel alius gravissimi mali*," the quinquennial faculties granted to the ordinaries of the United States permit greater leeway. Thus they may permit a nun to leave the enclosure to undergo a surgical operation, even though there be present no danger of death or any other great harm. This faculty may be granted only for such time as will be strictly necessary, and under certain precautions.[51]

Very often operations are preceded by special treatments of a prolonged nature. Since the quinquennial faculties are restricted for their use to the case of a surgical operation, they will prove to be of no value in such a case. Haring cites a case which made it necessary for a nun to undergo several X-ray treatments before she actually underwent the operation. Special faculties of one year's duration were granted the local ordinary to permit egress from the enclosure for such a purpose.[52]

A nun may certainly not be accompanied by another nun when

[51] Formula IV, 4—Faculties from the Sacred Congregation of Religious, n. 9—Bouscaren, *Canon Law Digest—Supplement* (1941), p. 33.

[52] "Mitteilungen,"—*ThPrQs*, LXXXII (1929), 362; "Kleine Beiträge,"—*Archiv für katholisches Kirchenrecht*, (Mainz, 1857—), CIX (1929), 584.

she leaves the enclosure to undergo an operation. Such a companion would undoubtedly give her great comfort, but that reason does not fall within the indulgence of the law.[53] As soon as it is prudently possible for a nun to leave the hospital after an operation, she must return to the enclosure. The local ordinary has no power to prolong her stay when it is not necessary. The judgment of the doctor will determine the time in this case.[54]

Necessary and urgent dental work which cannot be performed in the convent will present a sufficient cause for the local ordinary to exercise his quinquennial faculties and permit a nun to leave the enclosure.[55]

Coronata asks whether a community of nuns is obliged to leave the enclosure to attend Mass on a Sunday or other day of obligation when a priest cannot offer Mass in the monastery church.[56] Ordinarily this is not a cause which the local ordinary can approve as permitting egress from the enclosure. If the local ordinary possesses a special faculty in this regard he may exercise it. But even then the nuns need not make use of the privilege unless it is evident that in granting it to the local ordinary the Holy See meant to oblige the nuns to use it. The nuns may exercise a choice. Two positive laws are here opposed one to the other. That of enclosure observance is the more severe, as is evidenced by the necessity of a most serious cause to permit egress. Notable inconvenience will excuse from the obligation of attending Mass.

Can it be said that participation in public elections is a sufficient cause to permit nuns to leave the enclosure? Some authors admit this if egress of the nuns will avert a most grave evil.[57] Others either forbid it or state that such a problem should be settled by

[53] Goyeneche, "Consultationes,"—*CpR,* XIX (1938), 322-323.

[54] Jombart, "Consultations,"—*Revue des Communautés Religieuses,* IX (1933), 169-170.

[55] Creusen, "Melanges,"—*Revue des Communautés Religieuses,* III (1927), 134.

[56] "La Clausura delle Monache e l'obbligo della Messa festiva,"—*Perfice Munus* (Torino, 1926—), VI (1931), 430-432.

[57] Beste, *Introductio in Codicem,* p. 110; Schaefer, *De Religiosis,* n. 354; Vermeersch-Creusen, *Epitome,* I, n. 763; Coronata, *Institutiones,* n. 613, b.

Rome.[58] It seems quite possible that circumstances could be present which would warrant egress for this purpose. Civil laws may perhaps demand under heavy fines or penalties that all citizens exercise their franchise of vote; or offense may perchance be given if nuns refuse to vote at important elections. The vote of nuns may in given cases avert a great harm to the Church by defeating some inimical bill. Such cases could be admitted within the scope of the words "*alius gravissimi mali*" in canon 601.

It appears that a similar circumstance would be present if the civil law demanded that all women without exception register, *e. g.*, for defense purposes. The registration of aliens would beget a like circumstance warranting egress from the enclosure.

Ordinarily the Church will not dispense from the law of enclosure to permit nuns to leave the enclosure for the purpose of schooling. When a convent of Ursuline nuns in Graz found it impossible to conduct their school and award diplomas in accordance with State requirements unless some of the nuns attended courses outside of the enclosure, the Holy See decreed that thenceforth simple vows should be professed by the sisters and the episcopal cloister should be observed.[59]

The superioress of a monastery needs the permission of the Holy See to leave the enclosure for the purpose of being present with an extern sister during her dying moments. The local ordinary is not empowered to grant approbation to such a cause. It seems, however, that such a permission would readily be granted if the extern sister were in a house contiguous to the monastery.[60]

Regarding this phase of enclosure observance special faculties are possessed by Apostolic Nuncios, Internuncios and Delegates. In cases of sickness, or for other just and grave reasons, they may allow nuns to live outside of the enclosure for a time determined by their prudent judgment. This permission is granted, however, on condi-

[58] Oesterle, *Praelectiones Iuris Canonici*, I, 339; Sipos, *Enchiridion*, p. 371; Eichmann, *Lehrbuch*, p. 244, note 2.

[59] Haring, "Mitteilungen,"—*ThPrQs*, LXXXII (1929), 361; "Klein Beiträge," —*Archiv für katholisches Kirchenrecht*, CIX (1929), 585.

[60] Creusen, "Consultations,"—*Revue des Communautés Religieuses*, XII (1936), 70-71.

tion that the nuns shall always possess the companionship and assistance of their relatives by blood or marriage, or of some respectable woman. Wherever they live, be it at home or elsewhere, the nuns must lead a truly religious life dissociated from the society and companionship of men, as becomes virgins consecrated to God, and do nothing prejudicial to the law contained in canon 639, which regulates the duties of religious in their temporary leave of absence from the monastery.[61]

This faculty authorizes the Apostolic Delegate to allow nuns to leave their enclosure, to administer very important business affairs, to seek the health aids of mountain air or baths, and, with just reason, to vote.[62] Vermeersch expressed the opinion that these faculties of Delegates included the power to allow nuns to remain away from their convents beyond six months.[63]

A nun who goes out of the enclosure with the proper permission does not incur the censure of canon 2342, 3°, if she fails to return when the purpose for which she left the enclosure has been achieved. But a serious delay could readily import the guilt of grave sin.[64]

Article IV. Visiting Monasteries of Nuns

A study of the history of the cloistral observance has revealed the fact that punishments were enacted not only against those who entered the cloister of nuns, but even against those who visited the monasteries and conversed with the nuns. Detailed consideration has already been given to that legislation.[65]

The present legislation on this phase of cloistral observance is stated in canons 605 and 606, § 1. Canon 605 states that all those who have the custody of the cloister must carefully watch lest, dur-

[61] Cf. Faculties of Apostolic Delegates, Chapter V, n. 49—Bouscaren, *Canon Law Digest*, I, 184.

[62] Creusen, "Melanges,"—*Revue des Communautés Religieuses*, III (1927), 134.

[63] "Dissertatio,"—*Periodica*, XII (1924), (145)-(146).

[64] Cf. Schaefer, *De Religiosis*, n. 355, c; Biederlack-Führich, *De Religiosis*, p. 238; Coronata, *Institutiones*, n. 1979; Salucci, *Il Diritto Penale*, II, n. 257; Chelodi *Ius Poenali*, p. 105; Cavigioli, *De Censuris*, n. 133.

[65] Cf. *supra*, pp. 74-81.

ing the visits of externs, the discipline be relaxed and the religious spirit be weakened by useless conversations. Canon 606, § 1, warns religious superiors to insist upon the observance of the dictates of the Constitutions regarding the reception of visitors into the monastery.[66]

There is no indication in the canons of the Code that the severe enactments of the previous legislation are retained. In fact, a preponderant presumption points to a decided mitigation of that legislation. The same may be said of the *Instruction* which was issued by the Sacred Congregation of Religious. No mention of the former legislation is found in it.[67] Today, then, the former legislation may be disregarded, and the Code will serve together with the Constitutions as the norm of action relative to this phase of cloistral life. The former penalties no longer exist.[68]

What is to be said of the Synodal laws which, in relation to this matter, were enacted before the promulgation of the Code? Usually such particular enactments were simply a repetition of the existing common law. As such they must now be considered as abrogated together with the earlier common law. If, however, they were more than a mere restatement of the common law of that time and went beyond it, it will be difficult to state with certainly that they are abrogated by the more lenient legislation of the Code. The advisable procedure is that such statutes be mitigated and harmonized with the common law as it now exists.[69]

Many Constitutions were in existence long before the promulgation of the Code and contained regulations consistent with the existing common law relative to this question. What is their force at

[66] It is plain that these two canons refer to all religious communities. They are being considered in this place because of the link which they form with the former legislation. What is said in the way of interpretation may be considered as applicable to all religious bodies.

[67] Cf. *Instructio,* V.

[68] Cf. canon 6, 5°, 6°. Cf. also, Larraona, "Consultationes,"—*CpR,* I (1920), 369-370; Maroto, "Studia Canonica,"—*CpR,* VII (1926), 307-316; Schaefer, *De Religiosis,* n. 355, 9; Coronata, *Institutiones,* n. 613, d; Prümmer, *Manuale,* q. 229; Vermeersch-Creusen, *Epitome,* I, n. 762.

[69] Cf. Larraona, *loc. cit.*

present? If they were only a restatement, application or determination of that law, then they must be considered as no longer binding.[70] Approbation given to the Constitutions after the promulgation of the Code, however, constitutes them as particular law for the individual community. And the common law asserts that the dictates of the Constitutions must zealously be observed and accepted as the guide according to which this phase of observance in cloistral life will be preserved. Whatever, then, is found in these Constitutions subsequent to their approval must be observed.

Article V. Power of Local Ordinaries and Regular Superiors

The common law states the various penalties which are or are to be invoked against the obvious and more flagrant violations of the cloister of nuns. But it declares also in canon 603, § 1, that even though a convent of nuns be subject to regulars, vigilance over its cloistral observance pertains to the local ordinary who can punish with censures all those, including the regulars themselves, who are guilty of delicts destructive of the cloistral law. Many of the violations which strictly taken cannot be included within the scope of the present common penal law, may be punished by the local ordinary.

Relative to the monasteries of nuns over which they exercise jurisdiction, regular superiors may punish their subjects, including the nuns themselves, who are guilty of the cloistral violation.[71]

[70] Canon 489; Larraona, "Commentarium Codicis,"—*CpR,* IV (1923), 168-169; Maroto, "Studia Canonica,"—*CpR,* VII (1926), 315; Schaefer, *De Religiosis,* n. 355, 9.

[71] Canon 603, § 2.

CHAPTER VIII

EPISCOPAL CLOISTER

The preliminary draft of the law on the cloister which had been prepared for presentation to the Vatican Council required that the papal cloister be observed in the houses of the Congregations of men who professed simple vows. Though this command was not absolute, a just cause was necessary to render legitimate its non-observance. In the Congregations of women of simple vows, a complete or partial episcopal cloister was to be observed, in accordance with the ends of each Congregation.[1]

The Constitution *"Conditae a Christo,"* issued by Pope Leo XIII on December 8, 1900, ordained that in Congregations of women religious of pontifical approval, either the episcopal or the partial cloister was to be observed.[2]

Shortly after the promulgation of the Constitution *"Conditae a Christo"* the Sacred Congregation of Bishops and Regulars issued a guide to be followed in the practical formation of constitutions for Congregations of women religious prior to papal approval. This guide is known as the *"Normae"* of 1901.[3] Article 170 prescribed that a partial cloister determined by the Constitutions should be observed. Some portion of each house was to be reserved for the sisters. Article 171 permitted doctors, confessors and other indispensable persons to enter that part of the house which was thus reserved. Two sisters, however, were to accompany them. Article 172 stated that the bishop was to exercise vigilance over the cloister. Article 173 warned that any Constitutions which permitted men professors to enter the cloister and to conduct classes there for the sisters would not be approved. Article 174 prescribed that each

[1] Cf. chapters III, IV—*Acta et Decreta Conciliorum Recentiorum, Collectio Lacensis* (7 vols., Friburgi Brisgoviae: 1870-1890), VII, 680.

[2] § II, n. IV—*Fontes,* n. 644.

[3] *Normae Secundum Quas S. Congr. Episcoporum et Regularium Procedere Solet in Approbandis Novis Institutis Votorum Simplicium* (Romae, 1901).

time a sister left the house she was to be accompanied by a companion who was designated by the superioress.

The present law of the cloister relative to religious of simple vows is contained in canon 604. It pertains to all congregations, whether they be composed of men or of women, whether they possess diocesan or pontifical approval. Even societies which live in common but profess no religious vows are affected by this prescription of the cloister.[4] The confines of this cloister will follow the pattern of that which is established for religious who profess solemn vows. Exception is made, however, for the convents of women who profess simple vows. It will not be necessary for them to follow the enactments of canon 602 or the *Instruction* of the Sacred Congregation of Religious. Consideration has already been given to the question of the determination of their cloistral limits. Repetition here would be superfluous.[5]

Article I. Congregation of Men Religious

The cloister to be observed in the houses of men religious of simple vows bears a marked similarity to that of men religious of solemn vows. No common law censure is enacted, however, for its violation. Entry within the cloistral limits is forbidden only to women. Exception is made for the wives of rulers and their retinue.[6] The cloistral law of religious who profess simple vows is, however, somewhat mitigated. Entry of women into this cloister can be permitted by the religious superiors if just and reasonable causes are present. Since canon 604, § 1, makes no distinction, this permission may be granted even by the local superiors.[7] If this faculty is reserved to the major superior, that fact will generally be stated in the Constitutions. Such a reservation will not be contrary to the Code.[8]

It may be asked what will constitute a just and reasonable cause

[4] Canon 679.

[5] Cf. *supra*, pp. 114-115.

[6] Cf. canons 604, § 1; 598, § 2; cf. *supra*, pp. 127-137.

[7] Berutti, *Institutiones*, III, n. 118, II; Schaefer, *De Religiosis*, n. 363; Coronata, *Institutiones*, n. 614; Augustine, *Commentary*, III, 319; Vromant, *De Personis*, n. 385; Schaaf, *The Cloister*, p. 156.

[8] Cf. Schaefer, *op. cit.*, nn. 54, 6; 363, 2.

in this matter? Authors are generally content to assert that a mother may be admitted into the cloister to visit her son who is seriously ill.[9] Others go further and admit the giving of permission for entry to the close friends and relatives of the religious, to benefactors of the congregation, to the parents of pupils and to others.[10] Prudence, however, should be used in generally adopting this opinion. Its liberal use could easily lead to abuses. If the Constitutions state the reasons for which entry may be granted, they must be rigidly observed.

It will be recalled that the law of the cloister affects all canonically erected houses, even though they be not "formal" houses.[11] This law then will pertain to parish houses and houses of study. Extreme care should be exercised by superiors in permitting to women any access to the cloistered precincts of the house. It is desirable always that the necessary housework be done by lay brothers or by male help. Undoubtedly it will be objected that such work is not the work of men and that the results achieved by them are not comparable to those of women. Moreover, great difficulty is often experienced in obtaining lay brothers in this country. And it is the rare man who will accept work of this kind. This is all very true. And yet the law remains. In the houses of regulars such work must be done by lay brothers or male help. The strict penalty offers no alternative. The absence of any common law penalty relative to the cloister of the religious who profess simple vows should not be used as a pretext for disobeying the law itself. Except for the penalty, the two cloisters—that of the regulars, and that of the religious who profess simple vows—are practically the same.

The present discussion deals particularly with the question of the admission of women into those parts of the house which are reserved exclusively to the habitation of the religious. It appears that in order to permit women or sisters to perform the culinary duties,

[9] Cf. Vromant, *loc. cit.*; Beste, *Introductio in Codicem*, p. 411; Cocchi, *Commentarium*, IV, n. 104; Vermeersch-Creusen, *Epitome*, I, n. 760; Creusen, Garesché, Ellis, *Religious Men and Women in the Code*, n. 291; Bastien, *Directoire Canonique*, n. 267; Gerster a Zeil, *Ius Religiosorum*, p. 195.

[10] Augustine, *Commentary*, III, 319; Schaefer, *De Religiosis*, n. 363, 2.

[11] Cf. canons 597; 604, § 1; 488, 5°.

the kitchen could be placed outside of the cloister limits. A just cause for this is found in the expense which would be entailed in hiring chefs to do the cooking. Lay brothers who are skilled in the art of cooking cannot readily be found. The major superiors or the general chapter of the Congregation may establish the limits of the cloister, and they could feasibly place the kitchen and other necessary adjoining rooms beyond its ambit.[12]

There is, however, no justification in the law for the practice of permitting women to enter the religious house for any and all purposes. Such a procedure is equivalent to a general dispensation from the cloistral observance. But the cloistral laws form part of the general laws of the Church. Exceptions are permitted. But a just and reasonable cause must always be present.

Religious of simple vows are not permitted free and unlimited egress from the cloister. Canon 606, § 1, ordains that superiors will zealously enforce the prescriptions of the Constitutions in this regard. Sufficient commentary has already been devoted to this canon when it was treated in connection with the cloistral duties of regulars. The principles stated there will also apply to religious of simple vows. The same may be said of the interpretation concerning the absence from the religious house for a period of time which exceeds six months.[13]

Article II. Congregations of Women Religious

The cloistral law for sisters professed with simple vows is not so strict as the law of the cloister for nuns. The cloistral confines will generally be patterned after those which are observed in the houses of regulars and of men religious of simple vows.[14] It is not required

[12] Cf. canon 597, § 3.

[13] Cf. *supra*, pp. 172-177.

[14] This discussion prescinds entirely from the more rigid cloistral law of some sisters which follows very closely the cloistral design and regulations of nuns. Very often this strict enclosure will be preserved by sisters who are members of an Order the members of which by normal rule profess solemn vows but are allowed in some places to profess only simple vows. It matters not how similar to the papal cloister the enclosure may be. No penalty is attached by *common law* to its violation. Cf. Beste, *Introductio in Codicem*, p. 411.

that a grill be placed in the parlor. Moreover, there is no prescription forbidding sisters to enter, with permission, the parlor where visitors are. Those parts of the house, however, which are reserved exclusively to the sisters must be placed within the cloistral limits.[15] The enclosure limits will generally be determined by the higher superiors or by the general chapter in accordance with the Constitutions.[16] If, however, the Congregation is only diocesan in character, this right will generally pertain to the bishop.[17] Canon 604, § 3, implicitly gives the bishop the right to determine the cloistral limits in all the houses of Congregations situated within the diocese if he considers that the enclosure is not being properly observed.[18]

The prescription of canon 599 applies also to convents of religious professed with simple vows. Thus, if a convent has attached to it a school or a college for its own students,[19] or conducts other institutions in accordance with the proper ends of the Congregation,[20] at least a separate part of the building should be reserved, if possible, for the exclusive occupation of the religious, and this part will then be subject to the law of the cloister.[21]

Entry into the cloister of sisters is forbidden only to men. The exceptions which were conceded to monasteries of nuns in favor of certain privileged persons and in recognition of the needs of the nuns and of the monastery, are granted also to religious of simple vows.[22] Certain precautions must necessarily be observed when entry is granted. They are not mentioned explicitly in the canons. Those precautions, however, which are enacted for the monasteries of nuns may be applied by analogy to the convents of sisters professed with simple vows. The purpose of the law is the same in all

[15] Cf. canon 597, § 2; Bastien, *Directoire Canonique*, n. 266; Schaefer, *De Religiosis*, n. 363, 1.

[16] Canon 597, § 3; Bastien, *loc. cit.*

[17] Jardí, *El Derecho de las Religiosas*, n. 812.

[18] Canon 604, § 3: ". . . semper autem curet ut eadem rite servetur. . . ."

[19] Girls who are educated for admission into the novitiate.

[20] *E. g.*, colleges, parochial schools, hospitals, orphanages, etc.

[21] Cf. canons 599 and 604, § 2.

[22] Canons 598, § 2; 600. Cf. *supra*, pp. 181-198.

convents. No male persons should enter the cloister unless they are accompanied by at least two sisters.[23]

Canon 604, § 1, does not demand that the habitual approbation of the local ordinary be procured by the superioress before she grants entry to such persons. If, on the other hand, the Constitutions require this approbation, then it must be obtained.[24]

The permissible entry of men into the cloister of religious of simple vows is not restricted to the exceptions which are expressed in canon 600. For a just and reasonable cause the superioress may permit other exceptions. Unless the Constitutions rule otherwise, the permission of the local superioress is sufficient. Recourse need not be had to the local ordinary. There are some causes which are generally admitted as sufficiently reasonable to warrant such entry. Thus a father or brother may enter the cloister to visit a sister who is seriously ill.[25]

Mature judgment and prudence should be exercised in the granting of permissions. Whatever is stated in the Constitutions relative to this feature in connection with the cloister must zealously be observed. The rigid prohibition of the Church regarding the cloister of the nuns will serve as an adequate norm of action to temper any excessive generosity and broadmindedness on the part of superioresses in this regard. The cloister deserves primary consideration and its observance is to be preferred to the satisfying of the natural curiosities which are sometimes to be found in lay persons desirous of viewing the inside of a convent. A religious house should have and preserve its privacy.

The prohibition of entry applies also to the schools, hospitals, etc., which are annexed to the religious house.[26] A good cause coupled with the permission of the superioress is required to enter such places. Greater latitude, however, is allowed in granting permission

[23] Bastien, *Directoire Canonique*, n. 267.

[24] Bastien, *loc. cit.*; Schaefer, *De Religiosis*, n. 363, 2; Coronata, *Institutiones*, n. 614.

[25] Cf. Schaefer, *loc. cit.*; Bastien, *Directoire Canonique*, n. 267; Augustine, *Commentary*, III, 319; Cocchi, *Commentarium*, IV, n. 104; Beste, *Introductio in Codicem*, p. 411.

[26] Canon 599, § 2.

for such entry.[27] Vermeersch observes that in urgent cases the permission may rightly be presumed.[28]

The bishop must exercise vigilance over the cloistral observance and correct any abuses which may arise. In special circumstances and for grave reasons the bishop may enact censures against all those who are guilty of cloistral violation.[29] The primary duty of the bishop in this regard is the safeguarding of the cloister. This may often be fulfilled by the use of mere corrections and warnings. Recourse to severe penalties should not be had unless other means have failed or are deemed of little use. Frequent transgressions of the law of cloister accompanied by scandal would constitute sufficient cause for the enactment of penalties. When other means fail, censures should be employed.[30]

Sisters may not leave the enclosure without permission. This prohibition is expressed in canon 606, § 1. Reasons and causes are not given by the canon. Further, superioresses are exhorted to insist upon the observance of the constitutions in this regard. They will contain the causes for which egress may be permitted. It is worthy of note that canon 606, § 1, does not give to the superioresses the right to permit egress from the enclosure. Constitutions, then, which state that egress from the enclosure will be licit only with the permission of the local ordinary are not opposed in any way to the Code.[31] Strictly regarded, permission must be obtained each time a sister wishes to leave the enclosure. Canon 606, § 1, employs the words *"egressum . . . e claustris."* Since therefore the parlors are situated beyond the enclosure limits, permission to enter them at any time should be sought. Permission must be sought when sisters wish to go any place outside of the house. A strict interpretation

[27] Bastien, *Directoire Canonique*, n. 269; Cocchi, *Commentarium*, IV, n. 104; Vermeersch-Creusen, *Epitome*, I, n. 760; Creusen-Garesché-Ellis, *Religious Men and Women in the Code*, n. 291, 2.

[28] *Epitome, loc. cit.*

[29] Canon 604, § 3.

[30] Cf. Schaefer, *De Religiosis*, n. 363, 4; Coronata, *Institutiones*, n. 614; Bastien, *Directoire Canonique*, n. 270; Augustine, *Commentary*, 319.

[31] Cf. Vermeersch, "Dissertationes,"—*Periodica*, XV (1927), (64)-(65); Coronata, *Institutiones*, n. 614, c.

would also demand permission for the sisters to leave the house when their duties call them to the daily classes in the parochial schools. It seems reasonable to suppose, however, that general permission may be granted in such cases. Express permission, however, should be sought each time a sister desires to go to those places when duty does not demand it.

Article 174 of the *Normae* of 1901 prescribed that each time a sister left the house she was to be accompanied by a companion designated by the superioress. Canon 607 ordains that superioresses and local ordinaires must carefully watch that, except when necessity demands, sisters do not leave the religious house alone. The canon does not state that another sister must necessarily be the companion. A woman or a young girl approved by the superioress will sufficiently fulfill the regulation in this regard.[32]

Oftentimes it will not be possible to observe this regulation. The necessity of egress, then, will excuse from the law. Care should be exercised, however. The place to which the sister is going, the neighborhood in which the convent is located, the time of the day, the age and character of the sister, all these factors will exert their influence upon the lawfulness of solitary egress from the house.

Authors generally admit that oftentimes the nature of the work which some sisters undertake will necessitate their departure from the house unaccompanied. Sisters who are engaged in the care of the sick in private homes, or sisters who teach or attend classes in schools distant from their convent, may be granted permission to leave the religious house alone.[33] The regulation should be observed even in these cases, however, if it is conveniently possible.

Canon 606, § 2, prescribes that an absence from the religious house extending beyond six months' duration will require an Apostolic indult. Consideration has already been given to the interpretation of this canon.[34] That commentary will apply also in the case

[32] Bastien, *Directoire Canonique*, n. 273; Coronata, *Institutiones*, n. 614, c; Schaefer, *De Religiosis*, n. 364, 2; Beste, *Introductio in Codicem*, p. 412.

[33] Bastien, *Directoire Canonique*, n. 273; Beste, *Introductio in Codicem*, p. 412; Coronata, *Institutiones*, n. 614, c; Creusen, Garesché, Ellis, *Religious Men and Women in the Code*, n. 292, 4.

[34] Cf. *supra*, pp. 172-177.

of Congregations of women religious. The end of such Congregations will not demand, however, that its members be away from the community for any great length of time. It could happen, though, that a Congregation of sisters whose end is teaching could send one of its members to teach in a distant university where no house of theirs was located. In such a case no indult would be required, because the sister would be fulfilling the work of the Congregation. According to the interpretation of authors, a six months' absence from the religious house for such purposes demands no indult.[35]

[35] Cf. *supra*, pp. 173-174.

CONCLUSIONS

The following opinions are offered as conclusions resulting from the present study:

1. A canonically valid marriage is not a requisite for the enjoyment of the privilege which permits the wife of a ruler to enter the cloister. The opposite will be true, however, if scandal is thereby given to Catholics. The term "ruler" need not be taken in its absolute sense. His privilege may be invoked anywhere.

2. There is no canonical foundation for the interpretation that the penalty for the violation of the cloister is incurred by girls only when they have attained the age of fourteen years.

3. In practice, the opinion which is opposed to the admissibility of slightness of matter in the cloistral violation is the more acceptable one.

4. The penalty of excommunication is not incurred by anyone who merely detains within the cloister a person who has entered without permission.

5. An apostolic indult is not required when a religious is absent from his community over six months on work compatible with the proper end of his Institute. To destroy the coalescence of time when a religious has been away from his community almost six months, a month should be spent in his religious house.

6. It is most probable that the penalty of excommunication is incurred by those who introduce or admit into the cloister of nuns *any* children below the age of puberty.

7. The word *moniales* of canon 2342, 3°, has application only to nuns who have actually professed solemn vows. The interpretation of this word will derive not from canon 601, but from canon 2342, 3°.

BIBLIOGRAPHY

Sources

Acta Apostolicae Sedis, Commentarium Officiale, Romae, 1909—

Acta et Decreta Conciliorum Recentiorum, Collectio Lacensis, 7 vols., Friburgi Brisgoviae, 1870-1890.

Acta Sanctae Sedis, 41 vols., Romae, 1865-1908.

Acta Sanctorum Bollandiana, August, Tom. I, Parisiis et Romae, 1867.

Bullarium Benedicti XIV, 3 vols. in 4, Prati, 1845-1847.

Bullarium Diplomatum et Privilegiorum Sanctorum Romanorum Pontificum, Taurinensis Editio, 24 vols., et Appendix, Augustae Taurinorum, 1857-1872.

Bullarium Ordinis FF. Praedicatorum, 8 vols., Romae, 1729-1740.

Canones et Decreta Sacrosancti Oecumenici Concilii Tridentini, Romae: Ex Typographia polyglotta S. C. de Propaganda Fide, 1882.

Codicis Iuris Canonici Fontes cura Emi. Petri Card. Gasparri Editi, 9 vols., Romae (postea Civitate Vaticana): Typis Polyglottis Vaticanis, 1923-1939. (Vols. VII, VIII et IX *ed. cura et studio Emi. Iustiniani Card. Serédi.*)

Collectanea in Usum Secretariae Sacrae Congregationis Episcoporum et Regularium, Ed. A. Bizzarri, Romae, 1863.

Concilia Germaniae, quorum Collectionem Celsissimo Principe Ioanne Mauritio auctore et auspice Cl. Ioannes Fredericus Schannat primum coepit, P. Josephus Hartzheim continuavit et prelo dedit, P. Hermannus Scholl evolvit, auxit ac notis illustravit . . ., 11 vols., Coloniae Augustae Agrippinensium, 1759-1790.

Corpus Iuris Canonici, Editio Lipsiensis II (Richter-Friedberg), 2 vols., Lipsiae: Tauchnitz, 1879-1881. Editio anastatice repetita, 1922.

Corpus Iuris Civilis, 3 vols., Berolini, 1928-1929.
Codex Iustinianus, quem recognovit et retractavit P. Krueger;
Novellae, quas recognovit R. Schoell, et absolvit G. Kroll.

Decretales D. Gregorii Papae IX, una cum Glossis Restitutae, Romae, 1582.

Decretum Gratiani emendatum et notationibus illustratum una cum glossis, Gregorii XIII, Pont. Max., iussi editum, 2 vols., Romae, 1582.

Jaffé, Philippus, *Regesta Pontificum Romanorum ab condita Ecclesia ad annum post Christum natum, 1198, Editionem secundam correctam et auctam auspiciis Guliemi Wattenback curaverunt S. Loewenfeld, F. Kaltenbrunner, P. Ewald,* 2 vols. in 1, Lipsiae, 1885-1888.

Liber Sextus Decretalium D. Bonifatii Papae VIII, suae integritati una cum Clementinis et Extravagantibus, earumque Glossis restitutus, Romae, 1582.

Mansi, J. D., *Sacrorum Conciliorum Nova et Amplissima Collectio,* 53 vols. in 59, Paris, Leipzig, Arnhem, 1901-1927.

Monumenta Germaniae Historica, Gregorii I Papae Regestrum Epistolarum, Tom I, Pars 1, Libri i-iv, edidit Paulus Ewald, Berolini, 1887.

Monumenta Germaniae Historica, Legum Sectio II, Tom. I, Capitularia Regum Francorum, edidit Alfredus Boretius, Hannoverae, 1883.

Monumenta Germaniae Historica, Legum Sectio III, Tom. I, Concilia Aevi Merovingici, recensuit F. Maassen, Hannoverae, 1893; *Tom. II, Pars 1, Concilia Aevi Karolini I,* recensuit Albertus Werminghoff, Hannoverae et Lipsiae, 1904; *Pars 2, Concilia Aevi Karolini I,* recensuit Albert Werminghoff, Hannoverae et Lipsiae, 1908.

Pallottini, Salvator, *Collectio Omnium Conclusionum et Resolutionum quae in causis propositis apud Sacram Congregationem Cardinalium S. Concilii Tridentini Interpretum Prodierunt ab eius institutione anno MDLXIX ad MDCCCLX, distinctis titulis alphabetico ordine per materias digestas,* 18 vols., Romae, 1868-1895.

Potthast, A., *Regesta Pontificum Romanorum,* 2 vols., Berolini, 1874-1875.

Quaranta, S., *Summa Bullarii,* Venetiis, 1622.

Reference Works

Alphonsus Liguori, St., *Theologia Moralis,* 10 vols., Mechliniae, 1852.

Avanzini, Petrus, *De Constitutione Apostolicae Sedis,* 2. ed., Romae, 1874.

Ayrinhac, H. A., and Lydon, P. J., *Penal Legislation in the New Code of Canon Law,* revised edition, New York: Benziger, 1936.

Bachofen, Charles Augustine, *Compendium Juris Regularium,* New York, 1903.

———, *A Commentary on the New Code of Canon Law,* 8 vols., Vol. III, 5. ed., 1938; Vol. VIII, 5. ed., 1938, St. Louis: Herder.

Ballerini, A.-Palmieri, D., *Opus Theologicum Morale in Busembaum Medullam,* 2. ed., 7 vols., Prati, 1892-1894.

Bastien, Pierre, *Directoire Canonique a l'usage des Congregations a voeux simples,* 3. ed., Bruges: Beyaert, 1923.

Benedictus XIV, *De Synodo Dioecesana,* 2 vols. in 1, Venetiis, 1775.

Berutti, Christophorus, *Institutiones Iuris Canonici,* 6 vols., Vol. III, Taurini-Romae: Marietti, 1936.

Beste, Udalricus, *Introductio in Codicem,* Collegeville: St. John's Abbey Press, 1938.

Biederlack, Josephus-Führich, Maximilianus, *De Religiosis Codicis Iuris Canonici,* Oeniponte: Rauch, 1919.

Blat, Albertus, *Commentarium Textus Codicis Iuris Canonici,* 6 vols., Lib. II, 3. ed., 1938; Lib. V, 1924, Romae: Apud Angelicum.

Bonacina, Martinus, *Opera Omnia,* 3 vols., Venetiis, 1687.

Bouix, Dominicus, *Tractatus de Jure Regularium,* 2 vols., Bruxellis, 1867.

Bouscaren, T. Lincoln, *The Canon Law Digest,* 2 vols., and *Supplement (1941),* Milwaukee: Bruce, 1934-1941.

Bucceroni, Januarius, *Commentarii,* 5. ed., Romae, 1899.

Butler, Cuthbert, *Benedictine Monachism,* 2. ed., London: Longmans, Green & Co., 1924.

———, *Sancti Benedicti Regula Monasteriorum,* editio altera, Friburgi Brisgoviae: Herder & Co., 1927.

Cappello, Felix, *Tractatus Canonico-Moralis de Censuris iuxta Codicem Iuris Canonici,* 3. ed., Taurinorum Augustae: Marietti, 1933.

Cavigioli, Joannes, *De Censuris Latae Sententiae Quae in Codice Iuris Canonici Continentur Commentariolum,* Torino: Libreria Editrice Internazionale, 1918.

Cerato, Prosdocimus, *Censurae Vigentes Ipso Facto a Codice Iuris Canonici Excerptae,* 2. ed., Patavii: Typis Seminarii, 1921.

Chapman, J., *Saint Benedict and the Sixth Century,* London: Sheed & Ward, 1929.

Chelodi, Joannes, *Ius de Personis iuxta Codicem Iuris Canonici,* 2. ed., ab Ernesto Bertagnolli, Tridenti: Libr. Edit. Tridentum, 1925.

———, *Ius Poenale et Procedendi in Iudiciis Criminalibus,* 4. ed., a Vigilio Dalpiaz, Tridenti: Ardesi, 1935.

Ciolli, A., *Commentario Practico Delle Censure Latae Sententiae,* 4. ed., Siena, 1884.

Cipollini, Albertus, *De Censuris Latae Sententiae juxta Codicem Iuris Canonici,* Taurini: Marietti, 1925.

Ciprotti, Pius, *De Consummatione Delictorum Attento Eorum Elemento Obiectivo in Iure Canonico,* Pars I, Romae: Apud Custodiam Librariam Pont. Instituti Utriusque Iuris, 1936.

Claeys-Bouuaert, F.-Simenon, G., *Manuale Iuris Canonici ad Usum Seminariorum,* 3 vols., Gandae et Leodii, Vol. I, 3. ed., 1930.

Cocchi, Guidus, *Commentarium in Codicem Iuris Canonici ad Usum Scholarum,* 5 vols. in 8, Vol. IV, 3. ed., 1932; Vol. VIII, 3. ed., 1936, Taurinorum Augustae: Marietti.

Coronata, Matthaeus, Conte a, *Institutiones Iuris Canonici,* 5 vols., Vol. I, 2. ed., 1939; Vol. IV, 1935, Taurini: Marietti.

Creusen, Joseph-Garesché, Edward-Ellis, Adam, *Religious Men and Women in the Code,* 3. English ed., Milwaukee: Bruce, 1940.

D'Annibale, Josephus, *Summula Theologiae Moralis,* 5. ed., 3 vols., Romae, 1908.

De Meester, A., *Juris Canonici et Juris Canonico-Civilis Compendium,* nova ed., 3 vols. in 4, Brugis, 1921-1928.

De Siena, Paschalis, *Commentarius Censurarum iuxta Novum Codicem Iuris Canonici,* Neapoli, 1918.

Dubé, Arthur, *The General Principles for the Reckoning of Time in Canon Law,* The Catholic University of America, Canon Law Studies, No. 144, Washington, D. C.: The Catholic University of America Press, 1941.

Eichmann, Eduard, *Lehrbuch des Kirchenrechts auf Grund des Codex Iuris Canonici,* 2. ed., Paderborn: Druck und Verlag von Ferdinand Schöningh, 1926.

Fagnanus, Prosper, *Commentaria in Quinque Libros Decretalium,* 4 vols., Venetiis, 1696.

Fanfani, Ludovicus, *De Iure Religiosorum ad Normam Codicis Iuris Canonici,* 2. ed., Taurini-Romae: Marietti, 1925.

Ferraris, F. Lucius, *Prompta Bibliotheca, Canonica, Juridica, Moralis, Theologica necnon Ascetica, Polemica Rubricistica, Historica,* ed. Migne, 8 vols., Parisiis, 1863-1865.

Ferreres, Joannes, *Compendium Theologiae Moralis ad Normam Codicis Canonici,* 13. ed., 2 vols., Barcinone: Subirana, 1925.

Forcellini, Aegidius, *Totius Latinitatis Lexicon,* 4 vols., Schneebergae-Lipsiae, 1831-1839.

Genicot, E.-Salsmans, I., *Institutiones Theologiae Moralis,* 10. ed., 2 vols., Bruxellis: Alb. DeWit, 1922.

Gerster a Zeil, Thomas Villanova, *Ius Religiosorum in Compendium Redactum,* Taurini: Marietti, 1935.

Hollweck, Joseph, *Die kirchlichen Strafgesetze,* Mainz, 1899.

Hostiensis, Cardinalis (Henricus de Segusio), *Commentaria in Quinque Decretalium Libros,* 5 vols. in 3, Venetiis, 1581.

Ioannes Andreae, *In VI Libros Decretalium Novella Commentaria,* 6 vols. in 5, Venetiis, 1581.

Jardí, Antonio de la C., *El Derecho de las Religiosas según las Praescripciones Vigentes del Codigo Canonico y Civil,* 2. ed., Vich: Serafica, 1927.

Ladeuze, Paulin, *Étude sur le cénobitisme Pakomien,* Louvain, 1898.

Lehmkuhl, Augustinus, *Theologia Moralis,* 12. ed., 2 vols., Friburgi Brisgoviae, 1914.

Leitner, Martin, *Handbuch des katholischen Kirchenrechts,* 2. ed., 2 vols., Regensburg: Kösel und Pustet, 1921-1927.

Lucidi, Angelus, *De Visitatione Sacrorum Liminum Instructio S. C. Concilii,* 3 vols., Romae, 1883.

Marc, Cl.-Gestermann, F. X.-Raus, J. B., *Institutiones Morales Alphonsianae,* 19. ed., 2 vols., Lugduni: Vitte, 1933-1934.

Malnory, A., *St. Césaire, Évêque D'Arles,* Paris, 1894.

Migne, P. J., *Patrologiae Cursus Completus, Series Graeca,* 161 vols., Parisiis, 1856-1866.

———, *Patrologiae Cursus Completus, Series Latina,* 221 vols., Parisiis, 1858-1864.

Mocchegiani, Petrus, *Iurisprudentia Ecclesiastica ad usum et commoditatem utriusque cleri,* 3 vols., Ad Claras Aquas, 1904-1905.

Morison, E. F., *St. Basil and His Rule,* London, 1912.

Mothon, J., *Institutions Canoniques,* 2 vols., Paris: Desclée, 1922-1924.

Navarrus (Martin de Azpilcueta), *Opera Omnia,* 6 vols., Venetiis, 1618.

Noldin, H., et Schönegger, A., *De Censuris,* 32. ed., Oeniponte: Rauch, 1938.

Oesterle, Gerardus, *Praelectiones Iuris Canonici,* Vol. I, Romae: In Collegio S. Anselmi, 1931.

Ojetti, Benedictus, *Synopsis Rerum Moralium et Iuris Pontificii,* 3. ed., 4 vols., Romae, 1909-1914.

———, *Commentarium in Codicem Iuris Canonici,* 4 vols., Romae: Apud Universitas Gregoriana, 1927-1931.

Passerini, Petrus Maria, *Commentaria in Sextum Librum Decretalium,* 2 vols., Venetiis, 1698.

Pejska, Josephus, *Ius Canonicum Religiosorum,* 3. ed., Friburgi Brisgoviae: Herder, 1927.

Pellizzarius, Franciscus, *Tractatio de Monialibus,* editio novissima, Romae, 1761.

Pennacchi, Josephus, *Commentaria in Constitutionem Apostolicae Sedis,* 2 vols., Romae, 1883.

Piatus Montensis, F., *Praelectiones Iuris Regularis,* 3. ed., 2 vols., Tornaci, 1906.

Pirhing, Ernricus, *Ius Canonicum Novo Methodo Explicatum,* 5 vols. in 4, Dillingae, 1674-1678.

Pistocchi, Mario, *I Canoni Penali del Codice Ecclesiastico Esposti e Commentati,* Torino-Roma: Marietti, 1925.

Prümmer, Dominicus M., *Manuale Iuris Canonici in Usum Scholarum,* 4. et 5. eds., Friburgi Brisgoviae: Herder, 1927.

Raus, P. J. B., *Institutiones Canonicae iuxta Novum Codicem Iuris,* 2. ed., Parisiis: Vitte, 1931.

Reiffenstuel, Anacletus, *Jus Canonicum Universum,* 5 vols. in 7, Parisiis, 1864-1870.

Roberti, Franciscus, *De Delictis et Poenis,* Vol. I, Romae: Libraria Pontificii Instituti Utriusque Iuris, 1938.

Salucci, Raffaele, *Il Diritto Penale Secondo il Codice di Diritto Canonico,* 2 vols. in 1, Subiaco: Tipografia dei Monasteri, 1926-1930.

Sanchez, T., *Opus Morale in Praecepta Decalogi,* 2 vols., Parmae, 1723.

Schaaf, Valentine, *The Cloister,* The Catholic University of America Canon Law Studies, No. 13, Washington, D. C.: The Catholic University of America, 1921.

Schaefer, Timotheus, *De Religiosis ad normam Codicis Iuris Canonici,* 3. ed., Roma: S. A. L. E. R., 1940.

Schmalzgrueber, Franciscus, *Ius Ecclesiasticum Universum,* 5 vols. in 12, Romae, 1843-1845.

Sipos, Stephenus, *Enchiridion Iuris Canonici,* Pecs: ex typographia "Haladas R. T.," 1926.

Sobradillo, A. M. de, *Tractatus de Religiosarum Confessariis ad Normam Codicis Iuris Canonici Concinnatus,* Torino: Berruti, 1932.

Sole, Jacobus, *De Delictis et Poenis,* Romae, 1920.

Suarez, Franciscus, *Opera Omnia,* 26 vols., Parisiis, 1856-1866.

Swoboda, Innocent, *Ignorance in Relation to the Imputability of Delicts,* The Catholic University of America Canon Law Studies, No. 143, Washington, D. C.: The Catholic University of America Press, 1941.

Téphany, Joseph-Marie, *Constitution Apostolicae Sedis,* Tours, 1883.

Vermeersch, A.-Creusen, J., *Epitome Iuris Canonici,* 3 vols., Vol. I, 6. ed., 1937; Vol. III, 5. ed., 1936, Mechliniae: H. Dessain.

Vromant, G., *Ius Missionariorum, De Personis,* 2. ed., Louvain Museum Lessianum, 1935.

Wernz, Franciscus, *Ius Decretalium ad Usum Praelectionum in Scholis Textus Canonici sive Iuris Decretalium*, 6 vols. in 7, Tom. III, 2. ed., Romae, 1908; Tom. VI, Prati, 1913.

Wernz, F.-Vidal, P., *Ius Canonicum ad Codicis Normam Exactum*, 7 toms. in 8, Tom. III, 1933; Tom. VII, 1937, Romae: Apud Aedes Universitatis Gregorianae.

Woywod, Stanislaus, *A Practical Commentary on the Code of Canon Law*, 2 vols., New York: Wagner, 1925.

Principal Articles

Ciprotti, P., "Consultationes"—*Apollinaris*, IX (1936), 139-140.

Coronata, M., "La Clausura delle Monache e l'obbligo della Messa festiva"—*Perfice Munus*, VI (1931), 430-432.

Creusen, J., "Melanges"—*Revue des Communautés Religieuses*, III (1927), 134.

———, "Consultations"—*Revue des Communautés Religieuses*, XII (1936), 70-71.

Doink, P., "Pastoral-Fälle"—*Theologisch-praktische Quartalschrift*, LXXVII (1924), 119-121.

Ellis, A., "Annotationes"—*Periodica*, XXVI (1937), 83-84.

Goyeneche, S., "Consultationes"—*CpR*, II (1921), 47-48.

Haring, J., "Mitteilungen"—*ThPrQs*, LXXXII (1929), 361-362.

Jombart, E., "Consultations"—*Revue des Communautés Religieuses*, III (1927), 121-122.

———, "Cloture et Rigorisme"—*Revue des Communautés Religieuses*, XIV (1938), 83-86.

———, "Questio de clausura materiali regularium"—*Periodica*, XVI (1927), 48*-52*.

La Puma, V., "Acta et Documenta"—*CpR*, XIII (1932), 249; 345-346; XIV (1933), 33-37.

Larraona, A., "Commentarium Codicis"—*CpR*, IV (1923), 11-14; 168-169.

Maroto, P., "Annotationes"—*CpR*, V (1924), 140-141.

———, "Studia Canonica"—*CpR*, VII (1926), 307-316.

Schmidt, J., "The Juridic Value of the *Instructio*"—*The Jurist*, I (1941), 289-315.

Schweiger, P., "Questio Canonica"—*CpR*, IV (1923), 140-145.

Teodori, I., "Consultationes"—*Apollinaris*, V (1932), 108-112.

Vermeersch, A., "De Persona Morali"—*Periodica*, X (1922), (34)-(35).

———, "De commoratione extra propriam religionis domum"—*Periodica*, X (1922), (36)-(37).

———, "De Clausura Monialium"—*Periodica*, XIX (1930), 12*-15*.

———, "De religiosorum absentia sec. 606, § 2"—*Periodica*, XX (1931), 144*-145*.

PERIODICALS

Apollinaris, Romae, 1928—
Analecta Juris Pontificii, Romae, 1852-1868; Parisiis, 1869-1891.
Commentarium pro Religiosis, Romae, 1920—; ab anno 1935: *Commentarium pro Religiosis et Missionariis*.
Jurist, The, Washington, D. C., 1941—
Jus Pontificium, Romae, 1921—
Perfice Munus, Torino, 1926—
Periodica de Re Canonica et Morali utili Praesertim Religiosis et missionariis, Bruges, 1905—; ab anno 1927: *Periodica de Re Canonica, Morali, Liturgica*.
Revue des Communautés Religieuses, Louvain, 1925—
Theologisch-praktische Quartalschrift, Linz, 1832—

ABBREVIATIONS

AAS—*Acta Apostolicae Sedis.*
C.—*Codex* (Justinianus).
CpR—*Commentarium pro Religiosis.*
Fontes—*Codicis Iuris Canonici Fontes cura . . . Gasparri editi.*
Instructio—*Instructio de Clausura Monialium Votorum Sollemnium,* S. C. de Rel., 6 febr. 1924.
Mansi, *Sacrorum Conciliorum Nova et Amplissima Collectio.*
MGH—*Monumenta Germaniae Historica.*
MPG—Migne, *Patrologia, Series Graeca.*
MPL—Migne, *Patrologia, Series Latina.*
N.—*Novellae* (Justinianae).
Pallottini—*Collectio Omnium Conclusionum et Resolutionum,* etc.
PCI—*Pontificia Commissio Interpretationis.*
Periodica—*Periodica de Re Canonica et Morali utili Praesertim Religiosis et Missionariis.*
S. C. C.—Sacra Congregatio Concilii.
S. C. de Rel.—Sacra Congregatio de Religiosis.
S. C. Ep. et Reg.—Sacra Congregatio Episcoporum et Regularium.
ThPrQs—*Theologisch-praktische Quartalschrift.*

ALPHABETICAL INDEX

BIOGRAPHICAL NOTE

Garrett Francis Barry was born on March 1, 1909, in Norwood, Massachusetts. He attended Norwood High School and Boston College High School. At the completion of a year at Canisius College, Buffalo, New York, he entered the Oblate Novitiate, Tewksbury, Massachusetts. He pursued his seminary course of studies at the Oblate House of Philosophy, Newburgh, New York, and at the Oblate Scholasticate, Washington, D. C. He was ordained to the priesthood on May 30, 1939. In September of that year he entered upon graduate studies in the School of Canon Law of the Catholic University of America, Washington, D. C. He received the Baccalaureate in Canon Law in June, 1940, and the Licentiate in Canon Law in June, 1941.

CANON LAW STUDIES

1. Freriks, Rev. Celestine A., C.PP.S., J.C.D., Religious Congregations in Their External Relations, 121 pp., 1916.
2. Galliher, Rev. Daniel M., O.P., J.C.D., Canonical Elections, 117 pp., 1917.
3. Borkowski, Rev. Aurelius L., O.F.M., J.C.D., De Confraternitatibus Ecclesiasticis, 136 pp., 1918.
4. Castillo, Rev. Cayo, J.C.D., Disertacion Historico-Canonica sobre la Potestad del Cabildo en Sede Vacante o Impedida del Vicario Capitular, 99 pp., 1919 (1918).
5. Kubelbeck, Rev. William J., S.T.B., J.C.D., The Sacred Penitentiaria and Its Relation to Faculties of Ordinaries and Priests, 129 pp., 1918.
6. Petrovits, Rev. Joseph, J.C., S.T.D., J.C.D., The New Church Law on Matrimony, X-461 pp., 1919.
7. Hickey, Rev. John J., S.T.B., J.C.D., Irregularities and Simple Impediments in the New Code of Canon Law, 100 pp., 1920.
8. Klekotka, Rev. Peter J., S.T.B., J.C.D., Diocesan Consultors, 179 pp., 1920.
9. Wanenmacher, Rev. Francis, J.C.D., The Evidence in Ecclesiastical Procedure Affecting the Marriage Bond, 1920 (Printed 1935).
10. Golden, Rev. Henry Francis, J.C.D., Parochial Benefices in the New Code, IV-119 pp., 1921 (Printed 1925).
11. Koudelka, Rev. Charles J., J.C.D., Pastors, Their Rights and Duties According to the New Code of Canon Law, 211 pp., 1921.
12. Melo, Rev. Antonius, O.F.M., J.C.D., De Exemptione Regularium, X-188 pp., 1921.
13. Schaaf, Rev. Valentine Theodore, O.F.M., S.T.B., J.C.D., The Cloister, X-180 pp., 1921.
14. Burke, Rev. Thomas Joseph, S.T.D., J.C.D., Competence in Ecclesiastical Tribunals, IV-117 pp., 1922.
15. Leech, Rev. George Leo, J.C.D., A Comparative Study of the Constitution "Apostolicae Sedis" and the "Codex Juris Canonici," 179 pp., 1922.
16. Motry, Rev. Hubert Louis, S.T.D., J.C.D., Diocesan Faculties According to the Code of Canon Law, II-167 pp., 1922.
17. Murphy, Rev. George Lawrence, J.C.D., Delinquencies and Penalties in the Administration and the Reception of the Sacraments, IV-121 pp., 1923.
18. O'Reilly, Rev. John Anthony, S.T.B., J.C.D., Ecclesiastical Sepulture in the New Code of Canon Law, II-129 pp., 1923.
19. Michalicka, Rev. Wenceslas Cyrill, O.S.B., J.C.D., Judicial Procedure in Dismissal of Clerical Exempt Religious, 107 pp., 1923.

20. Dargin, Rev. Edward Vincent, S.T.B., J.C.D., Reserved Cases According to the Code of Canon Law, IV-103 pp., 1924.
21. Godfrey, Rev. John A., S.T.B., J.C.D., The Right of Patronage According to the Code of Canon Law, 153 pp., 1924.
22. Hagedorn, Rev. Francis Edward, J.C.D., General Legislation on Indulgences, II-154 pp., 1924.
23. King, Rev. James Ignatius, J.C.D., The Administration of the Sacraments to Dying Non-Catholics, V-141 pp., 1924.
24. Winslow, Rev. Francis Joseph, O.F.M., J.C.D., Vicars and Prefects Apostolic, IV-149 pp., 1924.
25. Correa, Rev. Jose Servelion, S.T.L., J.C.D., La Potestad Legislativa de la Iglesia Catolica, IV-127 pp., 1925.
26. Dugan, Rev. Henry Francis, A.M., J.C.D., The Judiciary Department of the Diocesan Curia, 87 pp., 1925.
27. Keller, Rev. Charles Frederick, S.T.B., J.C.D., Mass Stipends, 167 pp., 1925.
28. Paschang, Rev. John Linus, J.C.D., The Sacramentals According to the Code of Canon Law, 129 pp., 1925.
29. Piontek, Rev. Cyrillus, O.F.M., S.T.B., J.C.D., De Indulto Exclaustrationis necnon Saecularizationis, XIII-289 pp., 1925.
30. Kearney, Rev. Richard Joseph, S.T.B., J.C.D., Sponsors at Baptism According to the Code of Canon Law, IV-127 pp., 1925.
31. Bartlett, Rev. Chester Joseph, A.M., LL.B., J.C.D., The Tenure of Parochial Property in the United States of America, V-108 pp., 1926.
32. Kilker, Rev. Adrian Jerome, J.C.D., Extreme Unction, V-425 pp., 1926.
33. McCormick, Rev. Robert Emmett, J.C.D., Confessors of Religious, VIII-266 pp., 1926.
34. Miller, Rev. Newton Thomas, J.C.D., Founded Masses According to the Code of Canon Law, VII-93 pp., 1926.
35. Roelker, Rev. Edward G., S.T.D., J.C.D., Principles of Privilege According to the Code of Canon Law, XI-166 pp., 1926.
36. Bakalarczyk, Rev. Richardus, M.I.C., J.U.D., De Novitiatu, VIII-208 pp., 1927.
37. Pizzuti, Rev. Lawrence, O.F.M., J.U.L., De Parochis Religiosis, 1927. (Not Printed.)
38. Bliley, Rev. Nicholas Martin, O.S.B., J.C.D., Altars According to the Code of Canon Law, XIX-132 pp., 1927.
39. Brown, Mr. Brendan Francis, A.B., LL.M., J.U.D., The Canonical Juristic Personality with Special Reference to its Status in the United States of America, V-212 pp., 1927.
40. Cavanaugh, Rev. William Thomas, C.P., J.U.D., The Reservation of the Blessed Sacrament, VIII-101 pp., 1927.
41. Doheny, Rev. William J., C.S.C., A.B., J.U.D., Church Property: Modes of Acquisition, X-118 pp., 1927.

42. FELDHAUS, REV. ALOYSIUS H., C.PP.S., J.C.D., Oratories, IX-141 pp., 1927.
43. KELLY, REV. JAMES PATRICK, A.B., J.C.D., The Jurisdiction of the Simple Confessor, X-208 pp., 1927.
44. NEUBERGER, REV. NICHOLAS J., J.C.D., Canon 6 or the Relation of the Codex Juris Canonici to the Preceding Legislation, V-95 pp., 1927.
45. O'KEEFE, REV. GERALD MICHAEL, J.C.D., Matrimonial Dispensations, Powers of Bishops, Priests, and Confessors, VIII-232 pp., 1927.
46. QUIGLEY, REV. JOSEPH A. M., A.B., J.C.D., Condemned Societies, 139 pp., 1927.
47. ZAPLOTNIK, REV. JOHANNES LEO, J.C.D., De Vicariis Foraneis, X-142 pp., 1927.
48. DUSKIE, REV. JOHN ALOYSIUS, A.B., J.C.D., The Canonical Status of the Orientals in the United States, VIII-196 pp., 1928.
49. HYLAND, REV. FRANCIS EDWARD, J.C.D., Excommunciation, Its Nature, Historical Development and Effects, VIII-181 pp., 1928.
50. REINMANN, REV. GERALD JOSEPH, O.M.C., J.C.D., The Third Order Secular of Saint Francis, 201 pp., 1928.
51. SCHENK, REV. FRANCIS J., J.C.D., The Matrimonial Impediments of Mixed Religion and Disparity of Cult, XVI-318 pp., 1929.
52. COADY, REV. JOHN JOSEPH, S.T.D., J.U.D., A.M., The Appointment of Pastors, VIII-150 pp., 1929.
53. KAY, REV. THOMAS HENRY, J.C.D., Competence in Matrimonial Procedure, VIII-164 pp., 1929.
54. TURNER, REV. SIDNEY JOSEPH, C.P., J.U.D., The Vow of Poverty, XLIX-217 pp., 1929.
55. KEARNEY, REV. RAYMOND A., A.B., S.T.D., J.C.D., The Principles of Delegation, VII-149 pp., 1929.
56. CONRAN, REV. EDWARD JAMES, A.B., J.C.D., The Interdict, V-163 pp., 1930.
57. O'NEILL, REV. WILLIAM H., J.C.D., Papal Rescripts of Favor, VII-218 pp., 1930.
58. BASTNAGEL, REV. CLEMENT VINCENT, J.U.D., The Appointment of Parochial Adjutants and Assistants, XV-257 pp., 1930.
59. FERRY, REV. WILLIAM A., A.B., J.C.D., Stole Fees, V-136 pp., 1930.
60. COSTELLO, REV. JOHN MICHAEL, A.B., J.C.D., Domicile and Quasi-Domicile, VII-201 pp., 1930.
61. KREMER, REV. MICHAEL NICHOLAS, A.B., S.T.B., J.C.D., Church Support in the United States, VI-136 pp., 1930.
62. ANGULO, REV. LUIS, C.M., J.C.D., Legislation de la Iglesia sobre la intencion en la application de la Santa Misa, VII-104 pp., 1931.
63. FREY, REV. WOLFGANG NORBERT, O.S.B., A.B., J.C.D., The Act of Religious Profession, VIII-174 pp., 1931.
64. ROBERTS, REV. JAMES BRENDAN, A.B., J.C.D., The Banns of Marriage, XIV-140 pp., 1931.

65. RYDER, REV. RAYMOND ALOYSIUS, A.B., J.C.D., Simony, IX-151 pp., 1931.
66. CAMPAGNA, REV. ANGELO, PH.D., J.U.D., Il Vicario Generale del Vescovo, VII-205 pp., 1931.
67. COX, REV. JOSEPH GODFREY, A.B., J.C.D., The Administration of Seminaries, VI-124 pp., 1931.
68. GREGORY, REV. DONALD J., J.U.D., The Pauline Privilege, XV-165 pp., 1931.
69. DONOHUE, REV. JOHN F., J.C.D., The Impediment of Crime, VII-110 pp., 1931.
70. DOOLEY, REV. EUGENE A., O.M.I., J.C.D., Church Law on Sacred Relics, IX-143 pp., 1931.
71. ORTH, REV. CLEMENT RAYMOND, O.M.C., J.C.D., The Approbation of Religious Institutes, 171 pp., 1931.
72. PERNICONE, REV. JOSEPH M., A.B., J.C.D., The Ecclesiastical Prohibition of Books, XII-267 pp., 1932.
73. CLINTON, REV. CONNELL, A.B., J.C.D., The Paschal Precept, IX-108 pp., 1932.
74. DONNELLY, REV. FRANCIS B., A.M., S.T.L., J.C.D., The Diocesan Synod, VIII-125 pp., 1932.
75. TORRENTE, REV. CAMILO, C.M.F., J.C.D., Las Processiones Sagradas, V-145 pp., 1932.
76. MURPHY, REV. EDWIN J., C.PP.S., J.C.D., Suspension Ex Informata Conscientia, XI-122 pp., 1932.
77. MACKENZIE, REV. ERIC F., A.M., S.T.L., J.C.D., The Delict of Heresy in its Commission, Penalization, Absolution, VII-124 pp., 1932.
78. LYONS, REV. AVITUS E., S.T.B., J.C.D., The Collegiate Tribunal of First Instance, XI-147 pp., 1932.
79. CONNOLLY, REV. THOMAS A., J.C.D., Appeals, XI-195 pp., 1932.
80. SANGMEISTER, REV. JOSEPH V., A.B., J.C.D., Force and Fear as Precluding Matrimonial Consent, V-211 pp., 1932.
81. JAEGER, REV. LEO A., A.B., J.C.D., The Administration of Vacant and Quasi-Vacant Episcopal Sees in the United States, IX-229 pp., 1932.
82. RIMLINGER, REV. HERBERT T., J.C.D., Error Invalidating Matrimonial Consent, VII-79 pp., 1932.
83. BARRETT, REV. JOHN D. M., S.S., J.C.D., A Comparative Study of the Third Plenary Council of Baltimore and the Code, IX-221 pp., 1932.
84. CARBERRY, REV. JOHN J., PH.D., S.T.D., J.C.D., The Juridical Form of Marriage, X-177 pp., 1934.
85. DOLAN, REV. JOHN L., A.B., J.C.D., The Defensor Vinculi, XII-157 pp., 1934.
86. HANNAN, REV. JEROME D., A.M., S.T.D., LL.B., J.C.D., The Canon Law of Wills, IX-517 pp., 1934.
87. LEMIEUX, REV. DELISE A., A.M., J.C.D., The Sentence in Ecclesiastical Procedure, IX-131 pp., 1934.

88. O'Rourke, Rev. James J., A.B., J.C.D., Parish Registers, VII-109 pp., 1934.
89. Timlin, Rev. Bartholomew, O.F.M., A.M., J.C.D., Conditional Matrimonial Consent, X-381 pp., 1934.
90. Wahl, Rev. Francis X., A.B., J.C.D., The Matrimonial Impediments of Consanguinity and Affinity, VI-125 pp., 1934.
91. White, Rev. Robert J., A.B., LL.B., S.T.B., J.C.D., Canonical Ante-Nuptial Promises and the Civil Law, VI-152 pp., 1934.
92. Herrera, Rev. Antonio Parra, O.C.D., J.C.D., Legislacion Ecclesiastica sobra el Ayuno y la Abstinencia, XI-191 pp., 1935.
93. Kennedy, Rev. Edwin J., J.C.D., The Special Matrimonial Process in Cases of Evident Nullity, X-165 pp., 1935.
94. Manning, Rev. John J., A.B., J.C.D., Presumption of Law in Matrimonial Procedure, XI-111 pp., 1935.
95. Moeder, Rev. John M., J.C.D., The Proper Bishop for Ordination and Dimissorial Letters, VII-135 pp., 1935.
96. O'Mara, Rev. William A., A.B., J.C.D., Canonical Causes for Matrimonial Dispensations, IX-155 pp., 1935.
97. Reilly, Rev. Peter, J.C.D., Residence of Pastors, IX-81 pp., 1935.
98. Smith, Rev. Mariner T., O.P., S.T.Lr., J.C.D., The Penal Law for Religious, VII-169 pp., 1935.
99. Whalen, Rev. Donald W., A.M., J.C.D., The Value of Testimonial Evidence in Matrimonial Procedure, XIII-297 pp., 1935.
100. Cleary, Rev. Joseph F., J.C.D., Canonical Limitations on the Alienation of Church Property, VIII-141 pp., 1936.
101. Glynn, Rev. John C., J.C.D., The Promoter of Justice, XX-337 pp., 1936.
102. Brennan, Rev. James H., S.S., M.A., S.T.B., J.C.D., The Simple Convalidation of Marriage, VI-135 pp., 1937.
103. Brunini, Rev. Joseph Bernard, J.C.D., The Clerical Obligations of Canons 139 and 142, X-121 pp., 1937.
104. Connor, Rev. Maurice, A.B., J.C.D., The Administrative Removal of Pastors, VIII-159 pp., 1937.
105. Guilfoyle, Rev. Merlin Joseph, J.C.D., Custom, XI-144 pp., 1937.
106. Hughes, Rev. James Austin, A.B., A.M., J.C.D., Witnesses in Criminal Trials of Clerics, IX-140 pp., 1937.
107. Jansen, Rev. Raymond J., A.B., S.T.L., J.C.D., Canonical Provisions for Catechetical Instruction, VII-153 pp., 1937.
108. Kealy, Rev. John James, A.B., J.C.D., The Introductory Libellus in Church Court Procedure, XI-121 pp., 1937.
109. McManus, Rev. James Edward, C.SS.R., J.C.D., The Administration of Temporal Goods in Religious Institutes, XVI-196 pp., 1937.
110. Moriarty, Rev. Eugene James, J.C.D., Oaths in Ecclesiastical Courts, X-115 pp., 1937.

111. Rainer, Rev. Eligius George, C.SS.R., J.C.D., Suspension of Clerics, XVII-249 pp., 1937.
112. Reilly, Rev. Thomas F., C.SS.R., J.C.D., Visitation of Religious, VI-195 pp., 1938.
113. Moriarty, Rev. Francis E., C.SS.R., J.C.D., The Extraordinary Absolution from Censures, XV-334 pp., 1938.
114. Connolly, Rev. Nicholas P., J.C.D., The Canonical Erection of Parishes, X-132 pp., 1938.
115. Donovan, Rev. James Joseph, J.C.D., The Pastor's Obligation in Prenuptial Investigation, XII-322 pp., 1938.
116. Harrigan, Rev. Robert J., M.A., S.T.B., J.C.D., The Radical Sanation of Invalid Marriages, VIII-208 pp., 1938.
117. Boffa, Rev. Conrad Humbert, J.C.D., Canonical Provisions for Catholic Schools, VII-211 pp., 1939.
118. Parsons, Rev. Anscar John, O.M.Cap., J.C.D., Canonical Elections, XII-236 pp., 1939.
119. Reilly, Rev. Edward Michael, A.B., J.C.D., The General Norms of Dispensation, XII-156 pp., 1939.
120. Ryan, Rev. Gerald Aloysius, A.B., J.C.D., Principles of Episcopal Jurisdiction, XII-172 pp., 1939.
121. Burton, Rev. Francis James, C.S.C., A.B., J.C.D., A Commentary on Canon 1125, X-222 pp., 1940.
122. Miaskiewicz, Rev. Francis Sigismund, J.C.D., Supplied Jurisdiction According to Canon 209, XII-340 pp., 1940.
123. Rice, Rev. Patrick William, A.B., J.C.D., Proof of Death in Prenuptial Investigation, VIII-156 pp., 1940.
124. Anglin, Rev. Thomas Francis, M.S., J.C.D., The Eucharistic Fast, VIII-183 pp., 1941.
125. Coleman, Rev. John Jerome, J.C.D., The Minister of Confirmation, VI-153 pp., 1941.
126. Downs, Rev. Joseph Emmanuel, A.B., J.C.D., The Concept of Clerical Immunity, XI-163 pp., 1941.
127. Esswein, Rev. Anthony Albert, J.C.D., Extrajudicial Penal Powers of Ecclesiastical Superiors, X-144 pp., 1941.
128. Farrell, Rev. Benjamin Francis, M.A., S.T.L., J.C.D., The Rights and Duties of the Local Ordinary Regarding Congregations of Women Religious of Pontifical Approval, V-195 pp., 1941.
129. Feeney, Rev. Thomas John, A.B., S.T.L., J.C.D., Restitutio in Integrum, VI-169 pp., 1941.
130. Findlay, Rev. Stephen William, O.S.B., A.B., J.C.D., Canonical Norms Governing the Deposition and Degradation of Clerics, XVII-279 pp., 1941.
131. Goodwine, Rev. John, A.B., S.T.L., J.C.D., The Right of the Church to Acquire Property, VIII-119 pp., 1941.

132. Heston, Rev. Edward Louis, C.S.C., Ph.D., S.T.D., J.C.D., The Alienation of Church Property in the United States, XII-222 pp., 1941.
133. Hogan, Rev. James John, A.B., S.T.L., J.C.D., Judicial Advocates and Procurators, XIII-200 pp., 1941.
134. Kealy, Rev. Thomas M., A.B., Litt.B., J.C.D., Dowry of Women Religious, IX-152 pp., 1941.
135. Keene, Rev. Michael James, O.S.B., J.C.D., Religious Ordinaries and Canon 198, V-164 pp., 1942.
136. Kerin, Rev. Charles A., S.S., M.A., S.T.B., J.C.D., The Privation of Christian Burial, XVI-279 pp., 1941.
137. Louis, Rev. William Francis, M.A., J.C.D., Diocesan Archives, X-101 pp., 1941.
138. McDevitt, Rev. Gilbert Joseph, A.B., J.C.D., Legitimacy and Legitimation, X-247 pp., 1941.
139. McDonough, Rev. Thomas Joseph, A.B., J.C.D., Apostolic Administrators, X-217 pp., 1941.
140. Meier, Rev. Carl Anthony, A.B., J.C.D., Penal Administration Procedure Against Negligent Pastors, XI-240 pp., 1941.
141. Schmidt, Rev. John Rogg, A.B., J.C.D., The Principles of Authentic Interpretation in Canon 17 of the Code of Canon Law, XII-331 pp., 1941.
142. Slafkosky, Rev. Andrew Leonard, A.B., J.C.D., The Canonical Episcopal Visitation of the Diocese, X-197 pp., 1941.
143. Swoboda, Rev. Innocent Robert, O.F.M., J.C.D., Ignorance in Relation to the Imputability of Delicts, IX-271 pp., 1941.
144. Dubé, Rev. Arthur Joseph, A.B., J.C.D., The General Principles for the Reckoning of Time in Canon Law, VIII-299 pp., 1941.
145. McBride, Rev. James T., A.B., J.C.D., Incardination and Excardination of Seculars, XX-585 pp., 1941.
146. Król, Rev. John T., J.C.D., The Defendant in Ecclesiastical Trials, XII-207 pp., 1942.
147. Comyns, Rev. Joseph J., C.SS.R., A.B., J.C.D., Papal and Episcopal Administration of Church Property, XIV-155 pp., 1942.
148. Barry, Rev. Garrett Francis, O.M.I., J.C.L., Violation of the Cloister.
149. Bolduc, Rev. Gatien, C.S.V., A.B., S.T.L., J.C.L., Les études dans les religions cléricales.
150. Boyle, Rev. David John, M.A., J.C.L., The Juridic Effects of Moral Certitude on Pre-Nuptial Guarantees.
151. Canavan, Rev. Walter Joseph, M.A., Litt.D., J.C.L., The Profession of Faith.
152. Desrochers, Rev. Bruno, A.B., Ph.L., S.T.B., J.C.L., Le Premier Concile Plénier de Québec et le Code de Droit Canonique.
153. Dillon, Rev. Robert Edward, A.B., J.C.L., Common Law Marriage.
154. Dodwell, Rev. Edward John, Ph.D., S.T.B., J.C.L., The Time and Place for the Celebration of Marriage.

155. DONNELLAN, REV. THOMAS ANDREW, A.B., J.C.L., The Obligation of the Missa pro Populo.
156. ELTZ, REV. LOUIS ANTHONY, A.B., J.C.L., Cooperators in Crimes According to Canon 2209.
157. GASS, REV. SYLVESTER FRANCIS, M.A., J.C.L., Ecclesiastical Pensions.
158. GUINIVEN, REV. JOHN JOSEPH, C.SS.R., J.C.L., The Precept of Hearing Mass.
159. GULCZYNSKI, REV. JOHN THEOPHILUS, J.C.L., The Desecration and Violation of Churches.
160. HAMMILL, REV. JOHN LEO, M.A., J.C.L., The Obligations of the Traveler According to Canon 14.
161. HAYDT, REV. JOHN JOSEPH, A.B., J.C.L., Reserved Benefices.
162. HUSER, REV. ROGER JOHN, O.F.M., A.B., J.C.L., The Canonical Crime of Abortion.
163. KEARNEY, REV. FRANCIS PATRICK, A.B., S.T.L., J.C.L., The Principles of Canon 1127.
164. LINAHEN, REV. LEO JAMES, S.T.L., J.C.L., De Absolutione Complicis In Peccato Turpi.
165. MCCLOSKEY, REV. JOSEPH ALOYSIUS, A.B., J.C.L., The Subject of Ecclesiastical Law According to Canon 12.
166. O'NEILL, REV. FRANCIS JOSEPH, C.SS.R., J.C.L., The Dismissal of Religious in Temporary Vows.
167. PRINCE, REV. JOHN EDWARD, A.B., S.T.B., J.C.L., The Diocesan Chancellor.
168. RIESNER, REV. ALBERT JOSEPH, C.SS.R., J.C.L., Apostates and Fugitives from Religious Institutes.
169. STENGER, REV. JOSEPH BERNARD, J.C.L., The Mortgaging of Church Property.
170. WALDRON, REV. JOSEPH FRANCIS, A.B., J.C.L., The Minister of Baptism.
171. WILLETT, REV. ROBERT ALBERT, J.C.L., The Probative Value of Documents in Ecclesiastical Trials.
172. WOEBER, REV. EDWARD MARTIN, M.A., J.C.L., The Interpellations.

www.ingramcontent.com/pod-product-compliance
Lightning Source LLC
LaVergne TN
LVHW050253080826
844660LV00012B/631

* 9 7 8 0 8 1 3 2 2 3 3 7 7 *